The Super Traders

Secrets & Successes of Wall Street's Best & Brightest

Alan Rubenfeld

Foreword by Alan C. "Ace" Greenberg,
Chairman Bear Stearns

McGraw-Hill
New York • San Francisco • Washington, D.C. • Auckland
Bogotá • Caracas • Lisbon • London • Madrid • Mexico City
Milan • Montreal • New Delhi • San Juan • Singapore
Sydney • Tokyo • Toronto

McGraw-Hill

A Division of The **McGraw·Hill** Companies

This publication is designed to provide accurate and authoritative information in regard to the subject matter covered. It is sold with the understanding that the publisher is not engaged in rendering legal, accounting, or other professional service.

ISBN 1-55738-284-0   ISBN 1-55738-810-5 (paperback)

Printed in the United States of America

BB

   4 5 6 7 8 9 0

To
Alison, Jason, and Charles

Contents

Contents

Contents

NINE

Evan Schulman

Electronic Trading

227

Preface

When Harvey Shapiro of Institutional Investor approached me about getting together a group of Wall Street's Best and Brightest equity traders to write about how they perform their profession, it sounded like an exciting and hopefully painless venture. Little did I realize what was in store for me. Three publishers and five years later, the book is finally complete.

Getting this illustrious group of Wall Street professionals to sit down and write about their experiences was one of the most difficult endeavors imaginable. Fortunately, I had a very understanding group of executives from Probus Publishing behind me to encourage (i.e., push and shove) me to complete this ambitious project. What this book offers is the culmination of a lot of transcription, anecdotes and history of one of the cornerstones of the American system.

In dealing with traders, both during my tenure as Director of TraderForum with Institutional Investor and in the research and completion of this book, one theme repeated itself time and again. Without a doubt, the securities trader achieves a tremendous amount of job satisfaction. In fact, it goes beyond mere fulfillment; the traders in this book all believe that they were destined to this activity. It is a sense of self-worth I believe rarely attained in other walks of life.

My work with securities traders has given me an appreciation of the difficult conditions under which they must make split second decisions regarding thousands and often millions of dollars. Traders are sometimes maligned for the breezy manner in which they cope with the tensions inherent in their work. And they are also misunderstood. Securities markets are not merely lotteries for the rich. They are crucial

Preface

to the efficient functioning of the economy. And it is the traders, those who make the quick decisions on what to buy and sell and when to do so, who are on the front lines. Supply and demand are only abstractions until someone hits the bid or takes the offer, and the transaction is completed. Hopefully, this book will shed some light on how traders go about their work.

I must thank several individuals who helped bring this effort to fruition. During my five and half years at Institutional Investor, I had the opportunity to work with a uniquely creative group of individuals who always supported this extracurricular activity of mine. Much appreciation goes to Peter Derow, Judith Marcovitch, Heidi Merrill, Andrea Kern and the rest of senior management, both past and current, at Institutional Investor, for their consistent support of my efforts and providing a work environment that let me achieve and excel. Fran Sperato served as a transcriber extraordinaire who was quick to offer help at a moment's notice. Additionally, I must personally thank Diane Alfano for just always being there and for being the colleague and friend that everyone should find at least once in their career. My sincerest gratitude always.

I also must mention the over 100 members of TraderForum, Institutional Investor's membership organization for the buyside trading community. Its many members were never unfailing in their willingness to help me develop an agenda that helped to promote their profession. Many thanks to all of you for letting me be your "first call."

My hat also goes off to my associates at Merrin Financial, especially Seth Merrin and Scott Saber, who are both pleased to see this project finished so I can now dedicate 100% of my energies to marketing our new equity trading systems to the institutional investment world.

Finally, thank you Harvey Shapiro, my friend, confidant, and partner in crime, without whom I would not have been able to be put through such turmoil and agitation over the past five years. In retrospect, it was worth every moment.

—Alan Rubenfeld

Foreword

$\mathbf{P}$erhaps the greatest testimony to this country's aspiring to be a land of opportunity—a land of ambition, dreams, successes, and failures—is personified in the glory and greed of Wall Street. And for decades, the very soul of Wall Street has been the securities trader. Whether screaming on the floor of the stock exchange or sitting on one of the thousands of trading desks from San Francisco to Chicago to New York, this personification of risk, aspiration, and riches exists in countless transactions every trading day. And at the heart of this process lies the trader, engaging in securities combat, trying to squeeze out an additional eighth and a quarter for his clients on every transaction.

While securities trading has come a long way from meeting under the Buttonwood tree, the tangible and intangible qualities that make the difference between mediocre, good, and great traders over the decades have remained constant. Anyone can be analytical; anyone can memorize the symbols of the stocks he trades. That is irrelevant. A great trader must have the backbone to stay the course, to take calculated risks but not be afraid to take losses. If nothing else, a great trader is a fundamentally disciplined individual. Traders follow the advice of Davey Crockett, who said, "Be sure you're right, and go ahead."

Change is inevitable. It is inbred in the securities industry. If someone finds a better way of doing it—a better way to exploit an information edge or execute a trade, a faster way to contact a customer, or a more efficient way to transmit a confirm back to the client—it will be done. But how long will that edge last? Probably not very long.

Foreword

However, despite the whirlwind of change that has occurred in the securities industry over the past few years, what has remained consistent for the past four decades has been the calibre of individual who picks up the telephone to service the customer. He could be a block trader (such as myself), taking positions for clients in large blocks of securities that otherwise might take days or even weeks to accumulate. He could also be a sales trader, doing his best to put together natural buyers and sellers on 5,000 to 500,000 shares of a stock at any given time. Or he could be a buyside trader, controlling an organization's multi-million dollar commission budget and hiring those brokers who in his judgement perform the most capable execution given each unique set of circumstances.

Trading is a process that allows tens—or even hundreds—of millions of dollars to be exchanged over the phone. Forget about the handshakes. Traders exist in a world where one's word truly is one's bond. Yes, we have had our shares of Ivan Boeskys and Dennis Levines, but the fundamental nature of the profession is one of honesty and integrity. In what other industry can individuals call each other up on the telephone, quickly agree to a transaction valued at millions of dollars, and hang up, knowing in full confidence that the bargain will be kept—without contracts, witnesses, or even lawyers? The hundreds of millions of shares traded all over the United States each day are an affirmation of the character and honor of those who allow this system to succeed.

The contributors to this book are responsible for helping to ensure that the capital-raising function of the American economy works efficiently, effectively, and most of all, fairly. It takes years of practice and pain to become a good—never mind superior—trader. There are real skills to becoming a player in this game, and there has never been an alternative to experience to achieve it.

Traders come from all walks of life. Few of the old guard were Harvard MBAs. In fact, most probably never even went to college, or if they did, they went at night. Granted, that has changed dramatically over the past twenty years. I won't hold it against any potential employee if he or she has an MBA, but what we really look for among prospective traders at Bear Stearns are "PSDs"—poor, smart, with a deep desire to become rich.

You will also see that trading is a profession where "many are called, but few are chosen." It is a profession with virtually no shades of gray. At the end of each day, your performance is there in black and white for everyone to see. Did you hold that position a day, an hour, or even a minute too long, irrationally hoping that the price might miraculously turn in your favor? Did you act on some impulsive thought or unsubstantiated rumor, only to see it blow up in your face? If so, there's no hiding the results or shifting the blame; it is all there, counted to the penny. Make no mistake about it—trading is a ruthless profession.

In fact, if you can't separate reality from hope, then choose another profession. Calculated risks are one thing. Every businessperson takes calculated risks constantly. However, taking dumb risks is a surefire way not to be at the plate for your next at bat. A trader clouded by emotionalism is in the wrong profession.

The more things have changed in the past 40 years that I have been in the business, the more things have remained constant. Granted, the securities industry has gone through a revolution in countless ways— the dramatic increase in the volume of shares traded, the disappearance of countless brokerage firms (many of which were household names), the decline in commissions, the quantum leap in the use of technology and computer-generated analytics by traders, and the explosion in compensation for the entire Street. In spite of all the changes, you should realize that the qualities that make a great trader remain the same today as they did years ago under the buttonwood tree. In this book, these and other important issues have been all addressed to provide the reader with an insight into a way of life that is quite different from nearly all others.

What does the future hold? Just look at a "tombstone" advertisement from 25 years ago and you might find the answer. Scores of once-powerful firms from that period have been bought out or merged with other firms, or gone out of existence. The roll call is endless: E.F. Hutton, Kuhn Loeb & Co., Bache & Co., Carl M. Loeb Rhoades & Co., . . . the list could take up the rest of this page. Hundreds of millions of shares are traded each day with fewer firms and many fewer traders than there were even ten years ago. But while the number of traders entering the profession will undoubtedly decline further over the future (the Crash of 1987 virtually ensured that), there will always be opportunities for the hungry, the sharp, and the aggressive to become traders.

As you read about the personalities in the book and their individual convictions and philosophies, I think you will find that all of them share the traits of consistency, discipline and persistence—and it does not hurt to be born smart. The traders who have contributed their thoughts to this effort have mastered all of these skills and then some, and I think that they will shed some light on probably one of the most misunderstood professions in America. The capital markets of our country are a natural asset envied by the rest of the world. The traders play an important part in making them work.

Enjoy your reading.

—Alan Greenberg

CHAPTER ONE

JON NAJARIAN

The Options Trader

Once you have met Jon Najarian, it becomes quite clear that options trading was a career tailor-made for his statuesque physique. With the look of a middle linebacker (a position he played at the collegiate and professional levels), it becomes clear why Jon has been such an imposing—and highly successful—presence on the most active trading floor in the world—the Chicago Board Options Exchange. From his beginning virtually with no business background or trading experience, he has become one of the most prolific, and profitable traders on the CBOE. Jon runs his own highly successful market making and specialist firm, Mercury Trading.

But Jon's contribution to the options business does not end on the trading floor. He has represented the CBOE at forums and seminars all over the world, and is now very involved in the educational process of teaching both American and foreign investors the skills of derivative trading through his new organization, the Professional Traders Institute. Jon will highlight his story in this very amusing and educational chapter, and offers his insights into the combination of luck and skill that it takes to become a successful options trader.

The Bear Necessities

I came to Chicago in 1981 to play linebacker for the Chicago Bears. I knew the Bears were in a rebuilding phase, and I thought they were exceptionally weak at linebacker. Too bad they also figured that out and drafted a little guy named Mike Singletary. Fortunately for me, Mike held out as he negotiated his contract, but even my four week head start wasn't enough to keep me ahead of this superstar. Over the years I have enjoyed many hours of watching Mike Singletary win nine all-pro awards and help the Bears win the Super bowl, and I probably owe some degree of my success in business to the fact that his play helped convince me that my efforts would be better spent off the football field. Sometimes I look back at my brief time with the Bears, and I think about how the mental and physical toughness of college and professional football helped prepare me for the demanding life of an options trader.

When the Bears released me after four games, I had some decisions to make. Should I go north to play football in Canada? The idea was interesting, because it meant my football career wouldn't be over, but the pay was horrible and I would really just be putting off getting on with my life. I had played enough football and known enough athletes to understand how difficult it is to give up a sport that has meant as much to someone as football had meant to me. For me, football was a violent and passionate game. I had always played it that way. Even in the heat of competition it seemed I could observe the nuances of the offensive game plan and anticipate the next move of my opponent. I would miss the contact and camaraderie of football, but I also knew that whatever field I chose to enter after my gridiron career must have some element of competition and camaraderie.

The day after I was released by the Bears, my agent called me with a proposition: Would I stay in Chicago to clerk for him on the Chicago Board Options Exchange (CBOE)? He would provide an apartment in lieu of pay, but would allow me time to go to seminars and classes to learn the intricacies of options trading. He felt former professional athletes made good options traders. He reasoned that they were aggressive, able to think on their feet, and were used to being in a competitive environment. He had successfully brought two former professional athletes into the options business, and he said that with my head for numbers, options trading would be a piece of cake.

It sounded like a reasonable proposition to me. In my brief time with the Bears, I noticed that many fans who came to our 3:30 P.M. practices were stockbrokers and floor traders. The idea of driving a nice car and keeping brokers' short hours convinced me that a job as a floor trader could work out just fine.

Not Quite What I Expected

I arrived on the CBOE in mid-October 1981. The CBOE was created in 1973 by the members of the Chicago Board of Trade. They shortened the huge nine story ceiling of the Board of Trade by two floors to accommodate the new options trading floor. The old options floor was claustrophobic and noisy. There were hundreds of people dressed in just about anything but the three-piece suits I had expected to see. Some traders wore their ties slung down to mid-chest. Some had ties that were seemingly held together by mere threads. Although jeans were not permitted, most traders seemed to have a favorite pair of well-worn corduroys rather than Armani slacks. I quickly found that the only other rules of dress were a collar on your shirt, a trading jacket, and no sandals. These were not quite the images I had expected, but being a young man without a paying job, I appreciated the casual attire.

My 15 Minutes of Fame Were Up

My first day on the floor was very enjoyable. My agent introduced me to the members of his trading pit (Ford and Kerr McGee options), and I felt, to some small extent, like a celebrity. Part of the reason for my new found fame was my physical size. As I looked around the floor it became clear that the average trader wasn't 6' 2" and 235 lbs. As near as I could tell, most traders were 5' 10" and somewhere between 140 and 300 lbs. Some of the traders looked like tri-athletes and others like Hell's Angels. A majority of them seemed to be quite fit and in their early thirties.

And if traders came in all shapes and sizes they also came from any conceivable background. There were traders who had been bridge or chess champions. Some had been lawyers, others carpenters. One I met was even a former police detective. Some traders had Ivy League educations with graduate degrees, and others didn't even have high school diplomas. You could usually spot the new guys by two obvious traits: 1) they seemed to dress better than the veterans (who had nobody to impress), and 2) most new traders thought there was some secret to making a fortune in options that nobody else had thought of yet. For all their differences, they all seemed to have two things in common, they were very fast with fractions and understood a hell of a lot more about options than me.

I spent my first few weeks meeting traders, talking about football and getting acquainted with the intricacies of the trading floor. My temporary fame faded, however, and I began to dread going back to this loud, confusing menagerie. Months passed, and I became more and more discouraged about my ability to understand option pricing. The books on the subject were perhaps the best cure for insomnia I had ever read. Whenever it seemed there was a light at the end of the tunnel, the light turned out to be a train. I knew options couldn't be as perplexing as they seemed; it should be just like playing an instrument, or like learning a new language. They weren't learned by osmosis, but through practice and repetition. However, one also needs a good teacher. I was lucky enough to find two. One to teach me how to manage complicated arbitrage positions, and one to teach me the basics. Once I found them and put in the time, options did indeed become a piece of cake.

Option Basics

When I was a student in high school and college, the most enjoyable and successful instructors were those rare few who actually got into the subject matter and got their students excited about the subject. Alex Jacobson, the Head Instructor for the Options Institute of Chicago is such an instructor. His laid-back, comedic style of teaching basic option concepts has brought thousands of people into the derivative markets. Before settling down to teaching, Alex was one of the top option brokers for Merrill Lynch. Alex poured the foundation by asking his students "How many of you own a put option?" Very few hands went up. His description of how all of us really do own put options seemed to open everyone's eyes to basic option concepts. Alex started by saying that car insurance is really just a put option and that the components that go into the pricing of both the put option and car insurance are virtually the same. There are four basic components that are common to both car insurance and options: 1) Time, 2) Premium, 3) Deductibility and, 4) Volatility.

First, he told us to consider the component of *time*. To insure your car for three months is roughly one quarter of the cost of the yearly *premium*. If you wanted an insurance policy for just one day it would cost less than a policy for six months. Likewise, the put option with just one day to expiration will cost significantly less than an option with more life in the contract (Alex would wait until an advanced seminar to discuss the concept of time decay).

Next, is the *deductibility* factor. In both car insurance and the put option, the smaller the deductible, the greater the cost. A $500 deductible policy will cost much less than a $100 deductible policy because the insured will have to cover more out-of-pocket before the policy kicks in. In the case of the put option, the put buyer has the right to sell the stock at the specified strike price. If that put buyer wants zero deductible insurance, he purchases a put that is at-the-money. An example of an at-the-money put would be a 55 strike put, with the stock trading at $54¾. This put buyer will pay a healthy premium for his zero deductible insurance. If he wants to pay less for his insurance, he could purchase an out-of-the-money put as his hedge. An example of an out-of-the-money put would be a 50 strike put, with the stock trading $53. The buyer has the right to sell the stock at $50 regardless of where the stock falls to.

Finally, there is the concept of *volatility*. This is truly the most misunderstood component of option pricing. Volatility becomes easier to understand if you generalize it as an uncertainty or risk factor. For instance, volatility insurance is that a teenage boy is more expensive to insure than a married adult with two children. Insurance companies charge more because the boy is statistically more likely to get into an accident than the adult. For this reason, an option in a high-flying bio-tech stock will be more expensive than an option in a steady blue chip stock. Generally speaking, the price of the put option moves inversely to the price of the stock. It becomes easier to understand why when you remember that the put is the right to *sell* stock at a given price.

The antithesis of the put is the call option, which is the right to *buy* stock at a specific price. As the market moves higher, the price of calls usually goes up and puts go down. As the market moves lower, the price of puts moves higher and the calls lose value.

Additional Option Trading Basics

Except for special circumstances, an option contract is for 100 shares of an underlying stock or index. Buyers and sellers meet on one of our five options exchanges—the largest by better than a two to one majority is the CBOE, followed in descending order by the AMEX, the PHLX, the PSE, and the NYSE.

The market maker's function is one of the most maligned and misunderstood roles in securities trading. Basically, anyone can become a market maker. They need only register and receive a Broker Dealer number from the Securities and Exchange Commission (SEC). Next, they need to find a clearing firm that is willing to guarantee their trading account. This is no easy task, as the clearing firm receives only commissions from the market maker and takes on the risk of that individual's trading if he/she were to exhaust all their own capital. One of the final steps to becoming a market maker is to either purchase an exchange membership (currently trading for about $290,000) or to lease one. Approximately half the floor members in Chicago lease their seats.

Once the market maker has secured both the seat and a clearing firm, he/she is ready to trade. The SEC grants all market makers specialist margins. The reason for this extreme reduction in margins (as much as 99 percent) is given because the market maker has the responsibility of always making a bid and an offer for any customer order. In theory, the market maker should make the difference between the bid and the offer. The market maker also has near instant information dissemination and has the advantage of time and place to aid him/her in day-to-day trading.

Individual customers and institutions are represented on the floors of these exchanges by brokers. It is the option broker's responsibility to execute his customer's order by either trading with the market makers, or by competing against them for his/her customer. Market makers and customers create open interest by selling options and thus, obligating themselves to buy or sell stock at a specified price. Market makers receive specialist exemptions from Regulation T (a margin exemption) and thus, can carry enormous positions for as little as 1 percent margin. Traders also receive interest on the cash value of stocks they have sold short.

The Fundamentals of Trading

I found that even in our incredibly complex options market, very few traders really understood how to take advantage of options. Most traders carved out a niche for themselves and stayed there. One of the most basic obligations of a pit trader is that he or she must make a two-sided market in the options he or she is trading. The trader decides that the "fair value" for a given option is say, 2½. That trader would probably bid 2⁷⁄₁₆ and offer the option at 2⁹⁄₁₆. This most fundamental element of option trading is known as scalping. Some traders are strictly scalpers, that is a trader that reads the tape and discerns the exact moment to buy some options, and then attempts to sell them for a profit of as little as $6.25 per contract. This type of trader is known as a teeny scalper, since the $6.25 profit is ¹⁄₁₆th of $100. Traditionally, the teeny scalper trades 500 to 1,000 contracts per day and attempts to carry no long or short positions overnight. Typically, the scalper is the most risk averse of traders. By buying back all short contracts or selling out all long contracts before the end of the trading day, the scalper carries no inventory overnight, and thus, has no risk beyond that day's trading. Obviously, not every trade is a profitable one, but if the scalper is disciplined and covers his losses quickly, he can make a nice living for himself.

The Scalpers

I observed a large group of scalpers trade for several months and tried to learn how to trade in that style. I admired the good ones, how quick they were and how seldom they took on a bad position. When they did take on a trade that became a losing position, they quickly jettisoned the position and began anew. Traders that lacked the discipline to admit they put themselves into a bad position would became "married" to the position. These traders would inevitably waste time and miss other trading opportunities in an attempt to resurrect the position.

I learned from the successful scalpers that the key to their consistency was their ability to forget the price for which each trade was established and consider each trade as if it had just been created. In simple terms, if the trader would not have established the trade at the current prices, the trade would be eliminated, even if it meant taking a loss. In this way the scalpers would turn over their inventory on a more regular basis and thus, free capital for other trades. I convinced myself that there was much more to trading than just scalping, but this was definitely a skill I must acquire if I were to become a complete trader.

Position Traders

There was another group of traders known as position traders. Some of these traders would trade from the floor, but a majority of them traded from offices off the trading floor. I'm sure that some of them became position traders because they weren't fast enough to compete with the speedy scalpers. Others became position traders because they had a greater capital base, which allowed them to establish and hold large positions. Many of these traders came from competitive bridge or chess backgrounds. Some were former mathematics professors or even professional card counters from Las Vegas.

Position traders would search for disparities in option pricing and then create an arbitrage between one or more option classes and the underlying stock or futures contract. An arbitrage is a position established to exploit a mispriced option/stock/index/future relationship. The position trader sought to capture some theoretical edge as the relationship moved back to its real value. These positions were often quite costly to carry, moreover, the key was not only the position trader's ability to finance this cost, but his skill in managing the risk. Although not an absolute, a general rule of thumb is that the more difficult the arbitrage, the greater the profit potential.

When I started in the securities business the computer capacity and usage was quite low. With each passing year, the computers and programs written for them find these opportunities with ever increasing speed and efficiency. Some of the best position traders would return hundreds of percent on their portfolios. Most position traders understood that their edge in trading came from having the capital and spreading skills necessary to manage large arbitrage positions and not from "knowing" more than the market. Rarely would any of the successful position traders indiscriminately sell premium to make a quick buck.

Easy Money?

Unfortunately, the lure of easy money from selling naked option premium (calls or puts sold without a corresponding long to cover them) was a temptation some traders could not resist. If you could make several thousand dollars each month by selling uncovered options, why not sell more and make more money? The answer was quite simply that there were appropriate sizes for each type of trade, and it was the position trader's primary responsibility to make sure he could limit and identify his risk so that he could survive to trade another day. *Pigs get fat and hogs get slaughtered!* The temptation to make fast, easy money has sent many a trader looking for other forms of employment and a case in point was my agent.

One of the largest obstacles to my advancement as an options trader was that I didn't have a mentor. The options market can be very confusing, but with a little help from a reasonable teacher the questions can be quickly answered. Unfortunately, my agent had turned out to be one of the worst traders I ever observed. He barely knew enough to scrape by and certainly not enough to teach me anything valuable about trading. The only things I learned from him were how not to trade. When he did make money it was usually by selling naked options. (This trap has ended hundreds of promising careers, and is what some traders refer to as "the dark side.") He would always say, "Jon, these calls were made to be sold." For a short while in late 1981 he was right. But the classic trading proverb came back to haunt him. *"Pigs get fat and hogs get slaughtered."* If he could make $1,000 dollars a day selling ten straddles in IBM options (a position in which the trader sells both the call and the put of the same strike in hopes of capturing the premiums if the stock remains in a narrow trading range), why not double the size and make $2,000 a day?

Unfortunately, the stock didn't remain in a narrow range, and the position became very costly, very quickly. The last I heard from my agent he was one step ahead of the law, selling land deals in Arizona.

The Wake Up Call

If I were to become more than just a survivor among these cutthroat traders, I would have to be able to compete on their terms and to identify some special ability that would give me the necessary trading edge. I read every book I could find on trading. I sat through a seemingly endless stream of lectures and videotapes on options. I searched within myself to try to find that distinctive element I would be able to exploit to become a successful trader. When it seemed I was just spinning my wheels, I got my wake-up call to become a trader. My agent informed me that he was letting me go. WHAM! His words hit me like a 250-pound fullback. He said he decided I didn't really have what it took to become a trader. He suggested that perhaps it would be better if I were to look for another line of work.

Didn't have what it takes? Couldn't cut it? Those words lit a fire in me that still burns today. The next day I set out to plot my course and prove him wrong.

A Fresh Start

I approached a position trader named Tom Haugh, who had befriended me during the softball season, and asked him if I could work for him in exchange for some tutoring. He was kind enough to accept my offer, and I was soon off and running. I was overjoyed to finally have a mentor who could explain the intricacies of trading to me.

I spent the next four months running orders to various crowds on the floor, learning spreading, and becoming familiar with modern analytical machines that helped us price the options contracts. Basically, position traders like Tom seek to spread an overvalued or undervalued option against either the underlying stock or another option. These combinations of derivative against derivative or underlying stock are known as *spreading*.

Tom was both a great teacher and a skilled position trader. He was one of the hundreds of traders who had come to the CBOE from corporate America. Tom was a former senior financial analyst for Pullman Corp. In the early 1980s Pullman was absorbed into Wheelabrator Fry, and Tom used a compensation package as a springboard into the options markets. His ability to calculate risk/reward ratios and his comfort with fractions contributed to his success as an options money manager.

Tom taught me how to analyze the risk in a position and how to syntactically create protection that other traders might not recognize. He also was the first trader to point out to me that there were no dumb strategies, just inappropriate risks. I don't think I've ever met as voracious a reader as Tom. Many traders joke about Tom being the Cliff Claven (the postman on "Cheers") of the CBOE. He admits to being the largest depository of useless information in the northern hemisphere (Did you know that there are more phones on the CBOE than in the capital of the State of Illinois?).

In the entire time I've known Tom, I think I've seen him lose his cool only once. One of Tom's greatest skills is his ability to think on several different levels at the same time. Another would be his unshakable concentration and unflappable demeanor that have helped him become one of the top traders in the most active options pit in the world—The OEX 100. I still use many of the skills Tom taught me and I always try to make myself available to young traders looking for a hand because of the opportunity Tom gave me.

Getting Out on My Own

In the fall of 1982, I left Tom to become partners with Lee Tenzer. Tom had encouraged me to take the position of head trader for Lee because Lee's style of floor trading would further expand my knowledge of our options markets. Lee was another position trader who was tiring of the daily grind of floor trading. This is a common malady among traders. As they get older and presumably wealthier, they spend less and less time on the trading floor.

The trading floor in Chicago is a unique and intimidating place to work. It's basically a large indoor arena surrounded by video monitors that distribute stock and option prices also news from around the world. One of the first things a newcomer to the floor notices is the tremendous noise level. The racket can be deafening, ranging from a diesel engine idling (on a slow day), to a frenzied crowd at a football game. The second distinctive element you would notice is the variety of odors emanating from the assorted trading pits and traders. One pit might smell like stale cigar smoke, another like fish, yet another like rotten egg salad. Most traders have some sort of superstition, and unfortunately, some of those superstitions involve wearing the same clothes every day until their luck turns. One trader that used to work for me once came home, stripped in the middle of his living room, and proceeded to cut all his clothes into rags. Obviously, it had not been a good day!

All these factors contribute to the general ambiance of the trading floor. The traders scream, their arms flail, and they bounce up and down on their feet all day. At the end of an average trading day the trader's voice is strained, his feet and back hurt, and his head is still spinning with numbers and replays of lost opportunities. These conditions necessitated Lee's hiring of me and the establishment of our subsequent trading partnership.

Into the Pits

In the summer of 1983, I stepped onto the floor for the first time as a floor trader. Although I had been working on the floor for almost two years, the difference between trading on the floor and trading in an office upstairs was like the difference between day and night. Upstairs, you trade in relative anonymity. Your victories and defeats are visible only to you and your trading partner.

When you walk onto the trading floor as a trader, every move you make is seen by your competitors. The intimidation factor is intense, and perhaps that is part of the reason that floor traders empathize with professional athletes, whose actions are also constantly under intense scrutiny. I have seen several talented upstairs traders self-destruct under the constant pressure and harassment of the trading floor. The more aggressive scalpers will aggressively defend their "turf" (the area where they stand, usually in close proximity to the brokers) with verbal assaults, and by pushing, shoving, and generally making life as miserable as possible for the position trader.

I think my outgoing personality and poise under pressure helped me deal with the initial embarrassment and intimidation of the floor. Every month 10 to 30 new traders come to the CBOE to see if the streets are indeed paved with gold. Of these, only two to four will still be trading in one year's time. The new trader's hopes for beating these odds become even slimmer if he cannot find a trading crowd that fits his personality. You must realize that traders stand for from six and a half to eight hours within inches of each other. I would bet that the traders on the floor know the person standing next to them better than that person's wife or husband does.

Although all the traders are competing against each other for every trade, there is a certain camaraderie and character that each crowd develops. The personality of one crowd might be very outgoing, while the personae of another might be quiet and reclusive. Once a trader has developed his pit trading skills it becomes impossible for any crowd to shut him out, but at the start of his career, the more experienced traders can effectively eliminate the opportunities for each new trader.

Opening Night

During my first day as a pit trader, I spent most of my time watching, as the IBM crowd of 100 plus traders and brokers screamed, bounced, spat, shoved, and traded. Few people outside the securities business understand how much the individual option trader actually does trade. On any given day the IBM options crowd trades 30,000 to 50,000 options and about 600,000 shares of stock. A rule of thumb is that a busy options crowd will account for as much as 60 percent of the NYSE volume in their underlying stock. We can achieve these incredible numbers for two basic reasons: 1) our commissions are so low and 2) we get specialist margins.

The typical public customer pays a discount broker $65 to trade 100 shares of stock. A trader like me pays as little as $.02 per share or $2 for the same 100 shares. Our option commissions are likewise minuscule in comparison to the individual investor. We pay between $.20 and $.40 per option contract versus the public rate of about $10. Because the SEC recognizes us as specialists, we can carry a hedged position of 400,000 shares of IBM (or any other stock) with only $300,000 in our accounts (These discounted rates do come at a cost however, and that cost is a CBOE membership that can be purchased for about $290,000, or leased for about $4,000 per month!).

My Home at IBM

I was fortunate to choose the IBM trading crowd as the place I would call my home. I say fortunate because it was then, and continues to be the most active equity option pit in the world. The opportunities were greater in IBM, but the competition for trades was fierce. IBM was quite volatile in the mid-1980s and had enjoyed a run from $55 to $107 per share. I had already decided that rather than compete as a scalper, I would use my skills as a spreader to help support my floor trading.

By my second day of trading, I was looking for a spot to settle down in. I tried to work my way down to the front of the trading crowd, but found myself blocked by more experienced, aggressive traders. I waited until lunch for some traders to leave and then moved into their spots. During their lunch break I began to capture a greater and greater share of the orders from the brokers in the front of the pit. With each trade my confidence grew.

When the other traders returned from lunch, they quickly gave up any plans to shove me out of their turf. Instead they took places behind me. Because I am a large and animated man, it is exceedingly difficult to stand behind me and see the trading screens, and even more difficult to be seen or heard by the brokers in front of me. Consequently, from that second day until I left the IBM trading crowd in September 1991, I held that coveted spot in the front of the pit.

Any trader will tell you it's better to be lucky than good, and I was no exception to that rule. Scarcely two weeks after I began trading in the IBM pit, the stock made one of those moves that has earned it the nickname "Big Blue." The move started at $94 and, almost without pause, continued northbound for the next several weeks until it had established a new range in the mid-$120s. The trading opportunities in IBM during that initial surge and the subsequent consolidation were tremendous. The demands put upon me by the substantial increase in volume caused my floor trading skills to develop at an exponential rate. Soon I was making markets (bidding and offering options) in every option series and trading head to head with the big established traders. Since I had made a large amount of money over these first three months, I was becoming very confident in my trading abilities and quite comfortable in the inevitable showdowns with other aggressive traders. I never turned into a bully, but my initial success combined with my competitive spirit meant I wouldn't back down from a challenge.

The Pain Threshold

My quick evolution as a trader led to the inevitable bouts of overconfidence that every trader experiences, but rather than dwell on those defeats, I chose to analyze them and try to learn something from each setback. It is a common misconception that good traders don't make mistakes. Quite the contrary, I think good traders make mistakes every day. I've never met a trader that was so good that he never made a bad trade. We all make bad trades. The goal is to learn something from each mistake, and to limit the damage, and then to go on to the next trade. In fact, it was during this time in my growth as a trader that I formulated one of my primary rules for successful trading: my theory of a trader's *pain threshold*.

Everyone that has ever traded anything has recognized his or her pain threshold. Traders never set out to lose on a trade, but losing is as much a part of trading as death is a part of life. The key to successful trading is to keep your losses small and let your profits run. The single most difficult feat for a trader to accomplish is to take a loss. Maybe it's because traders develop tremendous egos, and taking a loss is akin to admitting they were fallible after all. Whatever the reason, the losses do come, and how you deal with them will decide how long you stick around and how much money you make. The key to my success is that I recognize my pain threshold and always trade within it.

For example, if I have a 100,000 share long position, can I deal with the loss of $1 in the stock? If the answer is yes, then I am within my pain threshold. If the answer is no, then I am outside my pain threshold. When I am outside my pain threshold it feels like I'm choking. My mouth becomes dry, I can't concentrate and most critically, I fail to see other profitable trading opportunities. Instead, I can only feel the pain of the loss. I liken this feeling to a being a horse with blinders on. The horse can only see straight ahead; the rest of his world is blank. The blinders are keeping him from seeing the complete picture.

When I'm outside my pain threshold, I reduce the position as quickly as possible to relieve the pain and allow myself the ability to again recognize the profit opportunities available to me. It has been my experience that even the worst trading days can be partly or totally overcome if you lessen the pain and concentrate on the opportunities to which the pain otherwise would have blinded you.

The Crash of '87

I would offer the readers two textbook examples of trading within my pain threshold. The first was the stock market crash of 1987. In the weeks leading up to October 19, 1987, the entire stock market, including IBM had become very volatile. The Dow had several 100 point up and down days, and "Big Blue" was acting as nervous as a long-tailed cat in a room full of rocking chairs.

Jon Najarian

Friday, October 16, was an option expiration day, and the Dow capped off a week of bizarre trading by selling off over 100 points, and closing on its daily lows. IBM had sold off with the market and closed just under the 135 option strike at $134½. Like so many of my peers, I thought both the Dow and IBM would experience a bounce on Monday the 19th. Was I ever wrong.

Monday, October 19th, I came into the IBM trading crowd the equivalent of about 25,000 shares long. That was over my pain threshold by 5,000 shares and the tone for the day was set early when IBM's opening price was indicated down more than five points. The tightness in my throat wasn't eased by the fear and panic I could hear coming from the OEX Index pit. A floor trader can tell the difference between fear and excitement, and the screaming I heard from the 700 market makers in the OEX told me this was not just fear, but panic. The S&P 500 futures contract went into in a freefall, and I could tell by the look in most of the traders eyes that nobody was going to get in the way of this train.

I called the firm that executed my stock trades in New York, and told them that I was a long seller of 30,000 shares of IBM down to $125 on the opening. They knew that this was a large order even for me and informed me that the stock "looked like it would open $131 or higher." I assured them I knew what I was doing and that I wanted to be guaranteed I got in on the opening print. I knew there was nothing I could do about the $100,000 loss on the opening, but I also knew this panic would provide opportunities that I would miss if I spent my whole day sulking or trying to fix my bad trade.

The stock finally did open at $129 and that was virtually the high for the day. By ten o'clock, the market was down more than 200 points, and I had already traded 150,000 shares of stock and about 20,000 option contracts. IBM was trading about $118 and nobody was picking the bottom yet. I have never experienced a better trading opportunity than during the down draft of October 19th. Professionals and public customers were liquidating their entire portfolios before my eyes. No sooner would I sell someone a put contract for 5½ than a broker would yell he'd pay 6½ for 1,000 more. As a position trader and a scalper the best you can hope for is a runaway market. People wanted options at any price, and it was up to the market makers to keep providing a two-sided market and to hedge our own risk so that we could continue to trade. For the rest of the day I tried to remain as short as I could, leaning as much as 50,000 shares short from $125 on down, but the brokers around me kept buying put options from me. Each sale of a put contract got me longer, so with each 100 lot put sale, I would hand signal my stock clerk to sell another 10,000 shares of IBM. Fortunately, there were far more opportunities in the options than there were in just selling the stock. My background in spreading allowed me to piece together call and put spreads that could take advantage of market conditions without adding to the selling pressure already panicking the market. The prices people were paying were crazy, but then none of us knew if we would even be able to open for trading the next day. Some traders couldn't take the pressure, but to their credit, most stuck it out through the most difficult and volatile market in history.

When the smoke finally cleared on that ugly Monday, I had traded 40,000 options and almost 250,000 shares of IBM stock. IBM had come in that Monday a $134 stock and had closed at $101! The Dow had lost over 500 points to close at 1,732. I sat in the pit for over an hour counting trades, and comforting friends. I always tell my younger traders that the second best feeling they can have is to turn a losing position into a winner. That horrible Monday, I had come in long over 25,000 shares of IBM and instead of losing money, I rang the bell. I had my biggest day as a trader, but rather than feeling like a champion, I felt numb.

All around me were traders and brokers, most of them my friends, with blank looks in their eyes and their mouths agape. Some had lost fortunes that took decades to build. Others had survived but would never be the same. Those of us lucky enough to have survived the disaster would have extremely heavy volume to trade against, but we all knew it would only be for a short time and that the fear of that day would keep the investing public away for years.

I'll be the first to admit that I have the best job in the world. I have always loved challenges, and for virtually all my life I have been a voracious reader. In my business those characteristics help give me the edge over my competitors. The fascinating thing about working in the markets is that they are affected by almost every detail of our lives: an earthquake in Argentina; a drought in Iowa; a nauseous President Bush at a state dinner in Tokyo. All these events can send the markets flying or diving. I remember reading the works of a Chinese philosopher that said, " Man can never do but one thing." As world markets have opened and free trade agreements proliferate, it will become less and less possible for an event that affects one market not to affect all markets. The United Airlines fiasco of 1989 was such an event.

The Crash of 1989

UAL had traded up over 300 percent as the stock became embroiled in one of our most frenzied takeover battles. In mid-October 1989, the stock was trading for about $280 a share and there were hopes that the $300 a share deal on the table would be raised yet again. Then on Friday, October 13, 1989, the bottom fell out of the UAL deal.

Late in the afternoon, it was announced that the bidders had failed to secure financing for the takeover. Obviously, the news was horrible for UAL shareholders, but the failed deal also sent shock waves through the market as traders feared the demise of the UAL deal signaled an end to the takeover mania of the 1980s. I was trading in the IBM options pit when I heard the scream come up from the UAL pit. For several minutes I wondered what was happening to slam the stocks so hard. Then I heard the fear of panic selling of calls and buying of puts. The tidal wave of selling was crashing all around me. Panic gripped the market, as stocks went into a freefall. With the haunting memories of 1987's market meltdown still fresh in their minds, traders, institutions and individual investors scrambled to dump their portfolios. It was difficult for me to get a market quote on IBM stock as the market swooned.

This crash didn't feel the same as October of '87, but the damage to professional traders' accounts was probably worse. The panic liquidation and volatility increase of '87's crash allowed traders to regroup and earn back some of their losses. Unfortunately, the volume and volatility of '87 never came, so traders that lost millions in '89's crash had little opportunity to recoup their losses.

Creation of the DPM System

Fortunately for me, in 1987 the CBOE had created a quasi-specialist system called our Designated Primary Market Maker or DPM system to augment our competing market maker system. Under the new system, the DPM would be responsible for maintaining a two-sided market (as all market makers are required to do), with one of the primary differences being the accountability of the DPM at all times. A normal market maker can wander to which ever crowd is busiest. The DPM must always remain at the station of his appointed stocks. The DPM would also be responsible for augmenting the CBOE's marketing efforts.

We had always felt that our competing market maker system makes the fairest marketplace for our valued customers. The only area this argument falls short of its intended goal is in the trading of newly listed products. Under our old system, the new listings would be brought into one of our traditional market maker crowds. The problem with this was that the crowd would pay more attention to the established and thus, more active, stock and pay little attention to the new listing. We needed to find some incentive for a market maker to favor the new listing business rather than trade in the established stock. The CBOE decided that the necessary enticement would be to guarantee the DPM a participation right of up to 50 percent on any option order traded in his allocated stocks. The success of this system has been amazing, and now at the CBOE, several of our busiest option posts are run by DPMs.

The Birth of Mercury

In 1989, I parlayed the profits and experiences of my nine years of trading into my own DPM, Mercury Trading. I decided on the name Mercury, because he was the Roman god of commerce and the markets and the protector of traders. I received my first DPM stewardship, of

Capital Cities Broadcasting, in December of 1989. Since then, I have expanded my DPM group to 14 stocks and the FTSE 100 put warrant. A majority of my stocks are NASDAQ OTC bio-tech or high-tech stocks such as Centocor, Borland, Biogen and Scimed Life Systems. Mercury trading now employs 14 CBOE market makers, 10 clerks, a technical analyst, and a full-time bookkeeper. From our humble beginnings with one stock trading just 150 contracts a day, we grew to become the most active DPM post on the CBOE, trading over 14,000 option contracts a day.

My Transition from Market Maker

My transition from market maker to DPM was a difficult, but exciting transformation. In my role as a traditional market maker, I always had other market makers and brokers to lean on. In our IBM trading crowd we had a great deal of camaraderie. I enjoyed joking with the other traders and brokers. When I made the move to become a DPM I was solo, out on a limb without a net.

The information exchange that takes place in the traditional market maker crowd was gone. So was the enjoyable small talk that helped pass the time on the slow days. As the sole trader on the other side of public and professional trades, I was also a sitting duck for the occasional inside information pick-off, or tape racer (a person who trades on news before it becomes public). In fact, in only my second month as a DPM, I sustained a six-figure loss when an unscrupulous customer traded ahead of the announcement of a substantial dividend increase on one of my stocks. I viewed this loss as yet another learning experience, albeit an expensive one.

Now when a trade like that shows up in one of my stocks, I tend to go along with the order, that is I supply the buyer a reasonable portion of his order, then buy the underlying stock in equal or larger proportion. In that sense I have become like the smaller fish that swim in and out of the sharks mouth. They take the scraps that drift from the sharks meal, but stay clear of his jaws. I don't pretend that I know it all. I realize that there are folks out there with research staffs in the hundreds, that sit in courtrooms with cellular phones. I don't expect to get my information as fast as these folks, but that doesn't mean I can't let their hard work help me make a profit.

Growth of the Mercury DPM

Since I started our DPM operation in 1989, I have found that my role has developed into two distinct job descriptions: 1) is that of a marketing person and 2) an options troubleshooter.

The marketing side of the job is easier and quite enjoyable, but it's not trading. Fortunately, I have a creative, outgoing personality, and I enjoy meeting and talking with people. I like contacting our big customers and networking with the heads of the large securities firms in New York or other wonderful cities across the U.S. Getting out to see what really is important to our customers has helped gain Mercury Trading the acceptance and success that we enjoy today.

My favorite role is that of a risk manager and options troubleshooter. Every morning I review our DPM stock and option positions with my traders. I take our positions apart and explain to our traders what our risks or potential rewards are in the positions. I layout a probable scenario for that day's trading, and then give the troops a game plan. After the opening, I determine which of our stocks is going to be the most active, and then trade that issue for the day. This gives me exposure to our entire trading operation, as well as the freedom to rotate into the active trading crowds that I do so love.

My first year goals were to increase the volume of business in my allocated stocks and to break into the black by the end of my first year. As with any new business, it was key for me to keep costs under control. As an individual trader I needed to carry only the expense of my seat and a clerk. However, the DPM business necessitated one additional trader and three clerks to help maintain our positions. Through the first six months of 1990, we crossed back and forth over that elusive break even zone. Just when it seemed we had a comfortable profit, it would be wiped out by some minor catastrophe.

Fallout from the Gulf War

As my DPM responsibilities grew, I added another trader: Michael Huffman. Huf is a very gifted trader, and a good friend. I chose him to be my number two man because I had watched him trade in the IBM pit for eight years, and I was impressed by his options knowledge and his composure. Then in July of 1990, my DPM group was faced with the greatest challenge of my young company's life: The Gulf War. Just days before Saddam Hussein's invasion of Kuwait, we had experienced our second six figure loss. The loss took three months of trading profits and left Huf extremely burnt out. The daily grind of trading, coupled with our recent losses had taken their toll. We decided that in his mental state he wouldn't be doing either of us any favors by sticking around, so he left on a much needed vacation.

The next day the selling pressure mounted, as concerns over how the U.S. could be drawn into another Vietnam panicked the markets. My ability to handle pressure would be tested severely, as I was left to trade our eight active stocks with only two young clerks. Those two clerks, Todd and Kevin were truly getting a baptism by fire as virtually all of our stocks went into a freefall. Whenever Todd is nervous, he chews his pen. I can tell how stressful the day has been by counting how many pens he destroyed, and Todd wasn't the only one who was nervous.

A panic ensued as firms and investors liquidated long positions. Our option volume tripled overnight. Our previously sleepy little pit had grown from trading 1,500 option contracts a day to well over 5,000! Fortunately I could draw on my years of active trading in IBM as well as two market disasters, to help me through all the craziness. Todd and Kevin did not have the luxury of such a background. I had to remain cool and calm or risk panicking my young apprentices.

The rumor mill on the floor kept cranking out doom and gloom about how bad the sell-off could become. There was talk among market technicians that the Dow could fall from its current 2600 level to under 1500 if the losses from the war mounted. Firms and individual investors reached for any protection they could get against such a calamity. These factors drove call prices into the sewer and sent put prices into the sky.

This volatility explosion caused the premiums in our options to double, triple or even quadruple. Puts that started the morning at $2¼ were trading $5½ even with the underlying stock unchanged.

However, as the DPM we had to supply that put protection for our customers or risk losing the business we had taken six months to build. One of the lessons I learned as a DPM is just how important and fragile trading relationships can be. We couldn't just walk away from our customers, and expect them to come back. It was a bit like having a gun to your head. Every day the put buyers circled our stocks like so many hungry sharks. On one hand we wanted to keep the customers we had sacrificed so much to get and on the other we wanted to survive to trade another day. I decided we could accomplish both goals of supporting our customers and living to trade another day, but it meant taking on an extreme amount of risk for a limited amount of time. Taking risk is part of the program you sign up for when you become a trader, but the risk of losing all my money seemed secondary to the thought of having to get a real job.

I decided to supply the put protection our customers were clambering for and sell the appropriate amount of stock against those put sales. This risky gambit left us virtually unprotected against an explosive upside move, but with the world on the verge of war, the upside was the last thing most traders were concerned about. Todd's pen chewing had reached epic proportions, and Kevin and I spent some sleepless nights commiserating about our hair loss due to fretting over our huge, risky positions, but our gamble paid-off handsomely.

The market found support near the 2450 level and put premiums and volatility's fell faster a lead balloon. We were able to buy back the options we had sold for tidy profits, and more importantly, we had not deserted our customers when they needed us most. There is a hardware store here in Chicago that has the motto, "The more we sell, the cheaper the price. The cheaper the price, the more we sell." True to that slogan, our increased option volume during that crazy July and August helped us to tighten our markets and entice even more customers into our options market rather than the underlying stocks.

Jon Najarian

One More Time

Some people would say my firm has been lucky to have so many *hot* bio-tech or high-tech stocks. I would have to agree, but all that interest in those stocks does carry a caveat with it: outrageously high volatility! For example, a majority of the stocks traded on the CBOE have volatility's ranging from 16 percent to 25 percent. These would be blue chip stocks like GE, MMM, MRK, and JNJ. The high-tech and bio-tech stock I trade range in volatility from 54 percent to 85 percent! Needless to say this huge volatility takes its toll on the nerves of me and my crew of traders. Strategies that are appropriate in lower volatility stocks have to be thrown out the door in these monsters of volatility.

Centocor (COQ) has been our hottest stock for the last two years. COQ is a genetic engineering bio-tech company. It has traded with a volatility of as low as 50 percent and as high as 200 percent. Obviously, Centocor has to make crazy, bizarre moves to justify this sort of volatility, and it does! I'll give you two examples of why trading COQ is like trying to stay on a greased rodeo bronco.

To the Moon

Late August, 1991, COQ was going before the FDA for phase two approval of its anti-sepsis drug, Centoxin. It was also embroiled in a protracted legal battle with its main rival, XOMA. A reporter for the *Wall Street Journal* quipped that perhaps the gallery watching the trial represented the largest contingent of cellular phones ever assembled. COQ was trading in the low $20s and speculation was running wild on both sides of the upcoming court ruling. We had customers betting on XOMA by buying puts on COQ as a surrogate for the calls that did not exist for XOMA, and we had other firms betting on Centocor, and buying every call offer.

All this uncertainty dramatically increased the volatility of COQ. This increase brought in speculative buyers, as well as the inevitable premium sellers. Premium sellers smell fear the way sharks sense blood in the water. Veteran premium sellers with deep pockets and strong stomachs came in and helped us supply our customers with the premium they so desperately wanted. Since we had the responsibility to take the other side of the trades, we let supply and demand set our prices. All the increased demand meant our volatility continued to soar, eventually peaking in the 150 percent level! I liked the odds of Centocor getting the nod from the FDA and told our traders to lean long in our positions, but to stay short as much premium as they could stand.

One of the misconceptions about what market makers do is that the public feels that we take the other side of their trade, and therefore, must be rooting against them. The trader may fade the public for a moment, but overall we don't stay in business just taking the other side of every trade and not hedging it. Quite often, you will find that the market makers are of the same opinion as the order they are trading against. Our ability to make money doesn't come from fading the order, but rather from our skill in assembling a hedged position.

Fortunately, we didn't have to carry our risky positions for too long. In early September, 1991, COQ got favorable news from the FDA. The stock surged through $30, and barely hesitated as it exploded through $40. With the news out, the premiums came crashing down to earth. Yet another old trading adage justified: Buy rumor, sell news. I think the volatility dropped over 40 percent in the first two days following the FDA announcement.

The trading was fast and furious. COQ became so busy that I pulled three traders and two clerks from our other stocks to help maintain an efficient market. On the opening surge from the FDA approval, COQ option trading became as crazy as any I have ever experienced. Mercury Trading accounted for 19,000 of the nearly 40,000 options that changed hands that first day. The traders and I were wiped out. Usual trading days are busy in the morning, slow around noon, and busy again on the close. This was no usual day. After the close our hands were cramped from all the writing of trading cards. That option re-valuation as well as the explosive move of the stock helped make Centocor the darling bio-tech of 1991.

To show just how quickly the worm turns, I'll describe Centocor's fall from grace. In early January of 1992, COQ finished its tremendous run, and peaked out in the mid $60 a share range. Investors started doubting Centocor's ability to continue its frenzied pace, and profit taking as well as short selling sent the stock down to the low $30s. Once again, COQ was in the center of a controversy. Several major houses had downgraded their estimates on Centocor. A few maverick firms were recommending accumulation of the stock for another run to $60. Again, fear and the element of the unknown drove up call and put premiums, as volatility spiked from 55 percent to 130 percent.

Traders will tell you that watching a stock trade day after day will give you a feel for that stock. If the stock starts to catch a cold, the trader should start sneezing. The feelings I was experiencing about the short term prospects for Centocor were becoming increasingly negative. It seemed as though the stock had fallen and it couldn't get up. I discussed my feelings with Todd Raarup, our lead COQ trader, and he agreed that the stock was acting pretty strange. We decided to keep an inventory of out-of-the-money puts on hand just in case.

Disaster did finally befall to poor old Centocor in the form of a rejection statement by the FDA. The FDA didn't like how COQ had conducted their phase three research for Centoxin, and was demanding a full re-testing. This news went over like a screen door on a submarine, and COQ hit the skids. It had closed trading on Tuesday, April 14th, as a $31 stock, and opened for trading Wednesday, April 15th as a $19 stock. I've traded in stocks that have made bigger drops on the opening, but none that had such heavy two-sided paper. It was unbelievable that we had folks buying and selling in equal portions. There was not the pure panic of the crash of '87, but the 45,000 options and 20 million shares of stock that traded were enough to even tell a novice that this was an unusual day.

We staffed COQ with every trader we could spare, and still had to borrow several of the CBOE's finest to handle the deluge of orders. Since we had as many buyers as sellers at the $19 level, the option premium level didn't expand, (as one would expect on a precipitous drop) and instead started collapsing. Call and put volatility's fell over 50 percent in the first few hours of trading. I was very proud of how our traders and clerks handled the pressure, and grateful that we were in a position to take advantage of the situation. Anytime a stock or a market moves that violently you are gratified just to survive, let alone make money.

Professional Traders Institute

One of the most enjoyable aspects of attaining a level of success in our options market was that people began seeking me as an expert speaker on derivative products. I traveled to Germany, France, Belgium, Holland, and Mexico to lecture on listed options trading, and OTC derivative arbitrage. I have also lectured across the United States, speaking to professionals and individual investors about the market maker's role in options trading. I was a frequent guest on the Financial News Network's weekly option report with Bill Griffith, and I even had a twice weekly show on National Public Radio addressing listeners' questions on options and the securities markets.

The notoriety is always nice, but there were several discouraging aspects of traveling and speaking on our options products. Perhaps the most disheartening revelation was that there were so few places investors could go to get competent advice and execution. To fill this vacuum of knowledge, Tom Haugh and I formed Professional Traders Institute in 1989. We began by acting as consultants to foreign banks and large U.S. firms and grew into giving seminars for individual investors across the country. In April of 1992 we began running two-day seminars in Chicago, for institutional and individual investors interested in learning more about derivative products and risk management. The response to these conferences has been tremendous. The most popular portions of the two-day event continues to be our mock trading exercise, in which the participants become market makers in a live simulation in the actual trading pits of the CBOE, and our option strategy sessions with actual market makers.

What Makes Me a Successful Trader

If I were to list the qualities that have made me a successful trader, the two most prominent would be that I can maintain my composure in pressure situations and that I can move the odds into my favor by creating hedged positions other traders might not see. I can keep a cool head and consider all my options rather than panicking myself into a dumb trade. I think keeping my composure can help calm my younger traders and mask a problem we might be having from other traders. I think any good trader can smell fear and panic in either the market or in his fellow trader. Once a trader has determined the vulnerability of some market (or market maker) he immediately sets out to exploit that weakness. Keeping a clear head helps ensure I will be the exploiter rather than the exploited.

When I began my career, that pressure was simply "could I make it?" When I had made it, the pressure became "can I keep making it?" When I experienced a setback in 1989, the pressure became "could I do it again?" I believe I can handle the pressure because of my ability to concentrate and focus on the problem. I don't accept any absolutes. There is always something I can do to affect the outcome. A good trader will not accept excuses or look for someone to blame. The focus should remain on goals and on charting the best course to achieve them.

Everyone of us faces pressure in our lives, and how we deal with that pressure can determine how far we advance or who we fall behind. I have already stated that I believe traders identify so strongly with athletes because we both face pressure on a regular basis. Whether it's a baseball player at the plate with the bases loaded, a basketball player at the free-throw line with no time on the clock, or a golfer lining up a putt for $200,000, the outcome is ultimately determined by how well these people deal with the pressure they face. There is nobody else to blame if they fail. If they succeed, there is instant gratification: absolute vindication: total euphoria. It's a feeling more addicting than any drug.

As a trader, I crave that feeling. I think all traders do as well, and that's why it's almost impossible to walk away from this job. I don't mean to imply anything as altruistic as saying that I don't trade for the money, but money isn't just keeping score, it's freedom. It allows us to live the way we choose to live. But, I know that money isn't the only reason that many of us choose to trade. We trade for the exhilaration of being in the center of the most exciting environment in business.

I've seen traders make multi-millions of dollars, leave the floor for a while, only to return to trading for that special feeling. Trading is an exciting, virtually all-encompassing job that can be very addicting and quite rewarding. I am grateful to be part of it.

CHAPTER TWO

ROBERT SCAVONE

The Specialist

The specialist occupies the most visible and controversial position of all professional traders. He is the center of the auction market, the traditional marketplace of American securities trading. It is the specialist's responsibility to maintain continuous, two-sided markets in equity securities by acting as both agent and principal in those stocks in which he is assigned. The specialist ensures that his markets are fair, orderly, competitive, and efficient, offering all market participants equal access and opportunity to trade. Robert Scavone has been fulfilling this role on the floor of the New York Stock Exchange for four decades. During this time, he has become the standard by which the NYSE floor specialist has been measured. Bob Scavone has seen it all, from the days of 10-million-share days to the full-tilt outrageousness of program trading and the nerve-wracking experiences of October 1987.

The New York Stock Exchange is one of the few places where a trader is looked upon purely for his production and not for his pedigree. Results are all that count on the floor. Bob started out on the lowest rung on the totem pole—strictly running orders and telephone messages around the NYSE—and rose to be one of the more experienced traders on the floor.

Since 1986, Bob has been the managing partner of Scavone, McKenna, Cloud & Co., a smaller but consistently highly rated specialist organization on the New York Stock Exchange. Among the stocks in which his firm specializes are CBS, Reynolds Metals, Golden West Financial, Boston Celtics, Banco de Santander, ConAgra, and Fiat, S.p.A., the well-known Italian automobile manufacturer, along with 25 other major corporations. Scavone, McKenna, Cloud has eight specialist partners and fifteen clerks, and their trading post is in the "garage" section of the New York Stock Exchange, built in 1929 as an extension of the original main exchange building constructed in 1903. Whatever it takes, Bob Scavone and the specialist community help to make the markets happen.

The specialist is a position of public trust that is open to constant and unrestricted scrutiny every business day. He or she is subjected to the stiffest standards of ethical and honorable conduct. Every trade a specialist executes is open to the light of day, observed by every trader: those on the floor of the NYSE, upstairs on the thousands of desks of the world's securities firms, and in the countless offices of money managers both in the United States and abroad.

In the pages that follow, Bob will describe the life of a specialist and the considerable, unique pressures under which he or she operates. This will give you a better understanding of the specialist's role in the transaction process. He also will address some myths that have evolved concerning how the specialist trader operates in the public arena, providing a competitive and quality marketplace for all investors.

The Making of a Specialist

I began my career as a page on the New York Stock Exchange in July 1948, running messages all over the floor for the brokers. In those days, it was shined shoes, white shirt, and neatness always. I paged for about a year, training to be a reporter for the Exchange. A reporter accounts all the sales made by the brokers. At that time we used pneumatic tubes, and all transactions were posted manually. A reporter inscribed the price and amount of shares on a piece of paper, placed it in a wooden tube, inserted it in a capsule in the tube, and shot it upstairs. That was how the sales got on the tape. I did this until the 1951 outbreak of the Korean War, where I then served in the U.S. Army from 1951 to 1953.

In 1953, my job was waiting for me, and I returned to my position as a reporter. By 1954 my hard work paid off, and I landed a job as a specialist clerk with Walters, Peck and Co., which later became Robb, Peck, McCooey & Co. In 1965, I acquired my seat with the firm, which by then had developed into a huge specialist firm. We had 20 seats, specialized in 100 stocks, and were responsible for approximately 7–8 percent of the total volume on the New York Stock Exchange. In 1982, I became president of Robb, Peck, McCooey & Co., and our growth continued. In November of 1985, I was bought out in a leveraged buyout by the firm's younger partners.

After the LBO, I retired for one month but couldn't stand the slow pace, so I joined the firm of McKenna, Cloud & Co. Two of my new partners soon retired, each receiving five-year payouts, and the firm's name was changed to Scavone, McKenna, Cloud & Co. We then proceeded to increase the size of the company, bringing in 11 new stocks, increasing our total accounts from 25 to 36 stocks, where we currently stand.

A Seat on the Exchange

The privilege to execute an order on the floor of the New York Stock Exchange is accomplished through getting a seat. The only way to acquire one of these 1,366 seats is to buy or lease it from another seat owner. The lease price is now about $90,000 a year. The price of a seat at the last sale was approximately $500,000. (Before October 1987 the price of a seat was $1.15 million.) But owning a seat does not mean you automatically make money—you must acquire customers.

When I started in the business in 1948, seats cost $125,000, but in 1973 and 1974, when things were very bad, they went down to $38,000 in panic selling, amid predictions of the demise of the Exchange. Seats cannot be used as capital, nor can they be used as collateral. When applying to buy a seat, you are thoroughly investigated by the NYSE and, in addition, prospective members must pass an examination administered by the Exchange.

Preparing for the Day

A specialist's day begins early. I'm up at 5:30, just to get a summary of what happened the previous business day and a flavor of the Japanese and European markets, which way the dollar is going in Europe and Japan, as well as the direction of interest rates, the price of oil, and the bond market. The market today is very interest-rate sensitive.

Most partners of specialist firms gather before the market opening at the New York Stock Exchange Luncheon Club, that former all-male bastion (In fact, it was just a few years ago that they put a women's bathroom on the same floor!) They review the previous day's activity and profit and loss sheets, which list each stock in which they specialize, as well as positions coming in, whether long or short. The P&L's display the daily, monthly, and year-to-date profit or loss, as well as the recording of dividends. The specialist reviews his positions that might be vulnerable during the upcoming day, and determines which long and short positions to cut back, if considered too heavy. I'm constantly reviewing positions that might be vulnerable in a down market, as well as checking any large positions that could be vulnerable on the upside. If one of my partners has too much inventory in proportion to the other partners, it is often recommended that he cut his positions by 20–25 percent wherever possible.

By 8:45, we begin the process of psyching ourselves and preparing our plans. We strategize on which direction the market is going to open and how we should react, and prepare for the inevitable surprises. There is nothing certain about which way the market is going to go, but at least we will have an opinion in which to examine our position sheets. We must be thoroughly prepared for the inevitable certainty of uncertainty.

All stocks don't commence trading when the bell rings at 9:30. Before the opening, there are numerous possible buyers and sellers, of many sizes, coming to the specialist posts to get a picture about the supply and demand for each stock and seeking out the possible range of the opening price. They then communicate this information back to their trading desks to see if their customers would be willing to pay slightly above or sell slightly below their original prices. So on any opening, specialists give buyers and sellers the opportunity to alter their original price demands, so they aren't "eighthed and quartered." Everyone has an equal opportunity to participate at the opening and get their trades on the tape. You can see why the specialists are so important, being the nucleus of the auction market. Every specialist aims for a fair and orderly opening in a stock, satisfying buyers and sellers to the best of his ability.

At the opening, many buyers and sellers often reduce some of their position, whether long or short. The specialist may not see a buyer's or seller's full hand at the opening. A broker will often execute a part of his order at the beginning of the day, then work the remainder of the order throughout the rest of the session. So instead of executing the block in a single transaction at one price, the broker executes at several prices, to prove to his customers that he took time and effort to attain the best possible execution.

Once that bell rings, every specialist is at the plate, and his managing partner can't tell him how to hit. One basic credo is to admit when you've made a trading mistake and to then alter your position with the least possible loss. Remember: he who trades on hope loses in despair. Within a reasonable amount of time, a trader knows whether he's right or wrong. For example, if you buy 20,000 shares and it is going against you, sell half the position and keep yourself in a more liquid position to buy again if the stock goes down further. In other words: face that lion or else you'll be eaten by him!

Robert Scavone

Showing the Hand

A specialist has to be on his toes because if a customer has a large block to sell, he might not think it is wise to show his full hand, as his position might overhang the market and scare away potential buyers. The customer might choose to piecemeal his order to the floor, starting with a 20,000-share slice to sell through Merrill Lynch, which we may buy for our own account. Ten minutes later, he might come with another 20,000 shares to sell through Prudential. Such a strategy inevitably places the specialist at a disadvantage, as he will never know if that 20,000 shares is part of a 1 million-share order.

Today, many specialist firms are cutting the commission rates, because the profitability of member firms is evaporating with the huge volume after the 1987 Crash. We realize the problem and the need for a cheaper execution. It is also our obligation to conform to what goes on in the industry, with many jobs being lost and decreasing profitability of member firms. On the floor of the NYSE, everybody tries to work as a team and help each other.

In the Ring

At the Exchange, the action is nonstop from the second you walk onto the floor. Besides scrutinizing his positions and those of his other partners, a specialist is constantly glancing up at the Quotron machine located over his head and monitoring its different indicators—the Dow Jones industrials, utilities, and transportation indexes. Other important markets to watch are foreign currencies versus the American dollar. But these are only some of the markets that a specialist utilizes. He also keeps a keen eye on short- and long-term bond indicators, the NYSE, the Standard & Poor's indexes, the Value Line index, and the oil index. These indicators give the specialist on the exchange floor a mixed bag of what is happening. We use the monitors to try to be 10 or 20 seconds ahead of the market.

At present, I see the stock market being driven predominately by two completely disparate factors—program trading and interest rates. With the American investment public essentially staying on the sidelines,

I believe that the market is approximately 50 percent driven by these two factors.

Making Money

Keeping positions liquid is an integral part of a specialist's trading strategy. Let's take an example. One recent day I found the Dow down at one instance some 40 points, coming back 12 and ending the day down 28 points. Now, because we traded intraday—something which specialists refer to as *fencing*—we tailored our losses, losing only $50,000, when our losses easily could have been $500,000. Our inventory going in was $15 million but we were able to reduce our position to $7 million by the end of the day's trading. Our strategy was to partially liquidate our holdings and prepare to buy additional stock in case of a selloff the following day. A good specialist maintains a reasonable amount of buying power, allowing him to be flexible and on the offense under unusual market conditions. If a specialist is overpositioned, he is forced to sell at the low points instead of being in a position to buy stock. A specialist has to remain flexible to minimize his losses, whether his stocks are going north or south.

A good example of maintaining flexibility would be the activity in one of our more active stocks, Reynolds Metals. Louis Spina, my partner, is assigned to trade Reynolds Metals. On a preceding day, Reynolds closed at 52⅜ in New York, and our position coming in was 20,000 shares—a $1 million-plus piece of inventory. But this is not an excessively large position for a liquid stock such as Reynolds, which has a daily trading volume of about 250,000 shares. If we were long 20,000 shares of CBS, which sells at about $200 per share, it would be a little heavy, since we specialize in over 30 corporations.

At the opening, we were able to sell our position at 52⅝ and 52½. The stock sold down to 52 and we then sold some stock short at 52¼ and at 52⅜. However, remember that a specialist can only short stock on plus or zero ticks. Subsequently, selling programs came in; we covered our short position and proceeded to be long 30,000 shares down to 51. That position was sold out at 51¼ and 51⅜. Later that day,

Reynolds plummeted as the Dow raced down 40 points. The stock dived as we bought 35,000 shares from 51 down to $49\frac{1}{8}$. We unloaded 20,000 shares up to $49\frac{1}{2}$, and the stock closed shortly thereafter at $49\frac{5}{8}$.

After the trading day, we ended up losing $5,000 on a 20,000-share opening position, marked down $3 and long 15,000 shares. Without a fencing strategy, this easily could have been a $100,000 trading loss, with a carryover position of over 50,000 shares. However, it is not uncommon for a specialist to lose $100,000 a day in one stock. But to lose $100,000 and still maintain an uncomfortably large position is not a judicious trading strategy.

It is unusual for a specialist to hold a continuing or even a flat position overnight. Generally, 80 percent of profits are generated through intraday trading. Many specialists might purchase 100,000 shares of stock and hold it for three or six months. But this technique ties up capital and costs the specialist in interest charges. Our philosophy is to keep the money moving. We are singles hitters, but often we'll go for the extra-base hit when the situation is favorable.

Keep It Moving

As a trader you keep your positions moving, whether you're right or wrong. When it's time to sell, price should not make a difference. If you are long 40,000 shares of a stock and you think you should be long 20,000, sell that 20,000 shares at any reasonable price. If the stock goes up, you profit on the remaining balance. If the stock goes down, you are in a position to buy more and average down. In a really frantic market, such as on Black Monday and Terrible Tuesday, what you had in mind was not the P&L sheet but basic survival. The most important factor in survival is inventory; you have to keep your inventory flexible. Most imperative is that this philosophy be consistent among all of your partners.

Each stock has its own liquidity formula. In those issues that are more liquid, a specialist will obviously maintain a larger position. Liquidity offers flexibility. In these situations, we would be willing to take a greater position at the end of the trading day. With stocks that do not offer a lot of liquidity, a good specialist would not want to have a closing position of more than 20,000 or 30,000 shares. With more liquid stocks, you could take on maybe 50,000 to 100,000 or more shares.

One of the specialist's trading philosophies is to link his positions in proportion to the average daily turnover; the higher volume stocks really dictate what position you should have in a stock. For example, CBS, one of our stocks, may trade 100,000 to 200,000 shares daily, and we would be on one side of the print an average of maybe 25 percent of the volume. Therefore, on a 200,000-share day, we could trade for our own account 50,000 to 60,000 shares, in and out. Keep in mind that a 20,000-share position in CBS utilizes $4 million of our firm's capital.

Rules of the Professional Trader

I like to keep the philosophy of trading rather simple:

1. Make the most amount of money with the least amount of risk.

2. Curtail your losses, without panic.

3. Continually move your stagnant positions around.

4. Become a student of research for each stock you trade.

5. Trade on fact and not on hope.

6. If you buy a stock and it goes up, sell it. And if it goes down, sell it.

7. Invariably, the first loss is usually the best loss.

As you can tell by these rules, the trader is always moving, just like a boxer. Even if you sell it too soon, it's not a major disaster; if you make a quarter on 20,000 shares instead of a half, it's not a major difference; if it goes down and you lose half a dollar or a dollar, it's not a major difference. As long as you are right more than you are wrong, you'll stay ahead of the game.

Rules for Avoiding Disaster

A good trader strives to avoid the big loss. If you take the big hit, it could take a few months to recoup. A specialist could convert his yearly profit into a loss with one bad trade. Therefore, the managing partner must maintain a consistency in his trading philosophy and approach, and the firm should follow his general trading standards.

I have been fortunate to have survived many major downturns or disasters in the market by adhering to these basic rules:

1. Do not increase your position too quickly on the down side, but increase your positions on the upside.

2. In bear markets, earnings and charts do not portray the true price value of a stock.

3. Take your loss, regroup, and start again tomorrow.

The Responsibility of Leadership

Today, more pressure is on the younger brokers who are trying to make a name for themselves by putting some quick points on the board. When you are older, you take the losses and mistakes a little more in stride. But even at my age, the business is evolving and I am still learning. As the firm's elder statesman, I try to share with my partners what I have learned through the years—how they should react under pressure and, most important, how to work as a team. Camaraderie in a partnership is extremely essential. We work together, play together, and are socially involved in the joys and crises of our existence.

The managing partners should educate their younger partners and share their expertise and experience. Remember:

1. There is always tomorrow and there is always next year. You never want to be knocked out of the box for good.

2. If you play too big, you play with scared money, and you will not trade rationally. You end up selling when you don't want to sell and buying when you don't want to buy.

3. Always keep yourself in a position to be on the offense.

Different Trading Approaches

No two specialist firms trade the same way. Some firms tend to be more active than their peers; some have better stocks than other firms. There are different trading philosophies for each stock because of difficult liquidity demands and because different stocks suit the public at different times. Some will carry an inventory in their stock for a longer period, only because they are better capitalized than other specialists. Obviously, it takes more capital to run larger firms. However, a smaller firm can proportionately be as well-capitalized as a larger firm. If you are stuck with a burgeoning inventory for a long period, interest charges will take their toll.

When the market is in a slow volume pattern, a specialist is often tempted to force trade. But forced trading in a low volume market is usually a losing trade. If you are wrong on a high-volume day, it is much easier to get out of position because the market is more liquid, giving you more opportunities to trade back and forth.

Staying Afloat

Specialists have capital requirements to maintain. Each morning, every specialist firm submits a capital report to the New York Stock Exchange, indicating its total positions and current buying power. Although specialists can trade with a 25 percent margin, the NYSE keeps a close watch on specialists' capital. It is to their benefit that the NYSE forewarn them as they approach a capital problem that could make them extremely vulnerable in cases of a sharp market decline.

A specialist strives to maintain his liquidity as the market is moving down. For example, you would sell $5 million of stock and buy $5 million back, still being long the basic $10 or $15 million inventory of stock with which you are comfortable. With a troublesome position, a specialist is forced to sell when he does not want to sell and buy when he doesn't want to buy.

Robert Scavone

Separating Truth from Fiction

Often, specialists are included on block trades. We try to accommodate the imbalances on either the buy or sell side of the block. Often, the large-block houses position with the specialists and we work as a team, trying not to hurt each other. Sometimes we make money together; sometimes we lose money together. We usually know who are on the trading desks upstairs, and they know the players down here; our communication is of both a business and a personal nature.

A specialist does not drive a stock down or up, because the NYSE rules prohibit a specialist from buying stock on a plus tick, as well as selling short on a minus tick, unless liquidating, and then with permission from a floor governor. It is incorrect to believe that a specialist dictates the price movements of a stock. Specialists are regulated by strict trading guidelines set forth by the New York Stock Exchange in order to stabilize the intraday action of the price of stocks. The specialist must live up to these rules and regulations or face the penalties. Many specialist firms have incurred the wrath of the Exchange, having their stock reallocated or their entire firm forced to merge into a stronger entity.

In all this trading activity, it is critical to remember that a specialist broker never acts as a principal when public orders could be filled at the given price. The specialist can never step in front of a customer's order when he is acting on his own behalf.

The Takeover Bomb

Being a specialist in a takeover stock can be a real killer. It is the specialist's obligation to maintain a market in a stock, and when there is an absence of buyers or sellers, he has to help provide the liquidity in the issue, even if it translates into taking a short position on an issue that is climbing on news of a potential takeover. Recently, one of our stocks was put in play. At the time of the announcement it was trading at about 17 and we were short the stock. Nonetheless, we opened it up $1\frac{3}{4}$ at $18\frac{3}{4}$, further extending our short position, which of course was our obligation. We covered the stock at 19, to minimize our loss, and the stock ran up to $21. In situations such as this, a specialist's job is to provide liquidity to the marketplace. We have to sell stock when nobody else wants to, which is exactly what occurred, and then begin trading from day to day to try to neutralize our losses.

Hopefully, this situation does not occur very often within any specialist's panel of stocks. In takeover situations, he tries to maintain a long position. If a higher bid arrives, he then has stock with which to supply the buyers, rather than being caught short.

In the event of a huge loss in one stock, the firm tries to minimize the loss through the trading profits in the other stocks in which they specialize. This is why position balance is so critical in the stocks in which we specialize. It is not practical for a single partner to carry a large percentage of the firm's capital. This is exactly why I maintain constant position checks among our partners.

The responsibilities of a specialist are continuous. Therefore, if a stock is for sale and there are no other buyers, he is forced to buy it in the context of the market, using his firm's capital and taking the risk of possibly owning a long position in a sinking market. But if that stock turns around and starts to move up, the specialist has to be a supplier of stock. This means selling 2,000, 4,000, even 5,000 shares at every eighth and quarter, making a real market. The bottom line is that the specialist constantly has to give up some of the unrealized gain in his portfolio. But that's the price he pays to keep his franchise — the cost of admission to be in the ball game.

The Team behind the Post

Clerks and specialists must think together as a single unit, because their constant communication tells the specialist what orders they have on the inside, and the specialists let their clerks know the action on the outside. Many times, I ask my clerks for trading ideas: "What do you think of the market, and which way do we go?" Naturally, only a specialist can execute an order, but a clerk also can get a gut feeling through his constant handling of orders in specific stocks. We work as a team; competent clerks are worth their weight in gold.

A clerk is not an apprentice. Some clerks, however, have been behind the specialist post for 20 years. Sometimes, specialist clerks work their way up the ladder such as I did, becoming a partner in a specialist firm. In this business, time does not really designate how good you are. When there is outstanding talent clerking behind the specialist post, it is only fair that they are brought out front for the benefit of all parties on the floor.

Many specialists sometime start out working as pages for the NYSE or as back-up clerks to specialist clerks. From there, they are usually promoted and become specialist clerks. It takes about four or five years of learning to accomplish the specialist clerk's job proficiently.

A specialist clerk is often the right arm of the specialist broker with whom he works on a daily basis. He must be extremely efficient and computer-oriented. A simple mistake can often lead to errors amounting to thousands of dollars; consequently, in busy markets all major trades are reconfirmed by the clerks.

The Specialist's Book

For many years the specialist's book was the specialist's exclusive domain. It is a recording of buy and sell orders that the specialist accumulates from the floor brokers, and the price and quantity at which each broker would like his order executed. But today, the book is computerized. Essentially, this new electronic book is now open to all the brokers on the floor and is distributed electronically to traders outside the NYSE. Personally, I view this as a very good idea because it gives all brokers a chance to have equal information. This information is then passed on to the public, including both the large institutions and Aunt Minnie in Utah.

Specialists also worry about the small investor; we want to bring the public back to this marketplace. We want to give them every opportunity to get the best execution possible because their 100 shares are part of the 5,000, 10,000, or 100,000-share pieces bought and sold by mutual funds, banks, and other institutional money managers.

The World of the Floor Broker

$2 Brokers

Besides the specialist broker, there are two other types of brokers on the floor of the NYSE—$2 brokers and house brokers. Many large brokerage firms on the Street employ additional $2 brokers when necessary. Two-dollar brokers usually maintain four to six accounts, such as PaineWebber, Merrill Lynch, Goldman Sachs, Pershing, and Prudential, and they are paid strictly for their execution. They are referred to as $2 brokers because years ago, they received $2 for every 100 shares they executed. Currently, their compensation is considerably below this $2 per 100-share level. They work extremely hard and under much duress, with their main duties being the communication of detailed information from the specialist to their account firms.

Some $2 brokers do extremely well and own their seats. Others have to lease a seat, which presently runs about $90,000 annually. They also have to employ a clerk and pay dues and other mandatory expenses. Therefore, a $2 broker who leases a seat has to make at least $150,000 a year just to cover overhead. But in low volume markets, many are not netting their monthly expenses. Two-dollar brokers work extremely hard, taking little time off. They are also under enormous pressure from their accounts off the floor, who are squeezing them for even lower execution costs. It is a pressure-filled existence, as their judgment and ability to attain the best execution possible for their customers are under constant scrutiny. There are some commission brokers who specialize in different areas of the NYSE floor. Often, one broker will work exclusively in the area of a certain specialist firm, executing orders for several members firms. By concentrating in one area, the broker will get a continuous picture of certain stocks, thus increasing his transactional opportunities. Walking away from the crowd for a moment can mean missing that big block. Seconds can be extremely instrumental in our business.

Death by Error. A $10,000 or $20,000 error is not uncommon for the $2 broker. In a busy crowd, amid 30 or 40 brokers screaming bids and offers, this independent floor broker has to be extremely accurate and double check each execution to avoid any errors, which could be sizable. If by mistake a $2 broker is on the same side of a trade, that is two sellers or two buyers are on the same side, it could cost a substantial amount of money. In fact, on October 19, 1987, a $2 broker experienced a $125,000 matching error during the intense trading volume and price fluctuations. He was on the same side as the opposing broker.

House Brokers

Not all floor brokers have the same trading responsibilities. For example, Merrill Lynch employs house brokers who deal solely in large blocks — 10,000 shares or more. These block orders also can be in the hundreds of thousands of shares. Others specialize in the smaller trades from 1,000 to 10,000 shares. Other orders often come through the automated Designated Order Turnaround (DOT) system. With the DOT system, brokerage firms electronically send their small orders (generally up to 2,000 shares) to the specialist post, where the specialist executes their order at the prevailing market price. Once executed, the order is electronically routed back to the broker's office. It takes less than 30 seconds from any part of the country, or even overseas, to execute a DOT order. The advantage of the DOT system is speed of execution and direct reporting back to the customer. Almost all program trading is done through the DOT system because all orders are executed at approximately the same time with the pressing of one button.

Turmoil in the Trenches

Specialists can also suffer their own share of fiascos. Six years ago, Cities Services, one of our stocks, was a prime takeover stock. There were many suitors: T. Boone Pickens of Mesa Petroleum, Occidental Petroleum, even Ivan Boesky, just to mention a few. The takeover situation went on for about two years, with the stock reacting in treacherous up and down cycles. And for about two years, at least two million shares were traded daily, and this was without the computerized trading strategies that exist today. The stock went from 22 to 48, back to 27, up to 54, and back to 26.

We were so busy, we had three or four of our specialists simultaneously handling the action, plus seven clerks processing the paperwork in the booth. The orders just flowed in all day. Each morning, we had to psyche ourselves up, as if we were a team preparing to play that big game. It was both a physically and mentally draining experience. We would often open the stock with a million shares either up or down $3 and proceed to trade another 3 or 4 million shares after that. This was one of the busiest crowds I have ever encountered. It was intense hand-to-hand combat with a crowd of frenzied traders. We were in the trenches with 100 brokers trading at once, and no place to run or hide.

Situations became chaotic anytime a piece of news came out that positively or negatively affected the takeover picture. Arbitrageurs were buying and selling millions of shares on the exchange on ideas, news, or just plain rumor. Because of the sheer complexity of the situation, I had my two biggest, huskiest partners stand beside me, acting as guards, because when 100 brokers came at me, they would pin me up against the post. And because of this intense trading, our firm's position was often not known until it was completed and confirmed an hour after the market closed. It was not uncommon for our position to be in error from 50,000 to 100,000 shares. Due to the five-day clearance procedures at that time, trading errors between brokers were in the tens of thousands of dollars, and sometimes more than $100,000. Thankfully, at present we have one-day comparisons, which minimizes the possibility of large errors.

One day in Cities Services we came in long; I think it was around 60,000 shares. The stock opened at 10:30 at 52. At 1:00 in the afternoon, when the stock was up $2, my clerk leaned over to me and nervously whispered: "Mr. Scavone, yesterday on the opening by error I paired off two 50,000-share sell orders," which meant we were long an extra 100,000 shares due to a clerk's error! "At what price?" I asked. "At 52!" This stock was now selling at 54½. Adding that to my opening position, I was then long 200,000 shares at 50. I turned around and said to my partner, Tony Napoli, "Tony—start selling and don't ask questions!" We sold the stock steadily making over $250,000 on the error. The employee who made the error was given a two-week vacation in Bermuda. Of course, if it had gone the other way, he would not have enjoyed where we sent him!

In the heat of battle, when the floor is in a frenzy, the specialist always strives to attain crowd control. Often, 50 or 100 brokers rush the specialist post, all trading a single stock. In times as this, the specialist shows his talent by maintaining a continuous and liquid market. In this type of frenzied atmosphere, whenever there is a sale, a quick loud quote in size by the specialist forces the hand of the other bids and offers in the trading crowd. Actually, this first loud quote with size shakes up the frenzied floor brokers. In other words, the specialist must "shock the crowd," forcing them to take a moment to look at their orders.

It is under this pressure that the professional trader shows his real talents. You can be excited, but you should never lose control of what you want to do. You cannot panic, and you must have a predetermined game plan in the event the stock should plunge or move up in an abnormal manner. The specialist must always maintain crowd control over the traders. He must be the lion tamer in the cage.

On another occasion, I came in on a Friday with a large opening position: I was long 85,000 shares of Cities Service—which was still in play—selling at around $48 a share at the time. That morning, I passed a Franciscan nun, Sister Teresita, whom I'd known for about 20 years, sitting by her familiar spot in front of the Exchange. Sister Teresita was there winter, spring, summer, and autumn, and we became very friendly. Every Friday morning, she would sit on her wooden folding chair, with her saintly look in her brown garb, rosary beads in her hand and the alms basket on her lap.

Every Friday morning I would pass Sister Teresita, give her a smile and a few dollars. This particular morning, the one where I had that large Cities Service position, I gave her a $10 bill and whispered in her ear, "Sister, for special intention." She nodded at me, and started to fervently pray with her rosary beads. I then confidently walked into work. But before the opening, we were hit with some extremely negative news; a few of the takeover parties withdrew their bids. Cities Services proceeded to open down 4½. I lost $350,000 that day.

On certain days, however, Sister Teresita would be at the PATH train station in the World Trade Center. The following Monday morning there was Sister Teresita with her alms basket, saying her rosary. She looked at me smiling and I walked over to her. I said, "Sister, one of your beads is missing!" The nun looked at me; she didn't know exactly what I meant but she got the general idea.

Trading Halts

As a specialist, you desire nothing more than the chance to be swept into that energy of the crowd, the million-shares-in-an-hour excitement in your stock. You do everything in your power to maintain that auction market, and the last thing you want is the trading in your stock halted. Not that it is a disgrace, but no specialist wants to be shut down unless it is by Exchange request, when some extraordinary news is about to become public.

Therefore, explicit to the operations of the Exchange are the rules and regulations by which every market participant must abide. We keep an eye on the floor with the help of our stock watch and surveillance departments. If anything unusual occurs, we never hesitate to bring in a floor governor. A floor governor might be called in when a stock is under heavy selling or buying pressure when there is no apparent news out. The governor could ask the market surveillance department to contact the company and ask for a comment on what is going on. Maybe there are merger talks beginning or breaking off; perhaps they are about to release bad earnings or cut the dividend, and maybe somehow the news has leaked out. Sometimes, all trading is immediately stopped because it gives the upstairs traders time to notify their customers of the news and to place them on an equal footing with the insiders.

So when there is extraordinary news pending on a stock, trading in that issue is often temporarily halted. In other words, they want Uncle Ernie in Utah to have the same shot as Bobby Scavone the specialist or the member firm traders on the upstairs desk. When the unusual occurs, it is the duty of the Exchange to notify the floor governors and to determine whether or not to halt trading. If the action ever really gets out of hand and crowd control is lost, any governor may take immediate action and halt trading.

All trading-halts news is published on the ticker tape, and after that, the specialist separates the incoming buy and sell orders. When sufficient orders accumulate, he publishes an indication on the tape as a wide quotation, which reflects the direction of the reopening. Within fifteen minutes of the published indication, the specialist then would telescope the first indication with a second indication with a closer spread, more reflective of the price area where the stock will reopen. The reopening price will reflect the buy or sell imbalances.

However, not all markets stop trading. When trading is halted, it is because it is in the best interest of the investing public. In some cases, the over-the-counter market continues their trading while the New York Stock Exchange and regional markets are waiting for new inseminations.

The Obligation

In many foreign exchanges, the specialists are dealers, not obligated to fill the differences; they have no obligation to risk their capital. We specialists, however, cannot walk away from the market—that is the difference. As we did on Black Monday, Terrible Tuesday, and Black Friday, we are obligated to maintain fair, orderly, and continuous markets and to act as principal when necessary to provide proper liquidity at all times. We take our lumps and accept the mandate to open a stock. By not performing his job, a specialist could lose the franchise in the security.

Some critics might argue that the market could be solely executed electronically—taking out the human interface. But that is certainly easier said than done. The reality is that the auction market system provides the best depth and liquidity and, most important, the best opportunity to fulfill an investor's stock buying and selling programs. This liquidity is augmented by the fact that all buyers and sellers are coming into a single, centralized marketplace. There are about 1,925 stocks listed on the NYSE, and not all are General Motors or IBM in terms of liquidity. What if you had a Capital Cities Broadcasting selling for over $400 a share, and there are hardly ever any substantial bids or offers in the book. Tell me how you can trade that electronically? You can't do it. Without the presence of the specialist, there would be an incredible amount of illiquidity in hundreds of Exchange traded issues. Even in Capital Cities Broadcasting, the specialist has a 3,000-share guideline which he is obligated to follow at certain levels.

Resolving Conflicts

The New York Stock Exchange is a self-regulatory organization. The well-qualified staff of the NYSE and the approximately 200 floor officials who are members of the NYSE all attend special classes on rules and regulations. The sixteen floor governors (composed of eight commission brokers and eight specialists), as well as four floor directors, all knowledgeable veterans elected by the NYSE members, share the responsibility of maintaining a market within the strict rules and regulations of the NYSE, providing the best execution for all customers, whether large or small.

Besides being managing partner of my firm, I am a governor of the NYSE. During the trading day, permission is needed for certain stop orders, trading halts, unusual pricing gaps, and many other situations that require official approval. The governing team is also responsible for resolving controversies between members, errors in prices or number of shares traded, instituting crowd control when some spontaneous information is disseminated, and maintaining overall floor etiquette.

The more serious errors or conflicts are referred to a panel of three governors or to a special arbitration committee, which can result in censures, fines, or both. All of these mechanisms help the Exchange to maintain broker integrity and public confidence in the auction market system.

Rating the Specialists

The reasons why customer satisfaction is paramount to the specialist can be summarized in one word — ratings. The specialists' rating system was the single most important instrument for creating this situation. Each quarter, all specialists are anonymously rated by their customers and the floor brokers, for their ability to create and maintain continuous and liquid markets in their stocks. The ratings play a significant role in the determination of new stock allocations on the NYSE, the life blood for every specialist firm. Many listings each year are lost to mergers and acquisitions, with approximately 150 new issues being listed each year. Every specialist firm fights tooth and nail for a new listing. But if you are poorly rated by your customers, you have almost no chance of picking up a new listing. Consistently poor ratings can be the death knell for a specialist firm.

Years ago, when I first arrived at the NYSE, an economically disadvantageous situation existed for floor brokers. They were at the mercy of the specialist for obtaining order execution as efficient as it is today. This rating system is extremely effective, creating a situation where floor brokers have effectively made the specialist firms totally customer-oriented. Through this transition, the apparent question is where we go from here? Specialists have a lot of criticism for the ratings, and of course, when you have a system in which you are anonymously rated every three months, you do everything in your power to attain distinguished results.

I believe in the ratings system, in terms of it being a watchdog for a specialist's credibility, integrity, and performance. But does this anonymous ratings system prevent specialists from striving to develop a personal rapport with their floor broker customers? Of course not. We still take our customers to dinner, ball games, and boat rides. That's the American way of salesmanship and the minute you say, "This is my customer," you become a salesman. And salesman do entertain. They entertain in every business in the world. But there are specialists who entertain and still get low ratings.

In the specialist rating system, there are five main functions which dominate the SPEQ ratings. There is a dealer function, a service function, competitiveness function, communications function and an administrative function. No specialist firms ever have a perfect rating as you are always going to have a couple of items that fall through the cracks, and the difference between first and last is generally within a few percentage points.

A floor broker frowns upon a specialist who is a buyer when he is a buyer, and who is a seller when he is a seller. Floor brokers want the specialist to make a contrary market. A specialist is usually a buyer on a market going down, a seller on a market going up. Ninety-two percent of the trades the specialist makes are against the flow of the business. They sell on plus ticks and buy on minus ticks. That is what the customer expects and demands from the specialist.

Everything's Negotiated

As with the rest of Wall Street, commission rates between floor brokers and specialists are negotiated. Most specialist firms differ in their billing rates. We may bill 15,000 shares, maybe 20,000 shares on a 50,000 share execution. That is a negotiated decision between us. When the specialist acts as principal (trading their own account), there is no bill. A member firm spends millions of dollars to develop trading operations, furnish offices, train registered representatives and traders, romance institutions, hire analysts, take advertising space and pay some incredible dollars to air a commercial during the Super Bowl. The above sales promotions generate orders that eventually come to the floor of the NYSE.

Why send orders to the floor of the New York Stock Exchange? Because the NYSE auction market system is the most liquid market and provides the best possible execution to both the buyers and sellers which is the reason why 83 percent of the total marketshare is generated by the New York Stock Exchange.

Lessons from the Crash

Looking back on October 1987, it is still difficult to comprehend the magnitude of what occurred or the magnificent manner in which the entire Exchange reacted during those dark days. We have to remember that on the previous Thursday and Friday, the 15th and 16th, the market dropped about 190 points. Therefore, going into October 19, the entire specialist community already had a tremendous buildup of inventory from the preceding two business days. So when all hell broke loose on Black Monday, our already heavy long positions were exacerbated even further, magnifying our already considerable losses. It did not make any difference if our firm would have possessed $1 billion in capital; nobody had enough money to sustain that market.

But those two dark days strengthened the camaraderie among the entire trading community at the NYSE. The Exchange staff, the clerks, and everybody else involved worked as a team to get through some very scary and sobering moments. But we all survived. And everybody involved was truly proud that he was part of the system that managed to prevail—despite the despair that surrounded us. It was a lesson for all of us involved, and it put the fear of God into many "experts."

The Crash taught a lesson to many brokers, not only in their trading but also in their living habits. Maybe the stock market should never have been selling at 2750 that summer. One thing we do know: many people were living in multimillion dollar houses and driving nothing less than a Jaguar when they should have been driving something less expensive and living in a $300,000 house. But the lesson was learned, and those who have survived are doing extremely well. They will prosper with the continuous innovations of the marketplace.

My remembrances of that one tumultuous week can be summed up with a single story. Tuesday, October 20, we were going into the morning session with an inventory of $50 million worth of stock—a staggering amount for our firm. Our firm was standing on the abyss of disaster. At 5:15 A.M. that morning, I called my partner, John DePiro. John DePiro is our premier trader, born and raised in the Bronx. He admits the closest he ever got to the Harvard Business School was by flying over it on his way to Canada. He answered on the first ring and immediately said: "Bob, what is it?" I responded: "John I just wanted to see if you were worried." And I hung up.

A Memorable Peril

One of my earliest experiences concerning the frailty of the specialist's lot in life occurred about 25 years ago, with the trading activity in Twentieth Century Fox. The stock was expensive—about $75 a share. My partner, George E. Robb, was probably one of the outstanding traders of all times. He was the specialist in Twentieth Century Fox.

During one day, the stock was selling at 73, and someone came in to buy 100,000 shares, a huge block in those days. George worked on the order all day and at the end of the session, he ends up selling the customer 30,000 shares short. The next day the stock is selling at 74, and the same buyer came in and bought another 100,000 shares. The stock closes at 75 that day and George had sold another 30,000 short, and he is now short 60,000 shares.

The third day, the broker comes in again to purchase another 100,000 shares. George is already short 60,000 but he still sells the broker 40,000. George is now short 100,000 shares. The stock is almost at 76 at this point.

On the following day, the floor broker comes to the specialist post and declares: "My last 50,000 to buy; where can I acquire them?" George responds: "I'll sell you the last 50,000 at 76½." Now George is short 150,000 shares at 76½. But fifteen minutes later, the broker comes back and announces: "I want to buy 100,000 shares." By this time, George is in a fitting rage. This mystery buyer was piecemealing his order, leaving George Robb very short and getting killed. George finds out the order is for the same buyer. He demands to speak to this mystery buyer, goes over to the phone, calls up this fellow and says: "Listen you son of a bitch, I thought you said this was your last 50." The buyer responds: "I lied." George says: "You want to know something? At least you're honest." And he hung up. Georgie lost a ton of money, but episodes like this occurred constantly!

Conclusion: I Could Have Been a Cop

Looking back, I almost never became a specialist. Before going into the service in 1951, I took the New York City police exam. Out of 17,000 applicants, I came out in the top 100, in both the written and physical sections. Upon returning from the service, I was called to become a policeman in New York City. I quit my job as a specialist clerk at Walters, Peck and Co. The next day, I awoke at 6:00 in the morning ready to go to the Academy. I looked into the mirror and contemplated: "Bobby, do you really want to become a cop?"

I sent the Academy a telegram, asking them to grant me a one-year extension. That morning, I proceeded back to the floor of the New York Stock Exchange and asked if could I have my job back. The partners very happily said: "We didn't think you were going to become a cop anyway, Bobby."

That was the best decision I've ever made. But to this day, my mother-in-law, who comes from County Monahan in Ireland, has never forgiven me. She reminds me: "Bobby, you could have been a police captain by now."

I think I would have been a pretty good cop.

CHAPTER THREE

JAY MANGAN

The Evolution of the Institutional Trader

Institutional or buyside traders carry out the final step on an asset management organization's investment process. After the investment idea has been created and a portfolio manager decides to act on it, buyside traders go into the market to transform the idea into reality. They are also often a catalyst of this process, because they are the pipeline to the Street for ideas, news, rumors, and opportunities.

Jay Mangan has had the unique perspective of watching the evolution of securities trading, both as the head trader of a large brokerage firm in the 1970s and as the director of equity trading at a major investment management organization for the past 10 years. Mangan has had a particularly long and colorful career on both the buy- and sellsides of Wall Street. Since beginning his career in Chicago in 1964 at A.I. Jablonski & Co., Jay has been recognized as one of the industry's most articulate spokesmen, never shying away from airing his opinion on a variety of industry related issues. He was director of Mitchell Hutchins' trading desk during the May Day revolution and the advent of negotiated commissions in 1975. After an extended hiatus from the business, when he became involved in local Connecticut politics, Jay reappeared on Wall Street in 1981, and has been running the equity trading desk of a major financial institution since his return. He has served on numerous industry committees, and is currently sitting on a New York Stock Exchange panel that is looking into the specialist system.

In this chapter, Jay will trace the evolution of the buyside trader, from the order clerk of the 1960s and early 1970s to the essential role he or she plays at many investment institutions today. Mangan has survived, and even thrived in, the turbulent 1980s and 90s, by redefining the role that the buyside trader can play, and by his unyielding determination to ensure the trading function as an integral asset of an institutional investment organization's research or portfolio management.

Additionally, Mangan also traces the evolving professionalism of the institutional trader, and how the trader must continue to strive to get his or her due for the value added brought to the table. For no matter how far the institutional trader has advanced over the past 25 years, he or she is still in the process of achieving full recognition within the money management profession for the contributions brought to the investment process.

The Continuing Evolution

Today, the transaction process has become a formidable responsibility unto itself. Despite a buyside trader's increased ability to impact on the investment mechanism, the transaction itself—the ability to access the markets and get the best price in the most advantageous fashion—has become fraught with peril. How and why has this era of perilous trading evolved?

The Age of Innocence

In the "age of innocence" of the 1950s and early 1960s, there was clearly only one form of transactional access—the auction market. In fact, the position of the institutional trader didn't really start to change until the arrival of the block trading business in the early 1960s. Before then, everything was based upon old school ties; salesmen got business from people at institutions because they were in the same fraternity, or because the brokers maintained big credit balances at their banks, or the broker sold their mutual fund shares, or they had good hockey seats.

The modern age of institutional trading only began after May Day, 1975. Before May Day, all a buyside trader could do was hire a broker to deliver his (female buyside traders—or sellside for that matter—were practically unheard of) order to the floors of a stock exchange where they would then be subject to the laws of supply and demand as determined by the specialist's book. This is all the open outcry system offered, and the buyside trader attempted to serve his client by trying to hire the most efficient brokers.

Then, efficiency was paramount: the buyside wanted a broker who was clearly a force on the New York Stock Exchange floor and to whom the specialist would give his best. That was about as far as a trader could go. Perhaps your broker might be given more of an ear by the specialist and the specialist might be willing—albeit very shrewdly—to provide his own capital to smooth out a transaction. And perhaps that would enhance your transaction. This was the only tangible and indirect way an institutional trader could add value. By definition, his role was limited.

The driving force in a brokerage firm's institutional trading organization, which then was known as an order room, was usually the institutional salesmen. He would stand in the back of the order room, jingling the change in his pocket and haranguing the order clerk, as the sellside trader was then called, to make sure he was calling his counterparts at the institutions often enough to provide the opportunity to give him an order. The sellside trader would never really ask for the order, but he would get on the phone enough to present himself to his client—in this case just another order clerk, his like number who, previously to that job, probably was a bank teller or an operations clerk. In fact, if you scratch any trader, buyside or sellside, who has been in the business 25 years or so, underneath you will find some very, very humble origins.

Building the Research Product

In the late 1960s, the first elements of the modern institutional brokerage process began. The first step was to develop a product: hire analysts and develop a research service that could be marketed to institutions. The second step was to develop an institutional sales force consisting of younger business school graduates, dynamic ex-athlete types, people who were really salesmen and not ex-retail brokers or ex-administrators who had old pals at famous banks. The final step was to build the cash register, the trading room (or more appropriately in those days, the order room), complete with order clerks who could generate commission revenues to pay for the product.

Efficiency was the heart of this process—offer the client a practical mechanism by which he could come and pay what was hopefully a specified price for the product that was being built and marketed. If you were inefficiently accessing the established auction market and didn't have good floor brokers, there would be sufficient reason not to give you business. Therefore, the first major concern the sellside addressed when building the institutional sales machine was to construct it to allow an efficient commission capture from the institutional side.

A Tenuous Existence

Before post–May Day institutional trading, any buyside trader's attempt to add value to the investment process took an incredible amount of courage. The only real way to accomplish this was to either hold a sell order out of the market, because you thought the market was going up, or to act more quickly and price the order, though that particular affirmation and the ability to price merchandise firmly, was not granted to the buyside trader until much later. The function in these days — make no mistake — was clearly a mechanical one, and if a buyside trader added anything more, it was really at his own peril. If he did better, he didn't garner any praise or benefit, neither financial nor psychic reward. And if he did worse, of course, it could only accrue to the tenuousness of his job within the investment function. There was a very sharp downside and a very limited upside.

Most were never recognized. The traders did it strictly for personal reasons: to provide, at least in their own minds, a degree of professionalism, of making money for the client, of being in the investment process. This was very much not a part of the structure at all. In fact, if he did wrong, the typical answer from the portfolio manager would be, "I told you to sell that stock. Why did you wait?" And if you did wait and you did do the right thing and you did sell it much higher, there would be no comment, no approbation, *nothing* from the portfolio manager. The timing of the order entry was considered luck, either good or bad. It would only be the personal satisfaction of knowing that you sold it at the right time. Of course, the client never knew.

The First Professionals

Twenty-five years ago, you could have counted on one hand the number of true traders on the buyside. Perhaps the group that best personified buyside professionalism was the Boston trading community. It was a closely knit group of traders who moved with a singleness of thought. Interestingly, this group of traders pushed one another to a higher level of performance, and instilled a great amount of peer pressure to abide by the high standards set by its leaders, Frank Mullin of Putnam, Tommy Thompson of MIT, and Miller Laufman, and subsequently Bill Devin, of Fidelity.

But what you were more likely to find were simply superior traders such as Ron Ivory of Morgan Bank, true professionals who were never really handed the mantle of professionalism that they deserved from their organization. Unfortunately, Ivory was recognized as important only because he was at Morgan Bank and controlled a lot of commissions. But Ron was one of those guys who took the personal risk of holding out an order or pricing an order and he just happened to have the talent and skill to be right more than he was wrong. So he really was the kind of trader who epitomized the highest level that you could aspire to in those early days. It's also important to note that Ron Ivory was also probably the least impressed or the least entertained guy in the business. Brokers almost sold their souls just to get him out to lunch. He immersed himself in the stock market and spent time with only those brokers he thought could most benefit his organization. Period. He really wasn't recognized by the industry; he was working in an era of mechanical trading. No organization gave the proper affirmation to its head trader that he deserved.

Clark Ridgely

The very first institutional trader to really become the kind of benchmark or watershed of the age of specialization on the buyside was Clark Ridgely. Clark was a trader at Channing American General in Houston, Texas, back in the early 1970s. He was probably the first securities trader ever to come out of Harvard Business School, certainly on the buyside, maybe on both sides. He thrust himself into an organization that first accepted him as having the ability, by dint of his education and background, to impact the firm's bottom line, and of having the smarts and the shrewdness to simply trade better than everybody else; he could get more eighths and quarters for his firm. That became an organization's first recognition.

Ridgely's superiors also quickly realized that since Clark was so sharp and so canny, he was even going to develop a better relationship with brokerage firms that would enable him to receive priority treatment. This was the second recognition of buyside excellence: the ability to get preferred treatment, the highly elusive first call, and the so-called use of capital, thereby greatly benefiting the organization's ability to execute at better prices with greater liquidity.

Much of this of course, was driven by an ability to pay. But professionalism also contains many unmeasurable factors: the manner in which you conduct yourself as a buyside trader; your treatment of the Street; the ability to treat your fellow workers as professionals; and the necessity of being honest, consistent, and having a good long memory about where the rewards should go. This was all something that Clark Ridgely achieved.

Back in 1973, Clark created a program in his organization by which he had a guest trader. With the strong support of his organization, he would allow some sellside traders, fairly well-known folks such as Jay Perry of Salomon Brothers and Bob Mnuchin of Goldman Sachs, to come out to Houston. The guest traders would actually run the desk for a day, taking the orders as they were passed on by the portfolio managers, being given a list of commitments, both real and moral, in terms of where the commission dollars ought to go, and going out there to try to get the best execution possible for the organization for that one day.

It was an enormous responsibility. Up until then, and even now to a certain extent, buyside trading desks were similar in conduct to a nuclear reactor in the hold of an aircraft carrier, in terms of the personnel who were allowed access. I can only say from my experience with Clark that it was frightening. I did all right, only because the function of getting a better price was something both the buy- and sellsides really understood. But being able to recognize responsibilities in terms of which brokers you owed, and then operating within that budget, that was really strenuous. In that regard, I was not an all-star. I would always err on the side of best execution and deviate from the list. And I think that is something I carry through to my current operations, that the trade is the thing.

The Buyside Powerhouses

Clark really innovated, showing the world that the buyside was someplace where a trader could be a professional, be rewarded, impact the bottom line, and do all the things that one didn't associate with the job. Soon other folks innovated by exploiting the sheer power inherent in their organizations. Frank Mullin of Putnam was and still is a great trader who really had a positive impact on his organization because of the power he earned and commanded within the firm. He was in the right place at the right time and he knew the right people, whatever the circumstances were. He turned out to be as powerful as any portfolio manager in his ability to get things done; he could use the velvet glove or the armored fist. So Frank Mullin became somebody you didn't mess with. You made sure he got the right reports; you made sure he got the first call.

Other people were powerful by dint of the sheer number of dollars they passed out, while others' power was based on their brains and the ability to outguess the competition, and their ability to intelligently access the Street. Some traders were powerful in terms of their ability to chisel the Street; they were probably the most hideous, the kind you feared because of their total lack of ethics. Unfortunately, they are far from an extinct breed.

The Dark Side of the Buyside Trader

While many traders used their power for their organization's benefit, others were autocrats who realized the power they wielded through commission dollars. Some surrounded themselves with a swarm of sycophants, where the name of the game clearly became receiving rewards for commissions given, whether in the form of hockey seats, airline tickets, or even money. Some of these were clear cases of abuse that resulted in litigation or jail terms. A spate of these episodes came to light in the early 1970s.

At this time, I was a broker for Jablonski & Company and, somewhat naively in retrospect, didn't know the boundaries of what one couldn't do as a trader, either sell- or buyside. You must understand there were limits on sellside traders as well. They were also essentially considered clerks, with no impact on the bottom line. But being an entrepreneur, I took a different perspective. When operating with a client, if I saw an opportunity to present myself in a better light, or if a client might even ask for some sort of favor or another, I was given the ability to perform because I owned part of the firm and I didn't have to ask anybody. So I, like many of my brethren, wandered through the mid-1960s and early 1970s, innovating my own set of ethical standards as I went along. But in defense of the trading community in these early days, not much had been stated clearly by the regulators or the firms themselves, as to what exactly a trader could and could not legally do.

For example, when I would make a trip to New York from Chicago to visit our clients, there was one fellow who never failed to take me out to his local supper club. He was part of an institution where the trader was not recognized as contributing any added value, and he was certainly not compensated anywhere near the rest of his colleagues. This trader would invite me to his club for lunch, where I would compensate him for the bill as the lunch would go on his tab as a member. He would then, unbeknownst to me, take that tab and present it to his organization as a business expense; he really did have his cake and eat it too.

To add insult to injury, on the way back to his office from one of these unique dining experiences, we would stop at a cigar store, where he would express his desire for a box of only the finest cigars. Another $50 expense. It turned out to be a costly lunch.

These were innocent times, but also dark times. There was a trader in the midwest who became very famous for his tricks. For example, he would take a broker to lunch, have a steak, and then ask for a raw one to take home! One of my clients used to take live lobsters home.

In retrospect, these episodes were sad; honestly, these vignettes were not dripping from moral turpitude. But even if a few traders accepted some minor form of graft or payola, there were plenty who represented their clients and organizations to the best of their ability, right down the line. They just viewed the little things received from brokers as fringes, not directly bearing on or relevant to the amount or the ability to do business with a certain broker. That very clearly is a difference.

There were two kinds of buyside traders. Some responded to the frills and let you trade with them a lot more easily than anyone else. They hit the bid a lot more quickly and flooded you with business. And there were the other guys who treated you just as tough as the next guy, but of course, availed themselves of all the fringes in the business. They somehow rationalized that this was their way of catching up: the hockey tickets, the French restaurants, the Broadway shows, and a live lobster to take home—they probably could rationalize it all.

The Buyside Duality

There were other abuses as well. There were, and clearly are, substance problems. There was infidelity and divorces. All this flowed from a frustration that existed on the buyside in the 1970s, where there was just too much of a dichotomy between the work environment and the trader's home life. On the trading desk, you were a king to be courted by the brokerage community; you could come to work and impact markets by the sheer weight of your numbers, impact socially on your brethren on the sellside by granting orders in large magnitude for various firms. After work, you could dine at "21," sit ringside at the best fights and on the blue line at the Ranger game, mix and meet movie stars whose husbands might be in the business, in short, to be surrounded by an atmosphere that was almost fiction.

But on the other hand, you'd have to go home at night to your blue collar neighborhood, to that little three bedroom Cape and your very ordinary wife and kids . . . to some great extent, it was almost an impossible existence for some. Again, it related to compensation and socialization. While you were a king to the sellside, you were often a schmuck to your own firm: "Buyside trader, you're not important. You're not part of the process. You're just a clerk — do what you're told. You're the last step in the process — just don't mess it up." And that was it.

Drawing the Line

The business eventually developed standards to identify what was and what wasn't legitimate. In the mid-1970s, the government regulatory bodies, through either renewed ardor for policing the industry or some glaring abuses that appeared in the headlines, developed an all-encompassing witch hunt that netted some very big fish, as previously discussed.

The New Abuses

Conferences and other boondoggles were eventually deemed fair game as long as you paid the airfare. Very quickly the world came to one thought. Perversely, the old style of abuses have disappeared in favor of the modern abuses — a total lack of morality — that have resulted in some incredible cases of insider trading.

Interestingly enough, most of the current spate of abuses have occurred on the sellside; although Ivan Boesky was clearly an exception. Today, buyside traders as a group are probably more professional and, perhaps, more honest than their sellside counterparts. That has to do with the change in compensation for the buyside trader, not with a burgeoning morality, but with improved compensation and with identification as a professional within the process. These are the important points. The buyside is being rewarded more appropriately. Many are deemed to be impacting the bottom lines and impacting the investment process, providing a psychic reward not previously acknowledged.

The Beginning of Broad Recognition

Incredibly, the real catalyst for the professionalism of the buyside trader was May Day, 1975, the beginning of the era of fully negotiated commission rates. Incredible, because the ability to negotiate rates was not and still should not be the benchmark of adding value to the process. Still, many buyside traders, less proficient or efficient, viewed this event as the real hook on which to hang their hat, in terms of adding value to the process. But their ability to negotiate eventually became a mechanical function. Negotiating the commission became a rather pointless exercise soon after May Day, as the rate very quickly sunk or rose based on the level of business.

Still, the rest of the world saw this as the first time there was a variable to the investment transaction, one that the buyside trader could easily impact. Ironically, the world did not realize nor care that this trader had had an impact on the process throughout these many years by buying and selling at the right price at the right time. May Day opened the doors to recognizing the buyside trader as a factor in the investment mechanism, even if it was something so mundane as negotiating rates from ten cents to a nickel.

The May Day Revolution

When May Day first kicked in, firms were aligned in different price levels with respect to their perceptions as to what their research product actually cost. Some firms were resolute and strove to keep that negotiated rate at a high level. The larger firms that committed capital, the Goldmans and Salomons of the world, were going to try to hold the rate at a higher level.

During the days leading up to May Day, all the major brokerage firms had meetings. They innocently thought that they could arrive at a new — perhaps slightly lower — rate level, even though it was fully negotiated, because they thought they could impose upon their clients the ability to recognize that their research product cost a certain amount — and that's just the way it was going to be.

When May Day finally arrived, it happened to be a particularly active day. Traders would holler over to me, "I have a 20,000 share trade; client wants to do it for 15 cents." There was a pre-conceived kind of level which did not want to go below. And that was an executive committee decision at our and other firms because we thought that if it just became a free-for-all scenario, we would simply be "devaluating the peso" every day, something we wanted to avoid. We wanted to make sure we had the level of profitability built into our trades and that our traders should fully understand that. As I recall, we didn't want to go below 15 cents, which quickly became the industry standard. But there were some institutions — and still are — that took particular pleasure in trying to back the Street up against the wall. They thought, and I think understandably so, that their value to their own organization was to really wheedle the brokers as far down as they could.

Shopping the Order

During the first few days of negotiated commissions, some clients shopped their orders from firm to firm. It is ironic that the markets then would stand still long enough for a buyside trader to be able to shop a 25,000 or 50,000 share order door to door. That was a fairly significant block back when total daily markets were still about 25 million shares a day. Yet a buyside trader could take that block to various firms and generically identify it: "I have a $50 stock, a big cap stock, an electronic stock (or however he wanted to describe it), and I want to trade it for x cents per share; will you do it?" The firms would just simply give a yes or no.

Because of this window shopping mentality, the Mitchell Hutchins desk established a series of hand signals and code words to smooth out the process so it didn't seem to the client, as it did in many other brokerage firms, that there was a management decision going on for every single transaction. That's what we did not want to portray. We wanted to depict strength, a oneness of thought, and an industry without price fixing or collusion. But within a week, the free fall was established.

Firms which had lower costs very quickly stepped in and brought the commission rate down to their own level. The age-old, time-honored way of competition is through price cutting, and that very clearly happened. Wall Street never was a club with regard to pricing its product to the client. It was always "Screw thy neighbor and capture that volume," which happened very quickly. An interesting aside on that fateful day was that Mitchell Hutchins brokered probably its largest transaction, a 400,000 share trade of a medium priced stock between a large New York bank and a Midwestern mutual fund. It was an important piece of merchandise, especially in those days; a 400,000 share trade was probably in the top ten of all transactions that had ever occurred up to that point.

It was also important to consider that we were able to trade it on this day only because clients were willing to be more flexible about the entire process. Not only was the rate really negotiated, the whole process became negotiated. Brokers thought more about all the various points of the transaction—how much an institution was willing to tell a broker about their ultimate size, how much you as an institution were willing to tell your broker about exactly how quickly or slowly you would like to trade. People thought in terms of negotiation—not in pennies per share.

Negotiation became a process unto itself. We could make both sides of a transaction see the significance of the trade, not in terms of price per share, but in terms of the sheer ability involved and efficiency for one client to buy his entire transaction, and of course, for a seller to be able to get rid of his entire holdings, both in one shot.

Jay Mangan

The Sellside Adapts

The driving force behind the broad-based professionalization of the trader therefore was not simply the coming of negotiated commissions, but the proliferation of alternatives to the traditional auction market mechanism of the laws of supply and demand. Markets developed through the 1960s and into the 1970s because the mantle of professionalism had been granted to the sellside trader, the former order clerk. He was recognized as able to provide incremental business by having relationships with his like number at the money management institutions. Being bottom-line driven, brokerage firms quickly recognized that increment and paid to attract it. They armed their sales traders with a liberal expense account and the ability to offer a little bit of a firm's capital to complete an order, to make it easy for the client to get all his business done today so that he didn't have to carry over an open order of a small number of shares to the next day. At first all that was somewhat innocent, but then some shrewd observers figured out that they could create their own markets and fulfill their own prophecy.

The capital facilitation game arose after the give-up was eliminated in 1968. Before 1968, it was legal for various firms to accept a commission from, say, a mutual fund, and to take perhaps 40 percent of that commission and put it into a so-called bank, to be distributed periodically at the client's request to certain firms or NASD dealers who sold their mutual fund shares. The mutual fund industry was very negatively impacted after the give-up was kicked out in 1968 because many funds didn't have front-end loads, just a selling concession. Until 1968, the real way you got the Mom and Pop shops in Keokuk, Iowa, to sell your fund shares was to give them a piece of the action. It was perfectly legal, and Bob Jablonski, Boyd Jefferies, and others had a fine time doing it. All they had to do was be members of the Detroit Stock Exchange, which allowed the give-up of 40 percent of the commissions on a per check, per firm basis.

But in 1968, the SEC, in its greater wisdom, decided that there was something immoral about the give-up and legislated against it. Bob Jablonski and I then went to Mesirow & Co. to create an institutional trading organization that, without any real particular driving mechanism such as the give-up, clearly depended upon some form of capital commitment. However, the rest of the world simultaneously recognized this.

These were more innocent days when, clearly, the big money was made through retail brokerage, investment banking, and syndications. But suddenly, the Wall Street world realized that: (a) there is an institutional business; (b) we can no longer get any part of it; and (c) we'd better find a way to access it. If Jablonski and Mangan could make all that money; if Jefferies, Bob Brandt, and Don Tomaso, Don Weeden and others were creating their little cottage industries of third and fourth market firms; if there was clearly enough to feed and populate those kinds of non-mainstream organizations, then clearly there must be a much bigger business than previously realized. Thus dawned the post give-up age, when suddenly those firms that had been benefiting by the give-up, discovered: "Gee, we better put a couple of clerks on the desk, call them traders, have them call these organizations and see if they can't get the business direct." That is how it started. It developed from there to the point of having relationships, complete with expense accounts, limousines, hockey tickets, whatever it took. But then the sellside realized that it took more than merely personal relationships. It took the ability to perform and produce a better transaction for the client. And that meant capital.

The Era of Capital Commitment

Capital committing started very humbly as an add-on, a do-the-client-a-favor facilitation. Firms quickly realized they could generate their own transactions by providing the other side to their institutional customers. Before this point, transactions were really dependent on finding the other side, whether it existed in the specialist's book or with another institution. The Street quickly realized you could almost drive the process by creating it. The entire transactional environment quickly became very sophisticated, and brokers started to commit large amounts of capital. Firms such as Goldman Sachs, Salomon Brothers, and Bear Stearns had always been risk oriented, and they were laughing all the way to the bank, because they were simultaneously creating and cornering the entire institutional business. Then in 1968, with the death of the commission give-up, the rest of the world—wire houses, retail firms, boutiques—got into the institutional business, developing it into a broad industry.

As the rest of the world discovered the miracle of capital commitment, brokers started hiring people who were particularly adept at taking risk. Maybe they had been former floor people, or they were just good sharp Italian kids from Brooklyn who liked to shoot craps. They were equipped with a part of the firm's capital and told to create incremental business. Well, the rest is history. It developed into a business unto itself, leading to the point where the industry is currently heading—toward total dealer markets.

I participated in this evolutionary process during my tenure at Mitchell Hutchins. In 1971, we realized we had a wonderful research product and, while we were thankfully getting paid for it, there wasn't any incremental business generated. We concluded that this increment could be obtained through some form of capital risk and that probably the best way to manage capital commitment would be: (a) to do it in the stocks we knew; and (b) do it with the clients we knew. That is a discipline that the Street has failed to come to grips with, I think, even today. I don't know that we did either, but at least that was our original idea.

As any block trader realizes, there are so many stocks out there to which you could commit capital and a proliferation of clients willing to accept your largess of capital, that it's almost impossible to be everything for everyone at the same time. Therefore, the sellside must maintain an "A" and "B" list of customers. Today, many firms are coming to grips with this reality and are developing their "A" list of clients. Because of the thinness of the commission dollar, there is very little difference between client and broker. The only thing separating us is a nickel a share. We're all at each other's throats, competing with one another. So clients are now picking their favorite brokers, and brokers are picking their favorite clients. We tried to do that back in the early 1970s: think of our favorite clients, those to which we would blindly almost commit anything, knowing that they had the ability and desire to repay if we were injured. Their ability was based in terms of sheer numbers of commissions they controlled, and their desire was based on the goodness of the relationship between our trader and their trader. So we made that cut, deciding who was the "A," "B," and the "C" list.

With Mitchell Hutchins being a research-oriented firm, we were forced to institute these kinds of disciplines. We could not be market makers to the world or market makers in all stocks. We then picked our best analysts, those who were most transactionally inclined, real-time analysts who knew what impact would occur tomorrow in the stocks. We placed our traders together with the analysts, creating a forced relationship: "I want you to be with this analyst; I want you to be his second skin." Starting with the morning meetings, there was at least an hourly update of the markets where the analysts appraised those particular stocks given to him by the trader, and what clients we had interested in his stocks. And there, at least once a week, we had a meeting by which the trader and the analyst got together to share thoughts. This environment helped to create a trader who was more capable in risking capital in those stocks. He developed a relationship with the analyst, and eventually the trader became a mini-fundamental analyst himself. Because he finally understood the ingredients that went into the fundamentals, he could put them together with the market forces and go one better than the analyst.

So the happy result then was fairly low capital risk with the clients in those stocks. Our commissions doubled the first year of our industry specialization coupled with capital risk. Nobody else was attempting anything close to it. We heard nasty comments from the specialists, "Who do you think you are? How can you specialize in our stocks? What are you talking about? This is against the law. . . ." The reaction was just incredible.

Well, it is safe to admit now that it was all done mostly with mirrors and very little capital risk. Mostly it was done through crossing stocks with Denny Engelman's list on the Midwest Stock Exchange. A transaction that started out as a capital risk ended up being absorbed by the market when it was finally presented to the floor, letting us off the hook. That, or we'd be lucky and find the other side when we got hit. Something usually happened to bail us out.

When this venture began, my partners stipulated that my budgeted loss was not to exceed 5 percent of committed capital, with the loss made up through enhanced commission revenue. The industry standard today is somewhere around 15 to 20 percent for capital risk. In fact, our worst year was 2 percent, and our commission business doubled. And the third year we made a little money through positioning, which caused another shrewd observation, which went along the lines of: "If you can make money kind of half-way accidentally, maybe if you really created a business of dealing, you could make money on purpose." Well, that is exactly what Salomon, Goldman and others are accomplishing. Markets have become so complex and large that you've got to have a huge cast of characters to be able to do profitable risk transactions today. You must have derivative traders to help control risk; you need the right analysts. It all takes a lot of horsepower, for these are not innocent times.

Thus dawned the age of risking capital to facilitate transactions. However, not only brokers took advantage of this burgeoning transactional environment. The ultimate client—the pension plan sponsor, the private client, the hedge fund—started realizing that the dawn of fully negotiated rates meant that the buyside trader could have an impact on the transaction process. The money manager started to realize: "Wait a minute, we can impact our profitability through superior trading skills. Boy, these eighths and quarters really add up to something. They are 12½ cents each. Maybe we better start having more professional clerks, call them traders now, arm them with the ability to impact our process, and even pay them too."

The Challenge of Market Access

The era of capital commitment also has created three distinct yet complementary markets that the buyside trader must learn to access to his advantage. In more innocent times, the only market that really existed was the auction market. In modern stock markets, because of the disappearance of the give-up and the coming of fully negotiated rates, the innocence of capital facilitation has evolved into a de facto dealer market, creating a second kind of access that a trader has at his disposal. This is the upstairs market-making capability of brokers, utilizing their own resources to commit to various stocks or groups of stocks, not as block facilitators but as true dealers. And the third adjunct to the specialist and dealer markets is what I call the negotiated market, that of finding the natural contraside of an institution's transaction through an upstairs sales force, whether it be another institution or market buyer of some substance that can accommodate the other side of the block: a non-dealer, but an investor of some sort, whether an individual or institution, which provides capital and interfaces with an institution to reach a mutually agreed upon transaction of price and size. Today, this can be accomplished with or without a broker intermediary, and can even be executed without any human interface, with one of the new electronic crossing systems.

With the auction, dealer, and negotiated markets, the modern buy-side traders must know how to efficiently access each of these markets, and quickly find out which of them is the right one for each transaction. No longer does he or she simply place an order in the hands of the broker and expect him to access the auction market in an efficient manner. Now the buyside trader has the ability to perform as a dealer himself.

Shading the Trade

The buyside trader, because of this evolution in markets, must remove the shackles of his previous order clerk mentality and begin to think in terms of a block trader. Sometimes it is good to hit that bid; sometimes it's better to wait and string out the block. That's really what block traders get paid for. And now the buyside must develop the block trader mentality. Both sides really have the same purpose at the heart of their existence, the ability to transact efficiently either for the benefit of their organization, their client, or the other side of a transaction, depending on who gets the order. In that regard, sellside block traders have the ability, through sins of omission or commission, to make things happen to benefit one side or the other of a transaction. That's how trades happen. They can still, even in this environment of large markets and large volume, rig markets and influence the market's direction. In fact, this can be accomplished now more than ever before, because of the tenuousness of markets, the sensitivity to information, and especially due to the whisper circuit. One can influence the direction of a tick now much more than ever before. In the innocent days when I was running sellside desks, to get a trade off dead center — in other words, if you had a buyer at 25 and a seller at 25¼ and never the twain shall meet — one of the only ways we could influence that transaction, notwithstanding the market's own action unto itself, would be perhaps to call a broker on a regional stock exchange and have him buy stock in New York to influence the action of the tick. If we're 25 to a ¼ and a 1,000 up, we'd get some regional broker come and take the ¼ offering in New York so that the 25 bidder might be influenced to pay the ¼ and do the trade. Today we call it "roughing up the market." Unlike in football, however, there are usually no penalty flags thrown on these plays.

This is all perfectly legal, because if the $2 broker on the regional stock exchange were to buy that stock for his own account and risk, without guarantees from you, without any kind of parking ramifications, then certainly, it's a business judgment on that broker's part: "Well, the guy wants me to affect that stock in New York. I have a reasonable chance of making some money here. Do I have a reasonable chance of getting a trade to print, a reasonable chance of selling it at a profit, taking all those things into consideration, without any guarantees?" It was legal.

Sure there was a nod or a wink, but let's put it this way: it probably wasn't in the spirit of the law. Maybe the letter, but certainly not the spirit. These kinds of unholy alliances still exist today.

Never Give Up Your Franchise

As a buyside trader, if I had only one piece of advice for my sellside counterpart, it would be to never give up your franchise: the people you cover, the clients and the relationships you have. It is a dynamic alliance that must be nurtured daily, or it will never survive. Your relationships can be so easily supplanted by another eager salesman. Another guy is always waiting to step in and be your best friend. So if you have one thing as a sellside trader, you have your franchise. You have your buddies at IDS and at Morgan and Chase, and you do everything humanly possible to keep them your buddies.

My personal relationship with a sales trader friend at a retail-oriented firm perfectly illustrates this friendship factor. He's really a close friend, he's family, he's very much involved. You get cut, he bleeds. I think it illustrates the near confessional approach to the business. This guy really is your priest or rabbi, and you're his. It becomes an association that is so close as to transcend the business. Clearly business is the grease that makes the machinery work, but with this person, it is really only the avenue for the close association. The business, the dollars, does not make any difference from one friend at an IDS or another friend at a Chase, though the income may be so disparate as to be incredible. He may be making $2 million a year from another institution and $100,000 a year from us. Doesn't make any difference. The association is still daily; therefore, the friendship is still nurtured.

And that friendship will always be there because the trust, the honor, and the honesty take the business relationship to a higher level, not just everyday dealing or accessing markets. You've got someone who is really working with and for you.

But a sales trader is in a precarious position, walking that fine line between the client and his own organization. He has to serve two masters. Besides never giving up his franchise, a sellside trader should never fall off that tightrope, the one that every sales trader walks when representing the firm on one side and the client on the other. You have to serve both masters equally. But if you err, always err on the side of the firm. Don't err on the side of the client. That's a sellside trading manager speaking. And I'm sure anyone you ask today will tell you the same thing. Maybe he won't admit it, but he's got to believe that.

But when you are talking about dealer markets, you're fooling with the firm's capital. Now you, Mr. Sellside Trader, must represent your client to the firm and your firm to the client. You can never err too much on the side of the client, and you have to inform your firm about your client's true intentions. You have to take advantage of the market anomalies that allow you to make some money at your client's expense when he is not fully informed of his markets and when he's likely to sell something to you half a point cheaper than he should. You should take advantage of the opportunity, because, without a doubt, someone will get the edge on you many, many other times. You've got to smooth the process out. If you've got a bunch of sales traders merely fronting for their buyside clients all the time, you're going to lose a ton of money. And that is an important facet the buyside trader must understand.

Do the Stock Gods Make Trades Happen?

The ability to shade a transaction one way or another has always been an ability of the Street. However, in the earlier days, I think many clients would either turn their backs, overlook it or, in most cases, just not be sophisticated enough to know that it was going on. There were many on the buyside who thought that the stock gods made things happen, that "it was wonderful that it was a quarter tick" and "isn't it great our trade happened," et cetera. Gee whiz, everybody was happy. Well, I always submitted that it was a sellside trader's divine-like role to be able to shade a trade one way or another and that he should have a long memory. He remembers whose turn it is next; that it was Fidelity's turn last time, and that this time it had damned well better be CIGNA's turn. The broker has to play that role of interlocutor on his desk.

Sacrifice the Smaller for the Greater

Therefore, the unwritten rule of the Street is that, based on the number of trades you have with specific institutions, there ought to be a certain number of times that the large client benefits at the expense of smaller accounts. In other words, you sacrifice the occasional accessor to "the greater good." That's always been the case on Wall Street. We were taught in theology class that when somebody wasn't a Catholic, that person wasn't necessarily going to hell, because he or she was in possession of invincible ignorance. That is, the person didn't know any better. Just take that and extend it a little bit into the brokerage business. The smaller firms that access a broker once a week or once a month — First National of Podunks — provide the cannon fodder for the greater good of the larger institutional clients.

The small fish provides the grist for the mill of the greater client. The J.P. Morgans and the Alliance Capital Managements of the world benefit by a socialism in the business that still very clearly occurs. There's no way a broker can claim that everybody gets equal treatment. Certainly not. A bigger client demands priority treatment, demands to be called first, demands that you disadvantage the smaller client. Why should the large accounts subsidize the cost of supplying all of the research these smaller firms receive from the brokerage community? Alliance Capital Management's price will, and should always, be better.

Choose Your Friends Wisely

To maximize their clout, buyside traders at smaller institutions have to be even a bigger hero to a smaller number of brokers. That's another part of buyside trading management. They've got to be able to understand who has the best resources on the Street for specific jobs. Who's a really good oil trader? Who's a really good purveyor of takeover information? Who's really good at guessing market trends? Who's really good at fundamental or technical analysis? They must pick the ponies and place their bets because they don't have the degree of generosity of larger institutions.

Looking at the development of the buyside trader, we now see a person who has to be capable of dealing not only in the auction market but in the dealer and the negotiated markets. This by itself implies a person who either has always been canny and clever and can just now extend his official abilities and capabilities within the organization, or it requires a newer, smarter person who can express himself to his organization and provide the access to the Street that the firm, by the nature of its commission dollars, should command. Large organizations should clearly have better access. That's just the nature of Wall Street. It's very much a bigger-is-better mentality.

The New Buyside Trader

The role of the new buyside block trader is to professionally represent himself to the Street, to his management, and to the ultimate client—the plan sponsor, the large net worth individual, the foreign government, whoever it may be. He has to prove that he is accessing these markets in an efficient and profitable method and contributing to the bottom line, whether it be in the form of negative market impact, an early research call, proprietary information, whatever it may be. Today it is mandatory to represent this concept to the client. The trader must command a marketing role, both within and outside of the organization, something that has never previously occurred on the buyside. He must be able to market himself to the Street, and prove that, even in an environment of a whole bunch of big fish, he is a prize catch. He must demonstrate that he's a desirable character who represents a deserving organization.

We now see the age of buyside marketing, which has never occurred before. The old game was to hold your hands out, catch the favors of the Street, and then turn them the other way and dump the commissions into the hands of the Street. It was only a two-way function. You didn't have to market yourself. You didn't have to dress well, you didn't have to express yourself, and you didn't have to be publicly visible. That's all changed.

Today, a buyside trader's charge is to represent his or her organization and its clients in a public manner with various trade and regulatory organizations, to get in print, be quoted, be public, be visible, be competitive, and be combative if necessary. I try to accomplish all this, and through our trading, I hope to be clever and canny, placing my organization's clients at an advantage, and utilizing the muscle of the organization, to organize and manage the Street.

The way to accomplish that is to get the first call priority treatment from the Street. This is the way to measure a trading room manager's ability on the buyside. The buyside must demonstrate to their own organizations that they are getting the full bang for their buck. If you're just turning your hands over and dumping out commissions, you're just an order clerk. The smart trader doles them out for value received and favors returned. Your organization can only know how well its performance is relative to its ideas, and relative to how many of the ideas are generated by the trading desk, and how many of those ideas are capitalized on by the trading desk. That isn't measured by outside functions. The trade itself may be measured in a kind of innocent way relative to the day's transactions, the previous day's transactions, and methodologies like that. But how well you're accessing the market and to what extent you're benefiting the organization can only be measured by your firm and that to a great degree is still being sublimated.

Most money management organizations recognize this value, though there is a social apartheid regarding the trader's role within buyside organizations. Many institutions realize the trader's value because they are rewarding traders at or near the level of its portfolio managers or analysts. But they're still not officializing the trader's full participation in the investment process. They are still not telling clients that they manage money with a skilled combination of trading, analysis, and portfolio management. Most likely, they're still saying that we manage money through efficient portfolio management and analysis. Trading is valuable, but is only represented to the client as a mechanical or last-step function, with little or no acknowledgement of added value, more likely as an unavoidable cost.

Is the Client Ahead of the Game?

The ultimate client—especially the pension plan sponsor—is one step ahead of the money manager concerning trading because the client realizes the money manager has been sublimated. Today, the pension fund client has had his nose rubbed in "the facts," according to the Abel/Nosers, SEIs and other consultants to the pension fund world, who have pointed out that trading costs impact the bottom line and are a factor to be monitored. Unfortunately, trading costs are often equated with commission costs, an attitude abhorrent to most professional buy-side traders.

But it is important to note that this almost prehistoric attitude of lowering the commission still exists as a value-added function in the minds of the pension plan sponsor. Many plan sponsors, still so innocent to the trading process, see only the commission as the visible part of that mechanism, and mistakenly place an inordinately high significance on it. They see the transaction purely in pennies per share and not in true trading efficiency or proficiency.

So suddenly, the whole process seems to be becoming short-circuited. The manager is no longer really the master of his fate in terms of how the client views his trading capabilities. The pension fund views the money manager based on his consultant's advice. The money manager has lost it here. He can always present his track record and all that type of marketing information, but in terms of professionally representing his organization top to bottom to the ultimate client, he's lost it because over all these years, almost every money manager has failed to develop his own internal system to measure trading. It's been done outside and beyond the manager's control. The manager has really missed a step.

Can this change? It can, but it's going to require that a manager put forward a record of trading performance to the client. It demands the final coming out of the closet, the ability to present to his client the full three-legged stool. Its going to have to require the manager saying to the client, "We have good portfolio managers and we are whatever kind of investors we are—value, momentum, whatever the hell we are—we've got these phenomenal analysts, superb Street resources, and we have these traders whose performance is measured in such and such a manner. We have finessed the market on these many occasions by our own internal measure. We have gotten the first call and have been able to get out of a block of stock on these many occasions." In other words, true measurement as you would measure a performance of a portfolio manager.

The Opportunities of the Transactional Environment

This also places the onus on the buyside trader to quantify his performance and value to his organization. This has been the problem with trading on both sides of the Street for too many years. Traders have maintained the belief that getting quality transactions is all done with voodoo, or it's magic or a secret. But the reality has to come out in the cold, clear light of day. The professional buyside trader has to identify and qualify his relationships in terms of what they do for him, in recognition of the fact that the buyside trader needs to be compensated in an official sense for the relationships that he's cultivated, for the accesses he's developed to the markets, and for the responsibility he has to his organization.

The buyside trader needs to be recognized for his multiple responsibilities: the ability to not only impact the investment process as the last step, but to be recognized also for the fact that he is very often the first step, developing the opportunity or discovering the trading concept through his good offices on the Street. The modern environment is one of transaction. Typically, the investment environment was to discover an idea, commit to it, and then finally transact. That has changed, probably for all time. In today's markets, an idea, its discovery, and its implementation, may all occur in a single motion, which has led to the development of today's hybrid portfolio trader or trader/manager.

The role model for this kind of professional was developed by the hedge fund. Hedge funds typically invest their own money, and they do it in a transactional sense that was previously considered less than value or good investing. There has been a prejudice against hedge fund trading and management over the years that has finally dissipated, based on the transactional nature of markets. We've become an environment of the bought deal. No longer do we have the lengthy process of determining investment appropriateness for the client and the long-winded development of investment techniques and targets. Clearly there are investment styles that will always remain, but the common denominator now has clearly become the transaction.

Into the Valleys

Markets have become too big, too fleeting, and too volatile not to access them to your own advantage. Clearly, clients are no longer happy with accessing markets in a kind of "look across the valley" fashion. They want their money managers to travel up and down the mountains now, down into the valleys. It's no longer good enough to be able to look on an annual basis and see that the Dow was at 2500 in January and at the end of the year it's at 2600, and to expect appropriate results in your portfolio. Very often the Dow could have been between 2500 and 2600, jumped up to 2800, back down to 1900, rebounded to 2200 and maybe finished at 2600, but you've missed all the transactional ability in the meantime. Clients are no longer happy with that kind of approach. The report card of the investment manager has been shortened from annually to semi-annually to quarterly and eventually, managers will be measured monthly. Sometimes, they already are. An environment of broad and volatile markets that can be more readily accessed by skillful traders trading on real-time information provides new opportunities for the client to achieve superior returns.

But what are the ramifications of all this? More turnover, bigger markets, and more volatility. Volatility with liquidity, if you can accept that, coupled with superior information flow. We will have bigger markets in terms of the ability to move blocks of stock, with the acceptance of volatility—in other words, the onset of true dealer markets and increased investment opportunities and pitfalls, depending on how you access the markets. We may be paying 7 cents a share or more, but at even 2 cents a share, traders will be paying, in transactional terms, a spread. Buyside traders should fully welcome dealer markets and be capable of accessing markets as a dealer. I'm fully prepared to accept a half-point spread in a stock as long as I have the full ability to access all parts of the market, and I am not hide-bound by my organization or my clients to only access one part of the market. This is something that flies in the face of modern stock markets, of the abilities of buyside traders to perform, to become dealers, to become trader/portfolio managers.

The Buyside Profit Center

This evolution of the buyside professional also offers the opportunity for him to impact his organization in ways which would have been thought incomprehensible just a few years ago. He can be a profit center for his organization, offering his services as a hired gun to his firm's current and potential clients. For example, buyside traders have the ability to buy and sell securities for their clients in confidentiality and anonymity on the Street.

The Directed Commissions Plague

My trading desk sits on top of a wealth of investment information: market data, technical research, economic advice, order flow, desirable blocks. I have the capability to be a valuable and strategic investment resource to countless individual and corporate clients. And I am far from being alone in this ability. Scores of other buyside trading organizations can also turn themselves into a strategic profit center if they look outward from their desks and explore the possibilities.

Yet what flies in the face of this is the earmarking of transactions, the proliferation of both soft dollars and client direction of commission dollars for their own benefit. This *must* stop because of the evolution of the market elements as pointed out earlier—auction, dealer, and negotiated. Any one of those markets can provide best execution at any one time. Not one of them can provide best execution all of the time. While everyone will never agree on a definition for best execution, it does exist.

To access markets appropriately, traders must be unfettered, capable of accessing the best one at the time, whether it be the dealer, auction, or negotiated market.

Conclusion: At the Crossroads

As we look at the state of the buyside trader today, we can see him at a crossroads. Never before has he had the opportunity to declare himself, through his actions and abilities, an equal in the entire investment process. The transactional nature of today's erratic markets is tailor-made for the individual who can take this turbulence and let his organization profit from his ability to effectively trade within it and conquer. The buyside trader also has the opportunity to unleash his entrepreneurial yearnings and truly *make money* for both himself and his firm.

The mantle of professionalism has been granted to the buyside trader. It is now up to him to prove himself worthy of shouldering the responsibilities and realizing the opportunities.

CHAPTER FOUR

JOSEPH APISA

The Sales Trader

Joseph Apisa is managing director and head of institutional equity trading for Gruntal and Co., a leading New York institutional and retail brokerage firm. Apisa began his career on Wall Street as a warehouse clerk for Reynolds and Co., gluing buy and sell order pads for the firm's traders on the New York Stock Exchange. From this rather inauspicious background, "an Italian Brooklyn boy with no money, from a relatively poor family, and limited education," Joe perfected the science of being a sales trader, a position he has mastered, having walked the mine fields for over 30 years at a host of illustrious organizations. In 1977 came the turning point of his career when he went to work for Mike Bloomberg of Salomon Brothers as a sales trader in their burgeoning equity trading division. Apisa left Salomon in 1987 to run Drexel Burnham Lambert's equity sales trading operation.

This chapter will explain the role of the sales trader in the entire institutional trading process: what it takes to be a true professional; how to get the business on the tape; and how a good sales trader learns to balance the demands of two competing forces—his client and his organization.

Why a Sales Trader?

The sales trader represents a brokerage firm's entire product to the institutional money management community. His responsibility is to comprehensively and professionally service the buyside across the United States. He is the messenger with the morning research call, the pipeline to the floor of the stock exchanges, the storekeeper with merchandise to buy and sell. If the sales trader is a true master of his craft, he also is a combination priest, rabbi, and psychiatrist, willing to take the most confidential of investment information and treat it with uncompromising loyalty. The sales trader is the middleman, the individual who must interface with both customer and his firm.

The evolution of block trading in the 1960s gave rise to the sales trader. In the early days of the block trading business, position traders talked directly to their customers. Eventually, this line of communications caused concern to securities firms, because they worried about the potential for abuse that might develop from this relationship. Too many problems were arising, and there emerged a need for someone to buffer the relationship between the customer, the trader, and the firm.

To confront this challenge, Wall Street created the sales trader. The sales trader became the link between the brokerage firm and the institutional investor, providing clients with his firm's research capabilities, its vast equities trading network, and the reservoir of liquidity that enables the institution to successfully react to the broker's investment recommendations. The sales trader is the person who knows all facets of every market, and utilizing this wealth of knowledge and industry structure, strives to create liquidity for his institutional clients. The sales trader must be a negotiator and a person who, through consistency at what he does, builds trust between himself and his money management customer. Consistency gets him the call and consistency builds trust. A sales trader walks a fine line between the firm for which he works and the customer he wants to keep. You cannot really dissect it—who really pays the paycheck—the firm or the customer. Without the customer you don't have the business; without the business, you can't work for your firm.

When an institutional customer comes into a firm and wants to buy or sell a big block of stock, it is the responsibility of the sales trader to initiate the pricing process and attempt to find the other side to complete the transaction. The primary objective for a sales trader is, through his negotiating skills and his access to various markets, to create immediate liquidity for his customer base while not damaging or destroying his firm's capital in the process.

A sales trader must maintain a daily equilibrium between customer and firm, practicing his craft constantly. He can learn the basics of the job in a few years, but it will take the rest of his career to perfect his skills and keep up with the constant innovations of the securities business.

Learning from the Veterans

A successful sales trader will always look to pick a pro's brain for little tidbits, compile them, and then couple them with his own abilities. Experience is the greatest teacher, and these skilled and accomplished professionals have a lot to offer. I learned at an early age that the older pro had already been to where I was going, so he had to know much more than I. So I listened.

The Transaction in Action

The sales trader finds an assortment of market forces, coupled with the internal dynamics of his own organization, working against him. For instance, a customer might come to the sales trader, wanting to sell a big piece of merchandise. However, the sales trader's own block desk might already be long the stock or own a position in this industry group when the customer order arrives. Or the sales trader's organization already might have enough capital committed and be hesitant about putting more on the line until they work out of some of their positions and, therefore, may be a seller themselves.

What then follows is a push and shove type situation: the customer's expectation of what he wants to get done at his price level, as opposed to what the position trader is willing to pay, which he obviously believes to be a valid price. To be successful, the sales trader must employ superior negotiating and people skills, enabling these competing forces to arrive at a happy compromise and a fair transaction for everyone. You must be a savvy businessman and also know what you are talking about because if you don't, you won't have any customers and you won't have a job.

When a client calls up and wants to sell 200,000 shares of XYZ Corp., the sales trader goes to the block trader, the individual who controls the position money and capital for the firm. The two then put their heads together and pick a price at which they can be relatively clean on the trade, a price that will make it attractive for the firm to find the natural other side of the transaction. Or, when the trader likes the stock, he may be willing to pay for the block because he detects an upside potential.

The Pricing Battle

The sales trader, if he's smart at what he does, has to know his customer and the parameters between which his customer wants to get his piece of merchandise sold or bought, and, just as critical, how he wants to get it done. And this has to be determined even before walking over to the block trader to initiate discussion. In other words, only after he has established the customer's intentions does the sales trader proceed to go to the position trader and begin the steps necessary to consummate the process. He checks the exchange floor to see if there are any sellers or buyers around, reviews how that particular group is trading, and sometimes even calls his firm's research analyst to see he how he likes the stock. Not until all this is done does he price the merchandise.

And of course, the price may not be exactly what the customer expects. For argument's sake, let's say 32 is the last sale in XYZ Corp. and the market is $31\frac{3}{4}$ to $32\frac{1}{4}$, meaning that the best price you can sell stock is at $31\frac{3}{4}$, and the cheapest purchase price is $32\frac{1}{4}$. The position trader might be willing to pay $31\frac{3}{4}$ for 50,000 shares or $31\frac{1}{2}$ for the whole 200,000 share block. The sales trader then must decide if it would be feasible to go back to present this proposal to the customer without getting him bent out of joint. Sometimes it's a tough call, but every sales trader does all in his power not to lose that trade to a competitor.

However, sometimes the prices to buy or sell are way below the last sale. Pricing the merchandise is key. Knowing where the buyers or sellers are located is crucial.

The Customer—The Key to it All

Know Thy Customer

The clever sales trader should, above all else, know his customer: know his needs, what it takes to motivate him to make that call, and what it takes to move his merchandise. Even at the same accounts, there could be several buyside traders who each have a unique way of operating; you have to know each individual. The sales trader must be sure that he befriends not just one individual, but the whole desk, and must make sure that he services those five people at that one institution as individuals, because they all have different styles. And he must zero in on the individual traders at each account to be effective when that customer calls, no matter which of those five buyside traders calls. The sales trader must maintain a tremendous flexibility to change his style, depending on to whom he is talking. To get that trade on the tape with as little damage to everyone involved, *know what that customer wants and needs*. The two often are not the same.

A sales trader also has to know how the customer expects him to perform. As a trader, you have to listen, but also you must sometimes stop your client from making mistakes. If you can prevent him from buying or selling a stock position at the wrong price or if you can supply him with a bit of information he has missed, then you are performing your job.

Solidify the Relationship

Sales traders are in a service business. But the relationship has to be deeper than that. Above all you must be honest with each client. And when something doesn't turn out right, don't try to cover it up. You must have the courage to say: "Something went wrong. How do we fix it and make it right?"

Once you've established this trust and rapport, there is not much that you need do except exercise your abilities. You will reach the point where your client will say, "I talk to this sales trader rather than those other 200 jokers because I have a relationship with him that I know won't be difficult. I must get the job done because I have to answer to my boss. When I phone this sales trader, he's going to give me 150 percent of his efforts. I think he's the smartest guy around; he knows where the bodies lie, who to call or not to call, and how to salvage a situation that maybe I messed up already."

But each day is different. A trader could perform ten magnificent feats of magic for a client but then have a single screw-up and be on the outs. It's often: "What have you done for me lately?" As a sales trader, you know that you have to go in every day, no matter how great you think you are, and prove yourself all over. You have to remain fine-tuned because everything changes, minute by minute. It's true: *you're only as good as your last trade.*

Wall Street Then and Now

There have been countless changes in the business during my career. The original "money partners" who traded on the floor of the exchanges are now all upstairs, concerned with administration, investing, investment banking, as well as trading. There also was a time when a high school graduate from blue collar Brooklyn could rise from the bottom and work his way to the top. Today this opportunity has disappeared. The business has become too complex and driven by so many different forces that were not present 30 years ago. Advances in technology and the speed of information flow, high-speed communications, overseas trading, derivative products, and other changes, have forever transformed the organization and structure of Wall Street.

All the above-mentioned factors caused an evolution in competition. In the early 1960s, very few firms played hardball. There were only a handful of Gus Levys and Cy Lewises in the business, going in for the kill at every opportunity. Today, the Wall Street credo is "take no prisoners," or else you are not in the game. It is a business of no mercy.

Joseph Apisa

Twenty years ago, a big block of stock was 5,000 to 10,000 shares. Volume, by today's standards, was minuscule on the stock exchanges. But as time went on, business grew, and the tape kept printing bigger and bigger blocks. During that period of time, commissions were high. The higher rates helped greatly in the pricing process, cushioning brokers against losses. We didn't have all the derivative products—futures, options, programs—forces that can move markets. In fact, the block business was a new venture for brokerage firms—the concept of the block trader negotiating with the customer—because the institutions themselves were not the major market force that they are today. Money managers just bought IBM and held it for six months; there were none of the market gyrations we see today.

To get business done at that time, customers paid full commissions. If you put a piece of stock on, say a block of 50,000 or 100,000 shares, which was enormous for that period, even if you did it down a point or two, the stock would most times trade back up because institutional buyers would come in and take advantage of the pricing opportunity. And if the merchandise didn't bounce back up, the fat commissions that the broker earned took out a lot of the sting from a bad trade.

That is all forever changed. Today, a desk could sometimes end up owning it all. Sometimes you find buyers, sometimes you don't, sometimes you find other sellers. The whole process is a lot more involved in regard to negotiation, technology, and size. There are more zeros and more risk.

The trading community of the 1960s was different. Back then, there was more camaraderie, because of the relatively diminutive size of the business. Twenty years ago, the Wall Street trading fraternity was small, and everyone knew each other, either on a professional or a social basis. Everyone was very careful of how they conducted themselves for fear that they would not live up to the standards required to function in the business. There was a tremendous amount of pride and loyalty in what you did. And much of that sense of honor has dissipated over the years.

In the "good old days," salesmen would pass along an idea or some information to the money manager through his trader, informing him of their intentions and asking if he would like to participate. Back then, to get a big trade done would take several days. During that time, you always had to maintain anonymity and be careful that certain people did not find out that you had a piece of merchandise for sale, or they would run ahead of you and start shorting it—even back then. But not with the vengeance that they do it today. But by the mid-1970s, everything started to get bigger and bigger: the positions grew, the prints had more zero's on the end, and the money under management exploded.

Before May Day, the securities business wasn't as cutthroat because of the commission structure. A broker could obtain up to 42 cents a share trading a piece of stock, thus offering a comfortable cushion for the pricing mechanism. So even when you were long and wrong, you always had the commission that ate up a lot of the loss, making it a completely different ball game. Sales trading was easier, in the sense that the entire scope of the market was smaller and people had yet to realize the potential of the liquidity to be found in this environment.

The Role of the Buyside Trader

In the 1960s, the buyside trader was only a minor part of the process. He merely parroted what his portfolio manager wanted to do within that marketplace. As the equities explosion continued in the 1970s, so did the buyside trader's role in negotiating the transaction. In earlier days, the account called the brokerage house, the position trader priced the stock, and it was put up on the tape. Take it or leave it—that's the way it was. Twenty years ago, the buyside trader did not negotiate. He just took the order and did whatever his portfolio manager wanted to do; he was not part of the process.

Because of the structural changes that have occurred in the institutional investment process, the head traders at many of these firms now are real traders, not order takers. In today's marketplace, the trader at your institutional accounts must be called upon and be included as part of the pricing mechanism if you have a piece of merchandise to buy or sell. For example, your position trader might be willing to sell a piece of stock at 31½, but the customer might only be willing to pay 31. Therefore, helping the customer also assists the position, and the sales traders find the levels at which the stock can be placed in the right hands and at which the firm does not have to be lugging all of the print. The buyside trader has become more valuable to the brokerage firm, in terms of the pricing mechanism for merchandise.

Some savvier buyside traders often function as investors, with money available to participate on prints. This development has fundamentally changed the role of the sales trader, something that many in the profession have failed to recognize. They are not merely order takers but an important part of the investment process, striving to get the best price possible for their organizations. This creates a more complex negotiating process, as the sales trader is challenged to deal with a real professional, not a mere clerk, on the other end of the telephone line. And if a sales trader does not treat the buyside professionals with respect and as equals, they have the power to make you look like a fool—or even worse.

The Morning Mayhem

The sales trading profession is definitely for early risers. Most dedicated sales traders are at their desks by 6:30 or 7:00 in the morning. Because of the globalization of the securities markets, finding out from their foreign departments what occurred overnight in Asia and Europe is essential for traders to be able to properly service their customers. Before a sales trader is on the phone with his customers, he must absorb all of his firm's new research and set up his day with regard to what orders he's working from customers, and he must make sure that yesterday's trades were properly processed overnight, with nothing left overhanging.

Sales traders also attend the morning research meeting, gathering all the latest information from their stable of analysts. Only after these steps are taken do they begin the trading call, where each trader goes through his positions—what he is both long and short, what new buy and sell orders have come from the foreign and branch offices, what he was working on the previous day, a reiteration of what was bought and sold, and what other stocks are needed going into the market that day. The trader must pay attention and focus on this information because this is how block lists are generated and how he is going to deliver the morning report to his customers.

A sales trader must focus intensely on the morning meetings because he will undoubtedly have customers who own these particular stocks about which his analysts are articulating. He must make sure that before the day starts, if there is some negative or positive news on a customer's position, this information gets put across to the customer's trading desk so he can relay it to his organization. Although there's a research salesman performing the same function for the portfolio manager, it is a sales trader's obligation to work closely with the research department and not shut himself off. Shut yourself off from the research and you are performing an injustice to your customer. Information flow is key in this business.

Consistency Builds Trust

Unfortunately, not all sales traders feel the same way about the research aspect. But it is crucial that an organization capitalize on it's individual and innovative style of research; it should be utilized as an integral asset. Part of the sales effort to get business from customers is presenting your product and bringing added value to the table. And although sales traders at other firms might not perceive it as important, I believe it is of crucial significance to make sure that every morning my customers are properly presented their morning call and a brief but comprehensive update of my firm's research. Keep it short and directly to the point. There isn't any time to pontificate. The good sales trader must be focused, disciplined, and consistent. Again, *consistency builds trust.*

But what is consistency? It is being there with the information, making sure the customer gets that information put over correctly, and enabling the account to act on that information. The more you call, the more you're in front of the customer, the more accurate you are, and the more you deliver in situations, the more trust you build. This is what gets you the call.

The First Call

The buyside always talks about the first call: "who's going to get the first call and the all-important information edge?" But the reality is that with any important information from the morning meetings, a sales trader is going to call all his important clients in a matter of five minutes, even though the market is not yet even open. The early call helps the customers make their decisions on what they should or should not do during the upcoming day.

Knowing who to call upon in certain specialty situations comes from dealings over the years with the individual customers and, again, knowing what their needs are and what they've been playing in recent weeks. A salesman's first call on one stock to one institution might be his last call to that same account in another stock. The sales trader must know in what stocks his customers have been involved and what they are looking for, and this comes only through the process of doing it every day and being dependable at what he does.

The Customer's First Call

Now what about the first call from the buyside? The first call that a sales trader wants during the day is from one of his customers who has a piece of merchandise that he wants to sell or buy. You want to kill for that "virgin call," when nobody on the Street knows about it but you and the client. For example, a customer wants to sell 500,000 shares of XYZ Corp., and he wants out now and does not want to wait for the sales trader to find the other side—another natural buyer—in the market. The broker makes his client a ½ bid—that is down a ½ point from the last sale, whatever it is. He might respond saying: "No, I'll only sell it ¼ point down from the last sale." You might not come together, and he will say: "Nothing done," and proceed to take the merchandise to another brokerage house.

But the last thing he wants to do is to make that second call, for fear that someone might have shopped his offering and that he wasted time while the marketplace is constantly changing. Perhaps when he first called, there weren't any sellers on the floor of the exchange, the stock was neutral with nothing going on. However, now somebody else walks in and wants to sell a big block of stock. This screws up his entire picture. The buyside trader wants to get his business taken care of with just a single call—one-stop shopping. Otherwise his risk escalates. And it is a sales trader's job to keep that call and not lose the order to a competitor. *He must know how to close a trade.*

The Art of Negotiation

A sales trader may not want to be put in a position where an institutional client wants him to make a bid for his 500,000 shares of XYZ. This is a big piece to come to the marketplace. But when a customer calls up his sales trader and places him in this situation, he could ask, "Is it all right to make a couple of calls? I have some accounts who bought this stock a few days ago. I have some smart calls to make." If the client is sharp, he'll agree, because if the sales trader finds a natural buyer, it benefits him. Because if he uses less of the firm's position money, it helps him get the liquidity that he needs at the price he wants. The more buyers a sales trader can find, the better he can price the merchandise for his customer because his position trader won't be carrying the entire position.

It can also work the other way. For example, if an institution is a seller, their trader gives the first call. The sales trader's position desk could like the stock and allow the sales trader to pay the customer's price. They take the chances and wait for the buyers to come in. That's good too. Let your block desk have it, based on their decision that they like the stock and they're willing to take the risk of a long position.

What is also critical to the transaction process is the negotiation of the commission. Most institutions pay 6 or 7 cents per share on a trade, but on big trades, before the print goes up on the tape, the savvy sales trader should make it a habit to negotiate the commission relative to the risk on the trade. And not many sales traders do enough of that. If you are going to make a tight bid for a big block of stock, do everything possible to maximize revenues.

And if a sales trader is putting up a significant portion of the firm's capital, the brokerage house deserves to get paid for its risk. This is something that both the buyside and the sellside have forgotten. Just to go on blatantly day after day taking risks for 6 or 7 cents a share and putting up capital is not the answer. Negotiate a commission relative to the risks involved, higher than 6 or 7 cents at times, depending on the risk and volatility of the transaction.

Walking the Tightrope

When an institution calls a broker, a sales trader must walk a fine line between his customers and his position desk. Once the customer makes that call, so begins the obligation to protect him. Whatever else occurs after the phone call, the privileged information that a sales trader now possesses must remain between the client and his organization. And above all, *never use this information against the client.* Unfortunately, not everyone on Wall Street upholds this standard.

When a sales trader is putting up a big print on the tape with millions of dollars involved, it is as intense as any situation could be. If a sales trader takes his customer out of a stock, 90 percent of the time, he gets away with the first print; he finds buyers and does not wind up carrying the position. If he has priced it right, he will find the other side of the trade, because the situation looks attractive to the potential buyer. Fifteen minutes after the sales trader puts the print on—800,000 shares of XYZ down ¾ of a dollar—he'll wind up clean because buyers came in, took the stock off his hands, leaving him a profit and, hopefully, with a decent commission; a good trade for everyone.

But a sales trader can also have another seller come in right after that print, also wanting to sell 500,000 shares. Then another institution sees the print go by, triggering them to act. If this occurs, you will have likely ended up, as we say in the business, "long and wrong." Ninety percent of the time you get away with the first print. It's the second one that kills you. This is exactly why it is so important for a sales trader to make the calls to his accounts to find the players prior to pricing a piece of stock. Unfortunately, it always doesn't work that way.

But let's say the right calls were made, and when you made a call to your customer looking for a buyer, you find another seller. That is why it is essential to know who to call when you get a piece of merchandise. Don't assume that the customer doesn't own it, just because it's not on the Spectrum system, which details the holding of institutional customers. Make the call anyway. You never know what the client has been in and out of in the last three weeks, and you're not privy to all their transactions. Maybe somebody bought the stock and maybe somebody sold the stock within the last month, and the transactions haven't hit up on the system yet. As a sales trader, you can never take it for granted that since it's not on the machine, you don't have to make that call. You get on the telephone anyway and let them tell you "we don't own it," or "we don't want to sell it."

If the salesman diligently makes those calls, maybe he can catch that second seller before he prices those 800,000 shares. But then he must go back to the first seller, and tell him, "I have another seller here so the price is going to be different now, because now I have 1,300,000 to do and not 800,000. The price cannot be the same for 800,000 as it is for 1,300,000 so we have to renegotiate everything." The business understands that, and the accounts understand that. Absolutely. It's out of your control, but you were doing your job.

On the other hand, the price for the 800,000 shares and the price for 1,300,000 could be the same. For example, the seller might have the buyers lined up, or his trader loves the stock so much that he will take it all into the firm's account. The key point to remember is that *each trade has it's own unique personality.*

The Keys to Victory

The difference between the ordinary sales traders and the successful sales trading professional is the ability to create a distinctive edge for a client. To make yourself outstanding and rise above the competition, you must work within the marketplace to generate both creativity and merchandise for your institutional counterpart. A sales trader has to commit to an idea and be willing to say, "I like this stock; I did my homework, spoke to the analyst, and he also likes the fundamentals and the outlook. I think we should buy this because it looks like the right fit. I might have a seller, I don't know if the price is going to be right, but I might have a seller here." That is the value added a sales trader must bring to his client.

And if you are good, you start to be right and begin to pile up some points: you pick this stock and make two points for your client. You make another point on this stock, calling the right shot. You start to build a track record. That is when they call you on the phone. Remember again: *consistency builds trust.* You can't be wrong too often, but there will always be situations that are out of your control, even after you have built your so-called track record up with a customer and gained his confidence. You strive to create something special between the two of you that the other sales traders cannot duplicate. If you're consistent and develop the long-term relationship with your clients, you'll be able to overcome any bumps in the road.

Therefore, if a major institutional client calls and wants to move a piece of merchandise right away, you can suggest to him, "Instead of trading the 800,000 between us, let's put 100,000 on so I won't have to be long with the remainder, and we'll wait to see what happens. Having a little patience should get us better prices because of the way the stock is trading, and I think I can do a $\frac{1}{4}$ or $\frac{1}{2}$ better for you during the course of the day just by working it." This comes only through being there for the client, being consistent, and being right a lot more times than you're wrong.

The Hedge Fund Mine Field

While a sales trader has an obligation to protect a seller who has hired him as his agent, there is also an obligation to other accounts, to tell them the truth. But when operating in a shark pool of hedge funds, a sales trader is working against major risk takers who are willing to shoot against him. There is a universe of difference when dealing with a pension or a trust client as opposed to a hedge fund. Hedge funds are in the business to transactionally make money, just as a brokerage firm. Just as a broker reacts to market information off the tape, about what's going on in an industry, hedge funds also react to stocks at a moment's notice. Hedge funds react to supply and demand in the marketplace at any given second. That is how they make their money. Their information flow is greater at times because of the high commission rates they pay brokers and because they are simultaneously well-placed into the infor-mation pipeline of numerous brokers. While most institutional accounts pay the usual 6 or 7 cents per share, a hedge fund might offer 20 cents.

And hedge funds also have a terrific turnover rate. As every sales trader knows, high commissions multiplied by fast turnover equals *big profits*.

It therefore takes a very special type of sales trader to cover the fast money player. You have to be both very knowledgeable and guarded on what you say and do not say. Discretion is the operative word. You must be incredibly cautious as to how you shop the firm's merchandise. The wrong call to a hedge fund can make everyone look like a fool. You have to make the right calls. If you push the wrong telephone button, you can get destroyed.

Years ago, hedge funds would hurt brokers; they would use their market intelligence edge to work against you. But over the years, sales traders have learned to build a solid rapport with these players. The sales pro who covers these particular fast money guys has to make an intelligent call to them and have a relationship with them so that they do not hurt your firm.

It is one of the toughest relationships on the Street to balance. For example, an institution could come and entrust you with their merchandise, and you can end up getting it all screwed up because somebody on your desk makes the wrong call, letting a hedge fund know the picture. Then the customer who trusted you is not going to be able to sell his stock unless you buy it. But if it's already down a point, he is going to have to sell it down another point to get out, or else do nothing, be very angry, and probably never call you again. At a minimum, it will be long time before you again hear from this disgruntled customer. Unfortunately, things do go wrong.

You Can't Fight the Market

However, what can and does go wrong are, for the most part, a function of the marketplace, and not of a mistake by anyone on either side, such as the previous example of trying to price 800,000 shares of stock; you send everybody out looking out for the buyer, but instead you find another seller. That is not something going wrong, but just an equitable repricing of the merchandise for all parties. You may also have a block to sell or to buy and someone shows up on the floor, and of course, you don't control them. Or perhaps after you've put on a good print and you're long stock, other brokers—who know you're long—start shorting against your long position and drive the stock down. By the end of the day when the market closes, you have a mark to the market loss without selling even a single share.

Thus, there are times when you are long on a print, you should just walk away and not show up on the floor for the rest of the day, depending upon what the stock is doing. If you're long, you might have to stay long rather than stand out there letting other firms know you are trying to get out. When the entire world knows what you are trying to do, they will jump all over your position. Come back tomorrow—the market will still be there (maybe!).

The Negative Selection Business

I never met any portfolio manager or trader who would sell a stock he thought was going higher. Sales traders are therefore by definition in a negative selection business. They know when a stock should be sold, so when an institutional seller comes in, they both already know the same story: it's time to get out! The institution wants its business done immediately and wants to know the price you will pay for its merchandise. There is a price for everything.

Getting Bagged

Often, the institutional customer has a better information flow than his sales trader. Therefore, you are going to occasionally get bagged by your clients. For example, you buy or sell a piece of merchandise from a client, and 15 minutes later news comes out and it all hits the fan. Then the arguments start. "That account knew it, that's why they called us. . . ." You start talking to the trader at the institution, but you are not sure if he did or didn't know. Sometimes it is obvious—he has taken you to the cleaners. But remember well: what goes around, comes around—especially in this business.

This is why it is so imperative to build a relationship with your account base. When they have a piece of merchandise they want to buy or sell, they often have some news or information that the portfolio manager passed down or that they picked up off their market screens, or they got a good piece of information from someone else on the Street. If your relationship is solid, they will tell you, "I hear they're going to come out with a lower earnings estimate in two days. That's why we want to get out. What would you pay?" Or, "I hear they're going to come out with higher estimates than expected. Where can we buy stock? Where would you short it to us?" That is where your relationships come into play. Above all, we are dealing here with credibility. But the word does not just stop on the brokerage side. It has to filter through to the customer side because a customer is only going to screw a sales trader once; once is enough.

How can a customer mess me up? Suppose he has shopped his merchandise around, and he does not tell his current call. Meanwhile, all the accounts in the country have seen it. The sales trader does not have virgin goods, and he's the only one on Wall Street who doesn't know it. He finds out only when one of his other customers says, "I just saw the piece of merchandise through another broker." The sales trader then finds out one of two things: either there is another seller around or, more likely, this piece has been shopped. "Oh yeah, I did show it." "Why didn't you tell me?" But this does not happen as much today, because the information flows are so great that you eventually find out everything.

After an episode like this occurs, you remember, and you don't put yourself in a position to be so accommodating until you come to a compromise. You're not going to keep doing business with that customer while getting killed. It does not work that way. What you want from a customer is a "win-win" situation. Everyone should benefit from the relationship.

The Soft-Dollar Bomb

Perhaps the greatest problem facing the business today is the explosion of soft-dollar arrangements within the securities business. The fact that every institution is giving an ever-increasing portion of their commissions to third-party vendors for so-called "research services" is killing the business. The ratio is approximately 1.7 to 1, meaning that for every $1.70 in commission business an institution does with a broker, the broker will give a $1.00 credit towards the purchase of a third-party research product. Even with narrowing spreads and a shrinking commission base, everybody is jumping into the soft-dollar business, seemingly driving the ratio down to zero. If the market volume does not come back close to pre-Crash levels, and the level of institutions using soft dollar payouts continues, there will be brokers out there, it's certain, doing this service for nothing just to gain market share. They will be paying institutions just to see their order flow, and losing money in the process.

There is going to come a time in this business—guaranteed—that the major brokerage firms which, over the years have put up principal capital to create liquidity for major institutions, will cease to provide this critical service. We are beginning to see this today. Full-service firms are not going to sit by and let these institutions give their commission dollars out to soft-dollar vendors, only to up and ask for a position bid or offer, and then disappear for three months. Nobody, including me, needs a customer like that. If this keeps up, the era of full net trading will be upon us before we even know it.

It does not pay for a major brokerage house to be block positioning for its clients and get only 6 cents a share to create liquidity, especially considering that it also provides these accounts with a research product for no compensation. If these accounts are going give their flow of business to the soft-dollar brokers, the major block houses will cease their capital commitment, and this will soon happen. Soft-dollar arrangements cut into the heart of the business. You have institutional accounts dealing with 115 brokers, and over one-half their commissions are obligated to soft-dollar payments. And the brokerage house that offers its complete research product wants to get paid for its ideas and labors, but is ignored. So when such an account wants to move a piece of merchandise, why should I pay them the price they want for 6 or 7 cents a share when I fail to see a good order flow of business?

You don't mind taking it on the chin and positioning stocks and shorting stocks and trading with an account if they in turn come back and give you some working orders, some agency business, and pay you back for your research, your quantitative services—whatever you are giving them—because that is the way business should be done. Yet it seems that the soft-dollar brokers are willing eventually to do business for nothing. It is all going to end; it has gotten to the point of lunacy. Once there is an abuse of a product, whether intentional or not, something gets done about it. You can't have an institution paying off their soft-dollar obligations with order flow while you are sitting there waiting to get paid for the services that you have rendered, and for which you should be but are not being paid, because the institution tells you, "Well, I can't because I owe all this money." Well, I'm sorry, but we positioned for you, took a risk for you, lost money on you, and you take research from me that makes you money. I deserve to be paid—plain and simple.

Institutions must rethink what their priorities are going to be: having their bills paid through a vendor or meeting their fiduciary responsibilities in executing their customer orders at the best possible price and providing the availability of a viable marketplace. It is time that the sellside stop covering the institutions' overhead.

People, Not Machines

There is good and bad in everything that comes down the pike. Technology has immensely enhanced the sales trader's capabilities with availability of information, enabling him to react quickly to market events. Technology has made the block trading business more acceptable for globalization than it was ten years ago. However, I don't care how much technology you put on this earth or where you put it. We are in a business that is a people business from the start, and machines can only interface and communicate when programmed to do so accordingly. The human element will always be a factor in this business. When you execute a trade, there are two reasons: sometimes you have to do a trade because it is a trading decision and a pricing decision; or you do a trade because it's a business decision, depending upon your customer and his relationship with you, your firm, and the availability of capital. Machines can't do that. Machines can only enhance, but not dominate. And as long as there are people to deal with, people want to deal with people, not machines. Technology is only an extension of human thought, not a substitute.

Closing Out the Trade

The greatest gift that any sales trader could have is knowing how to close out the trade. You can get the call; you can talk to your own traders; the market could be right, this could be right, that could be right; but if the sales trader doesn't know how to close it out—the big stuff, not the small stuff—the entire effort is wasted. The most important thing the trader can know is how to close that trade, how to get it on the tape, where everybody walks away satisfied.

To reach this level, a sales trader must constantly practice his craft. You have to be good at what you do, and that takes practice. Be aware of your experiences and use them to your advantage. And if you did something that really got you into trouble, make sure you don't get near it next time, and choose your words carefully. If a customer asks you a question, don't blurt answers that demonstrate you have no idea what you're talking about, because that will become your reputation. You don't want to be wrong.

Whatever It Takes

The role of the sales trader is continually evolving. Most important today is the realization that you can't be a good sales trader unless you are a good trader. Gone are the days where a sales trader could just blindly call his institutional accounts in the morning with his buy and sell lists. Neither can you simply provide the commodity-type maintenance research produced by the ton all over Wall Street and which is responsible for the needless waste of millions of dollars of paper annually. These are mechanical functions that can be better fulfilled by AutEx, Bridge, First Call, and a host of other electronic information services. The name of the game today is creating added value for your clients, providing them windows of opportunity to make money through your research, your execution skills, and your access to information. Your research must enable you to make some real money for your customers.

Besides being in front of the institutional client with a viable product, a sales trader must have the requisite skills to execute that strategy. Your organization needs a position trading capability, enabling you to provide your clients with liquidity and execution. And the good sales trader will always get more respect from the block traders at his firm if he can convince them that he knows what he's doing, that he knows the industries he's trading, that he knows his accounts, and that he sees the big picture as to what is going on with his clients. This way, the position desk will give the sales trader better service, and enable him to better represent himself and his organization to the institutional client. Again — and most important — a professional sales trader is also a good trader in any market.

Conclusion

I have known many people who were brilliant traders yet didn't come close to achieving the prosperity and accomplishments their skills warranted. And I think I know why. The key to success in this business is the realization that *you can't do it alone.* I believe that successful traders realize their shortcomings and take advantage of the opportunities to learn from their peers how to become not only a superior trader but also a better human being. My friends — including Tony Landi of Morgan Stanley, Geri Weiss of the NYSE (who coached me to pass my Series 7 exam!), my faithful buddy Marie Zefi, with all her help over the years, and my childhood pal Joseph DiMartino (president of Dreyfus Corp.) — and their continued support have been the essential difference for me between success and failure on Wall Street, and my family, for their help and understanding. I thank them *all* for believing in me.

I also learned along the way that the successful sales trader *must* be an innovator, because as soon as he lets up, there will be 100 other guys on the Street waiting to scoop up his valued customers. I've been in the business over 30 years, and I'm still learning something every day. If I ever wake up and don't feel like going to work, that's when I'll retire. Because if I don't do it myself, it will eventually be done for me. That's the reality of the Street. But nothing lasts forever, and you always know when your time is up.

Remember that the successful trader will survive through knowledge and with the ability to adapt to progress. But if you want to be a success at anything, the answer is simple: work hard and never, ever give up.

Remember, it's not easy. If it were, everyone would be doing it. Unfortunately, on Wall Street the yardstick for measuring success is how much money you make. This philosophy does not work. It is short lived. I've seen them come and go in my 30 years of trading, and most go home *broke*.

What really works is perfecting what you do, striving to be the best, and never, ever give up trying! — Oops! I said it again. "Yes, but at least I'm consistent! — Good luck!

CHAPTER FIVE

FRANK BAXTER

The Third Market

$\mathbf{T}$he third market for equities is the trading of exchange-listed stocks in an over-the-counter fashion. Frank Baxter is regarded as one of the leaders of the "second wave" of third market traders. As the brokerage industry moves toward the mid-1990s, the third market continues to attract a significant and increasing volume of equity trading in many issues traditionally traded on the floors of the New York and American Stock Exchanges. Additionally, many third market firms are riding the new wave of technology-assisted trading techniques and developing these esoteric strategies for their clients.

In this chapter, Frank Baxter describes the operation of his third market organization, Jefferies & Co., the leading financial institution in this expanding area. Frank has been the president of Jefferies since 1986, and during his tenure he successfully restored vitality and exuberance to a firm that experienced an exceptional amount of adversity when its founder and chairman, Boyd Jefferies, pleaded guilty to securities violations and was banned from the securities industry for five years.

Frank Baxter

Frank's discussion is limited to equity trading in U.S. equities, although a large third market exists in many foreign stocks as well.

What Is the Third Market?

A review of trading strategies would be incomplete without including the third market. Although this market has been around for over three decades, there is still considerable misunderstanding about it among professionals, and virtually no understanding of it by the investing public. Simply stated, the third market is the market in which equities listed on various exchanges are also traded away from these exchanges.

The first market has always been considered the exchange market—exchanges have been the major arena for trading securities for centuries. Those individuals interested in trading would go to an organized central marketplace where they could find their counterparts and have a chance of striking a bargain. All the orders were brought to one physical place, complete with particular auction market characteristics: willing market participants making bids and offers; a centralized location; and priorities given to specific trades.

The over-the-counter market is the second market. The OTC market is essentially a dealer market, historically serving largely a noninstitutional clientele. Most OTC stocks were securities that did not have enough of a public flow of buy and sell orders to justify the exchange listing and an auction market type environment. These issues needed the support of dealers, who were prepared to hold and position an inventory because there was an insufficient order flow to justify an auction market type of trading environment.

The second market's role has evolved as a result of advances in telecommunications technology, which obviated the need for a centralized place to trade. Broker-dealers set themselves up and invited traders to transact with them, first by telegraph and then by telephone. These dealers could be located all over the city or all over the world. Since it was a "dealerized" market, where the broker acted as a principal (or like a store keeper), it acquired its name: over-the-counter. Today, we see many companies—such as Apple Computer—that stay on the NASDAQ system as a matter of choice, even though their size, trading characteristics, and profitability would make them prime (and most welcome) candidates for the one of the more established exchanges.

The third market consists of transactions involving stocks which are listed and traded on exchanges, but using the features of the over-the-counter market. Third market broker dealers are contacted by other market participants by telephone. The market is a natural result of the evolution of communications and the institutionalization of securities trading.

The third market received its name in an SEC Special Study of Securities Markets, published in 1963. The Commission believed that the financial markets had changed considerably since the last study (which was after the crash of 1929), and they endeavored to understand the nature of capital markets during the early 1960s, when institutional investors were just beginning to increase in importance. In this study, the SEC gave a new name to this market, which had been previously described in the cumbersome fashion of "trading listed stocks over-the-counter."

Today, the third market in U.S. securities trades about 4 percent of the total composite volume of securities listed on exchanges. However, its impact is larger than its percentage of the volume, primarily because it restricts its trading to professionals and vigorously competes with the exchanges for their business. This competition from the third market exerts pressure on the exchanges to be open longer, to reduce the length of time that a stock has stopped trading, and to price more competitively. Also, when the exchanges are closed, which is 18½ hours a day in this country, the third market is the only avenue to execute a trade in the United States.

Early Markets, Early Players

The third market evolved because the structure of the auction market did not sufficiently address the needs of the institutions, large buyers and sellers of stocks, that wanted to trade. Institutions wanted to buy in size, to negotiate the trade, to transact privately, and to deal in a manner that did not expose their interests to the general public.

Utilities were the first significant group of common stocks to extensively trade in the third market. In the late 1930s, utility holding companies were required to consolidate into operating companies that were geographically contiguous to one another. However, other noncontiguous corporations needed to restructure, and many of these operating companies needed new financing. The major underwriters for utilities were Blyth and Co. and First Boston. Neither one was a member of the New York Stock Exchange, but both firms felt a responsibility to follow through and make sure that there was a viable secondary market. There was also profit to be made because they put the new issues of those operating companies into the portfolios of many of their institutional customers.

Interestingly enough, at that time, the NYSE accepted the concept that stocks listed on their exchange that developed institutional orientation could have a market away from the exchange, and that market was available to their own membership. They allowed their members to go off-board and buy and sell with Blyth & Co., First Boston, American Securities, and other market makers. No rules forbade such actions at that time, and so a third market in listed utility common stocks developed in the late 1930s and early 1940s.

Third market trading evolved in certain stocks because it was more efficient and offered a greater distribution of information. Adding to the move toward the third market was the burst of institutional interest in equity securities and the movement of the bank stocks to listing. Bank stocks had all been listed in the 1920s, and they became favorite vehicles of speculation. But when the Crash of 1929 came, major bank stocks experienced immense decreases in value, causing massive runs on their deposits. The investing public looked at this public display of prices and saw First National City Bank, Chase Manhattan, and other stocks sinking in value at a very rapid rate. After this experience, the banks considered the exchange market a speculative market, and they moved their stocks to the OTC market, where they would be quietly traded without a lot of publicity or fanfare.

The Father of the Third Market

One of the earliest and most successful third market firms was Weeden & Co., founded by Frank Weeden. Pacific Gas & Electric was the first common stock that Weeden began trading in the 1930s. By the late 1940s the firm began trading industrial common stocks. The reason Weeden started trading is that, for different reasons, two large groupings of its customers — institutions and nonmember broker-dealers — asked the firm to make a market. The institutions wanted to cut their commission expenses, which could be achieved by dealing on a net basis with Weeden. The firm made a standard half point spread, which saved approximately half the commission on either side of the market, whether the institution was a buyer or a seller.

For example, considering the commissions were 25 cents per share or more and that the spread between the bid and the asked was also 25 cents, a broker could compete if he could quote a market with a spread of less than 75 cents (two commissions and the exchange spread). The third market quote then was typically a quarter of a point on each side of the last sale on the exchange. If the last sale didn't change, which was often the case for utilities, third market brokers could make a lot of money taking a half point out of each trade.

The OTC broker had a different reason for dealing with a third market firm. Although he wasn't doing business with institutions on a regular basis, he might still have had a retail customer who wanted to buy a stock listed on the NYSE. And then there was no way that the OTC broker could make a profit off that transaction because no discount was allowed to another professional who was not a member of the NYSE. If the retail customer wanted to buy 100 shares of U.S. Steel at $50 per share, the OTC broker, a nonmember broker, had to go to Merrill Lynch and pay Merrill the full commission.

Theoretically, the OTC broker could charge an additional commission, but that would certainly discourage that investor from dealing with him, as opposed to going directly to Merrill Lynch. Or, he could do it for nothing and because he went to Merrill, hope he would get some business in return at some point in the future. Either way, it was not a promising situation.

Additionally, NYSE broker-dealers imposed a quarter point surcharge on odd lots on their nonmember customers. Adding this expense to the high fixed commission rates created an opportunity for the nonmember firms to realize huge potential savings.

Therefore, the OTC broker came to Weeden and said: "Look, if you would sell it to us at a price that is a mark-up from the last sale of half the commission, we can turn around and mark it up the full commission, and we make half a commission." To service this customer, Weeden made a market in these stocks. While these trades weren't huge, they were a source of good order flow. And the customers were delighted because there was no way they could get that advantage from a member of the New York exchanges.

Boyd Jefferies

The third market has been significantly influenced by Jefferies & Company for the past twenty years. Jefferies began its life on the floor of the Pacific Coast Stock Exchange in 1962. Boyd Jefferies was a floor broker on the P-Coast who astutely perceived the impending institutionalization of the stock market during an era when 75 percent of the volume was from individuals and 25 percent was institutional.

Today, these percentages are reversed, as many individuals have delegated their stock market decisions to professionals through investment vehicles such as mutual funds. More significantly, the working class has been represented in equity investment as pension funds have diversified their holdings.

Investor's Diversified Services (IDS) of Minneapolis purchased Jefferies in 1969 and was the critical factor marking Jefferies's entry into the third market. By then, Jefferies had grown considerably. One of the other restrictive rules on the NYSE then was that institutions could not be members. The membership feared that its customers, the institutional side of the business, would be transformed into its competitors. Therefore, to accomplish the purchase, Jefferies had to resign from its exchange memberships and join the third market.

The change was a good fit. No longer was the organization restricted by when, where, and how it could trade for its clients. However,

IDS wanted to put an end to the exchange's restriction of institutional ownership and sued for restraint of trade. IDS won the suit, and Jefferies felt compelled to rejoin the exchange. However, the firm had grown to appreciate the latitude of the third market and preferred to remain established in this sector. In 1973, Jefferies repurchased itself from IDS, and one of its first steps was to resign from the NYSE so it could provide a more flexible service to its clients. At that time, one of these services was anonymity, since third market trades were not printed on the tape as they are today. Institutions could acquire or dispose of a block of stock without anyone ever knowing about it. However, Jefferies retained its regional exchange memberships because those exchanges were more accommodative of professional business. In particular, they did not and do not require that every trade a member does be executed on their exchange.

Boyd Jefferies refined some ingenious ideas, such as the give-up, which assisted institutions in using a market that was designed to accommodate many brokers doing many small trades. The give-up came into existence because of the fixed minimum commission. The commission was so large that some firms such as Jefferies were willing to execute trades and share part of the commission with other brokers whom the client wanted to pay for such services as fund sales or research. The give-up made a mockery of the fixed commission system. It was obvious that the commissions were so high that there was room to pass out part of it to those who had nothing to do with the trades. The first regulatory reaction was to abolish the give-up rather than deregulate commissions.

Boyd is a unique individual. A lot has been written about his prodigious work habits and his searing focus on getting a trade done. The characteristic that stands out most in my mind is his sense that nothing is impossible. I often have said that he has no idea of the absurd. In the mid-1970s, we were trying to trade a large block of stock between a corporation and an institution. We could not get the two parties together on price. Boyd knew that the company whose stock we were trying to trade had done some business in the Middle East. Without a clue as to any of the sheiks or any players in the area, he prepared to head to Beirut to shop the block. The institution became so convinced that he might be successful that it finally paid the corporation's price, and Jefferies ended up engineering a 4 million share transaction! That was the largest dollar block the firm had done until that time.

Boyd would do anything for a customer. He gave us our sense of being client obsessed. He got into trouble by going too far in this pursuit. Without aggrandizing himself or the firm, he acceded to customers requests and performed services which were not legal.

In 1987, Boyd Jefferies pleaded guilty to a margin and recordkeeping violation. Boyd's fall was a great tragedy. The charges against him cannot be minimized, but neither can his contributions to the improvement of the U.S. capital markets.

Evolution and Competition

With the growing institutionalization of the securities business, other big third market brokers profited and thrived. Firms such as American Securities and Blyth & Co. would inventory and sell large blocks. But then a large block was 2,000 shares, while 5,000 shares was a very good block, and 10,000 was an exceptional size. This is how the third market evolved in the late 1940s and 1950s. But it was in the 1960s that the institutional business began to grow at a rapid rate — both absolutely and relative to the retail business.

By the mid-1960s, the entire institutional community began to be involved. The savings available were too attractive to pass up, so banks, mutual funds, insurance companies, and other money managers participated. Besides Blyth and American Securities, other major firms of the day such as First Boston, New York Hanseatic, and J. S. Strauss & Company—firms that couldn't or wouldn't join the exchange—entered the fray. The increased competition actually drew more clients and made it better for the entire securities business.

Ultimately, there were two-way markets in about 250 different issues—meaning that a customer could call a market maker and get a price in which he could either buy or sell a security. A typical market was for 1,000 shares, which was considerably larger than the exchange market of the day. 5,000-share markets were available for the best customers. 10,000-or-more-share markets were not uncommon. Most of the participants were well capitalized to be players in this market.

The SEC Seal of Approval

The 1963 Securities and Exchange Commission's Special Study—the report that gave the third market its official appellation—also offered a positive evaluation of the third market, commenting,

> . . . it appears to the Special Study that the advantages of competition generally outweigh any concern over impairment of depth in the primary market. . . . The challenge to the primary market represented by the third market calls for imagination and statesmanship in enhancing the usefulness of each, not for measures in the direction of destroying competitive markets.

The Special Study also concluded

> The rapid growth in recent years of an off-board market for trading listed common stocks has made this an increasingly important segment of the national securities markets. . . . Under existing circumstances, it appears that the over-the-counter market for listed stock has been beneficial to investors and the public interest.

The Exchanges Fight Back

Despite this unequivocal approval from the SEC, the 1960s and early 1970s was a time of constant struggle for the proponents of third market trading. The established exchanges did all they could to damage the credibility of the system and to drive these players out of the securities business. As previously mentioned, the bank market was primarily an institutional market, and one of the major players was the firm of M.A. Shapiro. In 1965, Chase Manhattan Bank decided to list, and they broke with the precedent that had been established since the late 1920s. That was not of concern to Mr. Shapiro, but he discovered that Rule 394 prevented members of the NYSE from dealing with him. Now these were traders who had been dealing with him and Chase Manhattan Bank for many years. There was no question about the service he and his firm performed or of his financial stature and integrity, but Rule 394 stipulated that a member firm no longer could deal with M.A. Shapiro in Chase Manhattan.

Rule 394 was put into place in about 1958. There was an overhaul of all NYSE regulations, and it was all presented to the SEC, which did not question the propriety of that particular rule. At that time, the SEC viewed the NYSE as a most effectively organized self-regulatory body, and the SEC, because of the concept of self-regulation and considering the dependence of the SEC on effective self-regulatory activity, did not want to do anything that would undermine the NYSE. They therefore viewed Rule 394 as an appropriate regulation, confining members to dealing in their own marketplace.

The New York Stock Exchange was increasingly concerned about the third market and the continuing market share loss to off-exchange trading. By 1971, this total went up as high as 7–8 percent, a very large change in percentage. But the absolute numbers were considerable too, as the volume of business was growing at a substantial rate at that time. So in the absence of any change in the NYSE's way of doing business or the demise of the third market, there was a clear trend toward the same thing happening in listed industrial common stocks that had happened to every other security that had become dominated by institutional buying and selling: government bonds, corporate bonds, municipal bonds, preferred stocks, and utility common stocks.

The exchanges clearly recognized this trend, and so followed concerted efforts by the NYSE to eliminate the third market. From 1968 until the 1975 Exchange Act, the exchanges demeaned the third market, throwing out an endless stream of arguments: "It's not in the public interest to have the fragmentation that's occurring to the marketplace; it's a private market; people don't see what was going on; customers are being advantaged; they don't disclose their transactions; we don't know what's going on. Believe me, customers get badly treated in that market."

Despite the findings of the 1963 Special Study, the exchanges still believed that the only "legitimate" market was being threatened by transactions taking place away from the professionals on the floor. They viewed this as contrary to the public interest, because the NYSE was responsible for maintaining a stable and continuous market. The third market lacked responsibilities, they used the public market to dump the inventories that they accumulated, and they tended to be a downward pressure on the market during difficult times and exaggerate movements in the marketplace.

The Martin Report

To extend the scope of the attack, in 1969 the NYSE engaged William McChesney Martin, former chairman of the Federal Reserve Board and a very well-respected figure, to look at what was happening to the structure of the securities markets. Well, people had forgotten that Martin had once been president of the NYSE back in the early 1940s. To nobody's surprise, one of Martin's recommended changes was the elimination of the third market. That represented the attitude of the NYSE: "We're the marketplace, we can't tolerate any other market-places, and we will use all our power and influence and resources to get the third market eliminated, because it's not in the public interest."

The Martin report set the stage for hearings by the SEC, which was then chaired by William Casey. Some felt that Casey had been appointed by the Nixon administration with the mandate to implement the Martin report and put an end to the third market.

Don Weeden—The Crusader

However, the third market community did not roll over and play dead under all of this pressure. They stood up and fought back. Undoubtedly, the champion of the third market cause at this time was Don Weeden, Frank's son. Don was a tireless advocate, promoting the third market through his testimony in front of the SEC at numerous opportunities, beginning in 1968 and on through 1974. He also testified at a Senate committee hearing on the third market that was chaired by Senator Harrison Williams of New Jersey, and at Congressman Moss's extended Congressional hearings.

But Don Weeden's efforts didn't stop in Washington. He also participated in a number of securities industry committees that were grappling with the problem of market structure and that were constantly advocating monopolistic practices in the business, which he argued were contrary to the public interest. Don fought incessantly against the industry's efforts to maintain artificially high levels of commission rates and to restrict competition in the area of market making and providing liquidity. The fixed commission structure was a prime example of those monopolistic practices. So was Rule 394, or the current Rule 390, because it did two things: it restricted the competition both on and off the exchange. The rule prevented members of the NYSE from dealing off-exchange, though the off-board market had better prices.

Don Weeden and other third market professionals argued for an elimination of both of those monopolistic practices, although the elimination of fixed commissions was contrary to their own interests, because the NYSE's fixed commission structure allowed third market firms to make markets inside of what the exchange brokers could charge.

Don spoke to every group and committee that would listen, and the rule was liberalized to the extent that a member could go away from the floor if he could convince a floor governor that he could get a better price that way. Of course, this proved to be an arduous task, and the member had to be pretty serious. After shopping around the dealers to see if there was a price that was better than the floor, the diligent broker had to point this out to a governor and get permission to go away from the exchange. This would be feasible in another environment, but it proved to be impossible in an environment where securities prices constantly fluctuated. So the concession was more in form than in fact.

Finally, after more fighting, mostly by Don, the rule was changed so that the member only had to prove that the price he was getting was better than he could get on the floor. At that time the rule number was also changed to 390. Two other limitations were also imposed: 1) the member could not act as principal; and 2) the member could not act as agent for both sides away from the floor. It still was not very easy to get a trade accomplished away from exchanges, because the busy broker had to call around to the various dealers to find the best price—there were no screens in those days.

The 1975 Exchange Act

Don's impact was also felt in Congress. The dominating premise throughout the Exchange Act of 1975 is the concept of promotion of competition: between exchanges, within exchanges, and between the exchange and the OTC market. In fact, the mandate for the creation of the national market system was a way to create a structure that allowed for the elimination of these protective and restrictive practices. It allowed an open field of competition that would operate in a framework that maintained the characteristics of the central marketplace, and to this extent, it was successful. Today, we have developed a composite tape and a consolidated quotation system. We have developed an ITS (the Intermarket Trading System) and have done 85 to 90 percent of what is necessary to have a national market system that would allow the elimination of barriers to trading. Unfortunately, the industry has not yet taken that last very critical step: the elimination of Rule 390 and the allowing of Salomon Brothers, First Boston, and Merrill Lynch to make markets in General Motors, IBM, and other stocks.

May Day and The Third Market

May Day 1975 brought the end of fixed commissions, and the putative reason for the third market ended. No longer was there necessarily a price advantage from dealing in the third market. Members could now charge what they pleased. If price savings had been the only rationale for its existence, by all logic the third market should have disappeared. Instead it grew. Some third market firms had become so strong and effective that clients continued to deal with them because they could get the job done.

Some big players such as First Boston and Blyth joined the exchange. Weeden and Co. continued to dominate the market. However, during the late 1970s, Weeden suffered some hard times with position losses, as spreads decreased and markets became more volatile. It eventually merged with F. S. Moseley. Now the company has reemerged, ironically, as a member of the New York Stock Exchange.

Price was no longer the primary consideration for dealing with third market firms. Finding the bids and offerings in the size that institutions now wanted was as important as the small price savings had been. Furthermore, being free of some exchange restrictions, such as when and where a client could deal, made the third market an effective complement to the rest of the system.

May Day worked. Our industry is an effective example of classic imperfect competition. In such an environment prices only go down, because there will always be an individual price cutter who thinks he can gain market share. But he is quickly followed by the rest of the competitors. Commissions per share plummeted. As the spreads narrowed, there was not the incentive to trade as principal, and the third market became more of an agency market than a principal one. Instead of primarily putting up their capital as principal, the third market dealers would try to put together blocks as agent for their clients. The brokers' capital was often still used, but the primary emphasis shifted to acting as an agent.

From Market Making to Agency Markets

Ironically, the evolution of the third market to more of an agency system made these brokers more helpful to their clients. Since third market brokers did not take large positions to compete against their customers, they could act as advocates rather than adversaries. During the 1960s and early 1970s, a market was quoted an eighth or a quarter around the last sale, net. What evolved after May Day was trading at one price plus and minus a commission just like everyone else. Instead of quoting a firm market, firms would negotiate from orders and indications.

In the old days, if a stock last traded at the price of $50 per share, a third market trader would typically put himself forward to buy shares at $49.75 per share and to sell them at $50.25 per share. Now the trader would attempt to line up the buyer and seller simultaneously. A price would be set that both sides would agree on, most likely the last sale

($50.00 per share), and a commission would be negotiated with both the buyer and seller (probably between five and ten cents per share).

The Third Market Today

The third market today is thriving. There are three firms that focus on third market business during market hours. They are Cantor Fitzgerald, Jones & Co., and Jefferies & Co. Additionally, Madoff & Co. services brokers with small orders. Jefferies and Co. is the largest of these brokers. When the exchanges are closed, many of the "bulge bracket" firms join the fray. In London, early in our morning, Goldman Sachs, Salomon Brothers, and Morgan Stanley are active, to name a few. Also, some of the Swiss banks are major factors in the pre–New York opening hours.

Two factors have increased the importance of the third market in recent years. First, the takeover era caused more stoppage of trading during regular exchange hours. So does late breaking news, which creates a demand for a market any time of the day or night. There have been instances where trades in the third market have resulted in a change of ownership such as in the case of Allied Stores and Cyclops.

For Allied Stores, Allied's management and Robert Campeau of Toronto were locked in battle for control of the company. Scores of clients offered sufficient shares through Jefferies to Campeau (who had dropped a tender offer), to give him control. In October 1986, Jefferies & Co. traded 25.8 million shares—48 percent of the company—in a single trade, enough to put Campeau over the top. After a harrowing few days in which a restraining order held up the transaction, the trade took place.

In Cyclops, enough of Jefferies' customers expressed interest in selling to offer control to Dixons, a British concern. The trade, which occurred late in the evening, was for 2.1 million shares—61 percent of the company.

The Third Market and Trading Halts

The influence of the third market firms has significantly influenced the NYSE treatment of stopped stocks—those stocks subjected to trading halts—over the past five years. In December 1983, trading in Warner Communications was closed for over two days when poor earnings were announced. Jefferies had a bonanza. The market began with two or three institutions expressing a desire to trade. We had one or two trades below the halt price, and soon the supply and demand started coming from everywhere. We were trading with institutions around the world, with company executives, and with brokers from everywhere.

Although most third market firms resist committing much capital to trading, the volume was so great that Jefferies & Co. committed more than we should, and lost considerable money on our position. However, the commissions we received compensated for the loss. Over the two-day period we traded several million shares of stock.

Luckily, Jefferies & Co. has been able to have a few more pay days like Warner. In addition to the business generated, we were able to develop new clients around the world.

Unfortunately for us—but fortunately for investors—the exchanges started shortening the length of their trading halts. Currently, it is unusual for a stock to be stopped for much longer than an hour because officials and traders on the exchanges realize that third market players such as Jefferies & Co. will gear-up immediately. This is one of the more obvious examples of the advantage of competition between markets. Today, regulators require a universal halt when the exchange closes down. We argued vociferously against this restraint of trade, but post-Crash hysteria prevailed.

Another significant fallout from the Warner episode was the burden placed on our back office. They were forced to work around the clock for the rest of that week, attempting to reconcile the trades. We realized that we needed to upgrade our securities-processing capabilities. Now, we can do similar volume in a couple hours time with little strain on our system.

Globalization—Here to Stay

The second factor that has enhanced the viability of the third market has been the continuing trend toward global markets. More and more trades are being done outside of exchange hours. Today, a German investor in American stocks might want to trade these stocks on the Tokyo Stock Exchange.

Investors in Europe and Asia want to trade in their hours rather than in ours. A 24-hour market is not a reality yet, but within a few years, continuous and liquid share trading in the world's equities should occur. Today, for trading of American shares, the biggest deficiency is having enough people on the buyside to want to trade around-the-clock. For non-U.S. shares, the morass of clearing systems is the biggest inhibitor, but with improvements now taking place in many overseas markets, this roadblock will eventually be removed.

My Story

The Journey to Jefferies

In 1974, I joined Jefferies & Co. as a salesman in the Los Angeles headquarters. There was another slump in the industry at that time, and people were leaving it in droves. The diehards who stuck around in the industry were depressed. Going to Jefferies was like a rebirth for me. Boyd and his crew were so committed to excellence and innovation, that almost every minute was exciting. The plan was for me to get some experience in Los Angeles and then return to San Francisco to open an office. But plans have a way of adjusting at Jefferies, and after a few months, I trudged my family across the country to take over the management of the New York office. At that time, we had about 30 salesmen and specialized only in the third market.

When I arrived at Jefferies & Co. in 1974, I had been with the third market for virtually all my career. I started working in 1961, about the time the third market received its name. After a brief spell at Bank of California in San Francisco, I joined Harriman Ripley, which, because it was incorporated and could not join the exchange, traded in the third market. Harriman was primarily an investment bank headquartered in

New York. I was not privy to their business strategies as a trainee, but they must have felt they needed to engage in secondary trading to give their investment banking ability more credibility. The man in charge of trading was Mac Tully, who had been at Weeden and went on to start third market trading at New York Hanseatic (then a major trading firm but now defunct). Unfortunately, Harriman didn't really have its heart in trading, and poor Mac never had much money to play with. Eventually, Harriman was absorbed by Drexel and Company, a few permutations before the late but certainly memorable Drexel Burnham Lambert.

In 1962, President Kennedy had a confrontation with the head of U.S. Steel over a price raise. In reaction, the stock market plummeted and so did volume on every exchange, including the third. The securities industry was slumping and I was subsequently "LIFO'd" (last in the door, first one out). But I was still enamored with the third market and landed with J.S. Strauss and Co. in San Francisco.

Jack Strauss had worked for Frank Weeden before striking out on his own in the 1940s. At that time Strauss was the number two factor in the third market, behind Weeden & Co. Mike Mallick and Mike Heflen, senior partners at Cantor Fitzgerald, an important third market firm today, joined Strauss shortly before and after, respectively, I did. Mike Heflen resigned to set up third market trading for Cantor in 1963 and Mike Mallick joined him about a year later. Many of the leaders in the third market today came from J.S. Strauss. Jack was always a maverick and still is today at the age of 92, as he actively trades for his own account in San Francisco. He instilled into many of us the quality of challenging the status quo.

I was hired to be an institutional salesman. Selling for a third market firm in those days was interesting, to say the least. At that time, the exchanges were put into the same category as motherhood and apple pie, so to talk of trading listed securities elsewhere was considered blasphemous. I was one of two salesmen at Strauss. Since the other one was not too highly motivated, I essentially had the whole country to choose for accounts. In the very early days, I would extol the cost savings of dealing in the third market. But as we improved our capabilities, our ability to get big trades executed for institutions was as important as the cost savings and became another effective selling tool. Despite propaganda from the exchanges, the service was good enough to earn the support of an increasing number of institutions around the country and, to a limited extent, abroad. I was one of the few sales traders in the business at the time. In conventional firms, the business was processed by upstairs salesmen and order clerks.

In late 1963, Strauss opened an office in New York. I begged to go along. I had wanted to give the Big Apple a try for a long time and I was not disappointed. The institutionalization of the market was attracting a group of talented young people into the business. There had not been much of an infusion of new blood since before the War. With the institutional volume increasing, our egos and incomes grew. In 1966, I was made manager of the New York office, and by that time we were dealing with most of the institutions in the area. In 1969, I returned to San Francisco to run all sales and trading.

An Early Start

The day begins early at the Jefferies headquarters in Los Angeles — 3:00 A.M. We have arranged with the local paper distributor to have early deliveries of all the major business newspapers. Early on, we concentrate on trying to look for undiscovered information that will affect markets or stocks. Even before then, one of what we call our "rockets" is already there, preparing the information sheets from which all the traders and trader/salesmen work, brewing the coffee, and posting a report from our London office, detailing what is going on around the world.

"Rockets" is the name that Boyd gave to the group. They are the guts of our organization. They record all trades and inquiries, interface with the various exchanges around the world, operate AutEx, scan periodicals for market-moving news, and try to find out which new research recommendations are extant. Whether a rocket stays in the rockets department or goes on to sales or trading, he or she is one of the best prepared individuals in the firm.

By 3:45 A.M. our foreign traders in London give an intensive report on all markets and market-moving events. The primary audience for that report is the team that trades and sells foreign stocks. But as the world has shrunk, frequently people are arriving in time to hear this report.

The next hour is quite free-form. If there has been news about a stock overnight or it is active in one of the overseas markets, we will try to get something started among the growing number of insomniacs at institutions or elsewhere who are willing to trade at anytime.

If, for instance, a bid for a takeover stock has been made since the previous day's close, there will probably be a buy interest coming from Europe and Japan. We call people anywhere in the world at anytime and update them about the news and prices. We have had trades executed with people on boats, in showers, airplanes, and many in cars. I was once giving a market to a client in his car. He started to give me a bid when the phone went dead. A few minutes later I found that he had gone into the Lincoln Tunnel. Fortunately, the market had not changed and we traded 100,000 shares.

During this period our trader salesmen exchange news or information they have heard overnight while calling on accounts. There is much free-form speculation about the meaning of the bits of information. At Jefferies, you can agree or disagree with anyone in the interest of truth. The military organizational structure is an anathema here. We want everyone piping in with whatever their insights are. The only stipulation is that a person's dignity is always respected and that fights must be conducted gracefully.

At 4:50, we begin our formal morning meeting. We start with an abbreviated update of the international situation from London. Next, we launch into an issue-by-issue review of every inquiry or order we have in the house. The trading director leads the listed portion of the meeting. The OTC director reviews the over-the-counters, and Jerry O'Grady covers convertibles. There are always people who would like the meeting to change in some way, but it seems to come back to the drudge of going over every name one-by-one, despite how long it has been in the shop. It is a bit like our morning Mass. If we don't go through the routine, we aren't as prepared as we should be.

By 5:30, the morning meeting is history, and we hit the phones in earnest. We call our accounts with our inquiries and an update of what has been and is going on in the world. We feel that we are a little better prepared than our competition because we have already been trading for a couple of hours, and our opinions and inquiries have been tested in the marketplace.

Each professional has a microphone-loudspeaker console in front of him. Any input that he receives from his clients that add to the information process is immediately put on the speaker and is instantly transmitted to his or her 150 plus colleagues in six domestic offices and in London. All day long, each of our offices sounds a little like Grand Central Terminal, except that instead of announcements for the next train, there are countless voices piping in with market intelligence, orders, inquiries, gossip, and anything else that might enhance the investment process of our clients. The traffic sounds (and is) chaotic, but that is how the business is created. We don't think of ourselves as a clearing house for orders. Rather, we like to feel that we create trades that would not have happened without our help.

We feel comfortable working in the subjunctive, constantly asking "what if" and trying to find the ingredients that will produce new buyers and sellers and agreement between them on price.

The Technology Advantage

Technology is one of Jefferies' important tools. It enables our traders to improve our service to our clients. An internal storage system records and classifies every inquiry for a stock. It alerts a trader when the price of a security deviates significantly from the price at which we received an inquiry, giving an opportunity to point the change out to the client and possibly creating a trade.

We can correlate all active and inactive inquiries with the portfolio of a client so that we can focus only on what he is interested in. We are linking our inquiries computer-to-computer with some sophisticated clients. Our goal is not to replace the human trader by automation but to greatly enhance his or her contribution.

Our Investment Technology Group has introduced an electronic matching service, POSIT, which trades 3 million shares a day. It has also introduced a new product called Quantex, which acts as a faithful electronic slave to the portfolio manager. Quantex monitors the markets, using the portfolio manager's directions and executes those instructions directly through the New York Stock Exchange's SuperDOT system.

The Client

Jefferies & Co. mostly relies on our clients for our input. Talking to over 1,700 institutions constantly, plus 6,000 corporations when appropriate, as well as most large individual investors, we see a window on the professional marketplace that is unique. Without compromising any single investor, we can spot trends and conditions before they become widely perceived. Because of our ability to get trades done without moving the market, clients may come to us at the beginning of a program. The biggest reason we are able to avoid moving the market is that we try hard to call only those who might have a genuine interest. Often, showing an order on an exchange will elicit the interest of speculative traders. Because our clients are more willing to open up to us, we can often note an accumulation of buyers or sellers before prices reflect a change in interest.

For some reason that I can't figure out, Jefferies's over-the-counter inquiry is an especially sensitive indicator. Recently, for instance, an astute observer of our OTC list could have predicted the decline in technology stocks in advance as they saw the build up of sellers in that sector.

The clients who are most helped by us contact us early in their decision process, long before they decide to act, to use our input to reinforce or challenge their conclusions before they are committed. For instance, a client may indicate that he is expecting to invest in the market, a sector, or a stock. We might reply that we have seen many people going the other way, and perhaps he might reexamine his premises. He will probably go ahead with his original plans, but he would be more cautious in execution. Any information that Jefferies & Co. receives is used only for our clients' benefit, and clients' identities remain confidential. Neither the firm nor its employees can trade on such information. Our profit comes from the service we render to our clients.

Like other brokers, Jefferies & Co. is paid a commission for its brokerage services. But unlike other firms, we do not provide a research product; our clients are paying us for our market intelligence. Unfortunately, we are paid a little less commission per share than the regular full-service broker.

Stopped Stocks

Although it is not the majority of our business, the trading we and other third market firms engage in that receives the most attention is when we deal in a stock that has stopped trading for some reason. In reality it is only about 5–10 percent of our business. When a trading halt occurs we are deluged with calls from institutions, arbitrageurs, and brokers. We feel that keeping a market available to professionals is an important service. To handle this surge of business, we have developed for those who concentrate in this area a second speaker system as well as an electronic book. It has been instrumental in shortening prolonged delays on exchanges. It helps in pricing, as indicated by how close the exchange openings are in price to our market. It allows the pros to hammer out the right price.

The exchange market closes and our off-exchange market starts when a significant piece of news breaks. Usually, if the news is good, Jefferies's first calls will be from arbitrageurs bidding for the stock and trying to acquire some merchandise. At this point, the firm might use some firm capital to provide an offering side of the market. Shortly, the market will move to a point where sellers are interested, and we mostly act as agent from then on.

When we are trading stopped stocks, the market really is international. A book may be coordinated from New York, Los Angeles, or London, depending on the time of day and personnel availability, but the bids, offers, and transactions are coming from all over the world. Jefferies & Co. endeavors to use as little capital as possible so that the ultimate buyers and sellers will set the price. When the stock reopens, our activity slows considerably. Institutions feel that risk arbitrage trades are no-brainers when the exchange is open, and they use this commission business to pay their bills, a dubious and perhaps somewhat expensive approach.

When any piece of merchandise comes in, we have procedures to determine who should see it. We can go from showing it to no one and just waiting for the other side, to blitzing our whole client list. Jefferies

& Co. emphasizes constantly that when a client commissions us to complete a trade, it is a sacred trust. We must try to find the right amount of exposure and the right accounts to show the order. We are always qualifying accounts so that we will only show them merchandise that they can act on. We avoid anyone that makes a living running ahead of orders.

This strategy has become more necessary in the past couple of years, because there has been a significant increase of short-term trading money coming into the marketplace. This has been fueled by general liquidity and perceived opportunity. These opportunities derive from increased market volatility.

In addition, I believe that the execution measurement systems promoted by consultants encourage institutions to excessively expose their orders to the marketplace, making them easier targets for short-term traders.

Another piece of business for which we got a lot of print is in the so-called street sweep. This is when a major percentage of a company changes hands in a market transaction. This can only occur when there is a lot of stock in professional hands such as the arbitrageurs, and it requires clients who can act quickly and are predisposed to selling the stock. It also requires a buyer who has already cleared Hart Scott Rodino restrictions that say that a buyer can only buy a rather small percentage of a company before clearing further purchases with the Federal Trade Commission. The only so-called street sweeps in which we have been involved were the aforementioned Allied Stores and Cyclops. In both cases, they were initiated by sellers, so the "sweep" analogy is strained. The only time street sweeps can occur is when the buyer has FTC approval and has no tender offer extant, and the stock is in weak hands, such as arbitrageurs.

Merger Mania

Like many other major Wall Street players, Jefferies has been involved in all recent mega-merger trading activity. In the RJR Nabisco battle, there was a lot of interest in the stocks abroad, so we had to trade almost around-the-clock. Jefferies was also the leading trader of the junk pre-

Frank Baxter

ferred stocks and bonds that came out of the deal, because our clients —
the arbitrageurs — were the major holders and our institutional clients
were the major new investors.

The Time-Warner situation was a tough one to trade. There was
no strategy that could exploit all possible outcomes. If Paramount won,
Warner's stock would suffer. If Time won, as it did, its own stock would
suffer.

Friday the 13th

The Friday the 13th massacre of October 1989 was a good test of our
system. There was a little less than an hour left of trading when it was
announced that United Airlines could not arrange the financing for its
$300 a share tender offer. The stock had been shut down pending the
announcement. It was trading at 280 at the time of the halt. Shortly after
the announcement, American Airlines, which had a $120 bid from Don-
ald Trump, was shut down at $89. All stocks fell sharply with the cold
realization that the major fuel for the strong market — the takeover movement — was no longer going to be able to receive instant liquidity.

Very quickly, other stocks subject to takeover rumors were shut
down by the NYSE. In response, our London office got markets going
in United and American at $280 and $80, respectively. Trading was brisk
with us, as the stocks never reopened on the exchange. When the market
closed at 4:00 P.M., the Dow Jones Industrial Average was down 190
points, almost 7 percent in a little over an hour.

Many of our customers did not want to go home, and we were very
busy trading until around 7:00 P.M., when things slowed. Our London
office picked up the mantle at 5:00 A.M. on Saturday, and while there
were a lot of telephone calls, there was not much trading over the
weekend. The business that was done was mostly around the closing
prices on Friday.

Activity turned brisk again on Monday morning at around 5:00
A.M. The pace was very active until the exchange opened, then it let up
a bit. We didn't have time for our regular morning meeting. Although
the activity was not as intense as two years before, it seemed even lighter
because of the operational improvements. We achieved 100 percent
accuracy on all trades.

138

POSIT and Portfolio Trading

An important area that our subsidiary, the Investment Technology Group, has recently devoted a lot of time and resources to is the trading of entire portfolios, mostly for passive investing clients. We, with BARRA in Berkeley, have developed a system we call POSIT—Portfolio System for Institutional Trading—that enables clients to input their entire program, looking for the other side. Institutional traders enter into their personal computers the names of the stocks in the portfolios they would like to buy or sell, and the time of day that they would like to trade (which determines the transaction price). The information is then sent to POSIT's VAX computer, which matches the appropriate trades. Execution and clearing are then performed automatically.

We think the program has implications for all professional investors who have multiple stocks to buy or sell. POSIT represents an electronic clearing house between buyers and sellers. If another side to a trade can be found, there is no market impact, and the commission can be relatively small. It is not the right market for all trades. No market is. But it is a valuable vehicle for a certain part of every institution's business.

Our job is to offer the right blend of tools to maximize the effectiveness of the professional trader. We have done transactions of up to $100 million on POSIT. If they are done during the trading day, they are reported on the tape. If they are done when the tape is not running, they are reported to the NASD. About 20 percent of the orders entered are crossed. That is a very good result, considering the ease and speed of entry and the cost savings when you have a hit. POSIT volume has tripled in the past year.

My vision is that when any trader has a program, a significant number of stocks to buy or sell at once, he or she would automatically run it through POSIT first to see if he could get a fit, and then consider letting our trader salesmen work on some of the residual. That thought gives me very pleasant dreams. Since so many people now restrict the words "program trading" to index arbitrage, perhaps we need a new word to replace the old general definition.

Frank Baxter

Conclusion: The Future Looks Bright

Although we were in a slow market period in 1988 and 1989, the future for the third market looks bright in the 1990s. Investors are rejecting the regulations of exchanges that are designed mostly to retain business rather than to provide flexibility to the professional investor. Professionals should be able to trade when and where they wish, and the third market fulfills this objective.

The third market, coupled with the automation of the transaction process that allows computer-to-computer dialogue to set up trades that can be negotiated by humans, provides limitless opportunities for those, like us at Jefferies, who are obsessed with service, committed to change, and love innovation.

Jefferies will continue to look for products which can be traded third market style. Recently, we started a high-yield bond trading and sales operation. Since these bonds trade a lot like equities, we are very optimistic about our value added.

It has been suggested that third market trading firms are not much different from our major competitors who are exchange members. In a superficial sense, that is true. We go after about the same clients and trade in about the same stocks. We think the difference—now and forever if we keep working at it—is that we offer the only marketplace exclusively for professionals where they can feel assured that they are dealing with those who understand the rules and protocol of professionals.

It has also been suggested that exchanges might wither away and all trading will be third market style. I hope that is not the case. Professionals need diversity and competition. I doubt that the exchanges of the future will have hundreds of highly paid people running around floors, if there are floors. There should still be, though, places where like-minded people meet. Exchanges are also a vital nexus between the professional and the less frequent investor.

Whatever the market structure of the future, I am confident that there will be room for third market mavericks like Jefferies. And I hope to keep leading the charge.

CHAPTER SIX

VICTOR SPERANDEO

Assessing Risk to Exploit Market Trends

Victor Sperandeo is President of Rand Management Corporation, a money management firm in New Jersey. Since 1966 he has been involved in the stock, bond, commodities, and currencies markets as a trader and money manager. Mr. Sperandeo is also an advisor and consultant to a number of institutional clients. His opinion is often quoted in the financial press and he frequently appears as a guest lecturer. Vic is also the author of Trader Vic—Methods of a Wall Street Master. A native New Yorker, he studied economics and finance at Queens College.

"Trader Vic's" reputation as a prophet of the stock market was immeasurably enhanced when he correctly predicted and capitalized on the stock market debacle of October 1987. In this chapter he discusses how he—an extremely successful hedge fund trader—uses his ability to identify and exploit market trends for the benefit of his shareholders. As this chapter reveals, Sperandeo's goal of "staying at the table" is achieved through diligent conservation of capital by deducing the appropriate risk of the given economic and financial profile of a market, much like a poker player or an insurance actuary. Once that risk is analyzed and assessed, the trader must rely on emotional discipline to maintain the statistical advantage.

"For surely we are not . . . now simply contending in order that my view or that yours may prevail, but I presume that we ought both of us to be fighting for the truth." —Socrates

Searching for the Truth

A trader's business is to profit by correctly identifying the truth. To achieve this, he must integrate a rigorous understanding of the odds, the markets and their instruments, statistical and technical analysis, economics, politics, and human psychology into all trading and investment decisions.

I continually struggle to be correct, without struggling to be completely free from mistakes, using my independent judgment to the best of my knowledge. When I make a mistake, I analyze it. Then I integrate new facts and principles into my decision-making process to avoid repeating the mistake. Although uncertainty is always present, trading isn't guesswork. It is a process of applying knowledge of the past and the present to determine future probability.

People call me a trader—someone who only plays the shortest term trends. In truth, I am part short-term trader, part intermediate-term speculator, and part long-term investor. I'm really a money manager who manages risk. If there is one fatal flaw in this business, it is allowing isolated information to drive investing or trading decisions—in other words, committing money without knowing *all* the risks. Systematic knowledge of complex economic and marketplace interrelationships is a prerequisite for assessing risk.

The Tools for Success

As a teenager, I became intrigued with cards and the potential to profit by knowing as much as possible about the game. To win at cards, you have to play the odds, and to know the odds you have to remember what's been dealt. I therefore studied books about gambling, odds, card counting, and other facets of the game. I also learned memorization techniques from my good friend and famous memory expert, Harry Lorayne.

I also learned something about risks and risk management when I realized what deceptions card sharks could perform. To avoid being cheated during games, I learned how sharks manipulated cards. These lessons would have future value when analyzing the true purpose of government economic policies.

Learning the Ropes

In January 1966, I surveyed *The New York Times* employment section and found that the highest-paid people were physicists, biologists, and securities traders—$25,000 a year! Since I was already proficient at gambling and understood more about odds than analyzing atoms, I began on Wall Street as a quote boy for Pershing & Co.

Although I knew nothing about the stock market, I understood odds. Figuring that these skills applied to trading, I set out to learn exactly how; I needed more knowledge. I studied the markets the same way that I studied odds and memorization techniques. I also memorized the symbols for all the approximately 1,500 NYSE listed stocks. During a job interview with Ricky Bergman, a partner at Filer Schmidt & Co., I demonstrated this skill. Impressed, he hired me as an options trader in January 1968.

At Filer, trading over-the-counter options was an opportunity to learn how to read the tape and gain experience at pricing and leveraging. In those days, there was no such thing as a reasonable firm quote for options contracts to a buyer. Typically, a customer would call several dealers for prices and then place an order. But there was no guarantee that an order would be executed. The idea of a single broker-dealer offering guaranteed contract delivery at a reasonable quoted price simply hadn't occurred to anyone yet.

Making a Firm Market

Recognizing a new business opportunity, I joined several other options traders to establish Ragnar Options Corp. Our radical new approach of offering reasonable firm quotes worked. If we couldn't buy an existing option contract to fill an order, then we sold it ourselves. Our competitors thought that we must have had tremendous capital to take on that level of risk. Actually, all we did was take some small losses to secure high volume and continued profitability. The willingness to take losses was totally alien to the business at the time. Within six months, Ragnar was trading more OTC options than any other single dealer in the world.

Things got more competitive when the Chicago Board Options Exchange (CBOE) standardized the options business in 1973, but Ragnar bought three seats and traded its own capital until 1977, when Weeden & Company, in effect, merged all the Ragnar personnel into their operation under very favorable conditions. I managed their options department and became their block trader in the "glamour stocks." Unfortunately, Weeden got into financial difficulty in 1978 and stopped doing business nine months later. After Weeden, I started trading for Interstate Securities in any market that offered potential: stocks, options, bonds, futures, commodities, currencies—whatever was judged to be a good value with low risk.

In 1979, I founded Hugo Securities, a private trading partnership still in existence. As an independent, I traded several accounts concurrently on a 50–50 profit/loss basis. Now, after 24 years, if I have any specialty, it is managing risk in any market.

The Dinosaurs of Wall Street History

Because my specialty is managing risk, I haven't become a Wall Street dinosaur (at least not yet!). The dinosaurs are extinct because they couldn't adapt. Similarly, relying on just one specific trading method has ended many Wall Street careers. If a trader's only ability was intraday trading, then the arbitrary volatility that program trading introduced into the intraday trend in the early 1980s might have made him an endangered species. Why?

Program trading renders normal price movements irrelevant because, at any moment, a program can hit and upset what was once predictable from reading the tape. It is impossible to second guess the manipulators and costly to be on the wrong side of their programs. I did a lot of profitable intraday trading until late 1986, but it required an adeptness and intensity that was extremely difficult to maintain. Instead of trading three times a day, I was trading from ten to thirty times a day.

The stresses were incredible and the odds against me were increasing. It was like playing poker with a known bottom dealer. In response, I shifted my major focus away from short-term to intermediate- and long-term trends, trends I'll explain about later.

Clear Objectives

My professional objective has always been to be in business for myself. I set out to make money consistently and to establish a method of managing risk to achieve my goals and objectives.

From 1971 to 1989, in managing my own money and that of a few partners on a professional basis, I have never had a losing year. In fact, from 1978 to 1987 I had a documented 67.8 percent compounded annual rate of return.

Staying at the Table

The key to winning consistently over a long period in this business is to constantly keep the odds in your favor. Suppose you are sitting at the right side of the dealer in a five-card draw poker game with a $10 ante, there is $50 in the pot after the deal. If the first player bets $10 and everyone else calls, then there is $90 to be won if you call and win. The potential reward at this point is 9 to 1. Assuming you have four hearts and want to draw a flush (a probable winning hand), the odds are 5.2 to 1 of drawing a heart. With a risk of 4½ to 1 and a reward of 9 to 1, the odds are clearly 1.7 to 1 in your favor. Over the long-term, if you maintain this kind of strategy, you will win twice what you will lose. Of course, if you pull a flush on the draw, you will then have to make another bet which will be based on your reading of the other players and your assessment of their behavior. But to win over the long-term, you must limit your losses and stay at the table.

Luck can be only partially controlled. However, I learned how to get that small amount of control from a book by Joan Didion. In the book a character says, *"You can't win if you're not at the table."* In other words, you can't win at craps unless you're at the craps table. The secret of being lucky is to give yourself enough chances to be lucky—to roll the dice enough times to make your point, even if you don't roll seven on the first roll. You may crap out a number of times, and each time hurts. But you keep rolling, and *"if you have even a modicum of talent, you will make your point, even if the bet is small at first. . . ."*

On Wall Street, staying at the table means staying in business. The smart trader approaches trading as a business, and a prudent business-man wants first to cover his overhead each month and then achieve a steady growth in earnings. So, rather than striving for the big hit, a trader should endeavor to be in business year after year and make consistent profits. My goal is to protect capital first and then to consistently produce better than average returns.

Preservation, Consistency, Pursuit

Therefore, I base my trading and investment philosophy on a hierarchy of three principles: (1) preservation of capital, (2) consistent profitability, and (3) the pursuit of superior returns. They are basic in the sense that they underlie and guide all investment decisions. They are hierarchical because each carries a different weight in my investment strategy — they ascend from one to the other. That is, preservation of capital leads to consistent profits, which make the pursuit of superior returns possible.

Preservation of capital is the foundation of my investment philos-ophy. In evaluating risk/reward, risk is the *prime* concern. Before asking "What potential profit can be realized," a trader should ask, "What potential loss can I suffer?" I focus on accumulating profits without exposing capital to a high degree of risk. Before taking a position, I require at least a 1 to 3 risk/reward ratio. When the risk/reward of remaining in any financial market is poor, I go into cash, despite the contemporary wisdom.

For example, when Iraq invaded Kuwait, the Dow dropped to 2710.64 on August 6, 1990, from a July 16th high of 2999.75. This was a 9.6 percent drop! Since the market could have reversed and gone to new highs if Saddam pulled out, the amount of decline needed to "invest" in shorts (instead of to trade) would be another 28.8 per cent. This would have created a 3 to 1 risk/reward ratio. But, in 96 years of history, there have been only five declines totalling more than 38.4 percent without an important rally in between; only a 2 percent likelihood of occurrence. Since a typical (median) decline amounted to 11.5 percent, this was a very poor short based on Saddam's whim. Consequently, I do not compete with the averages or with the performance of others. This isn't merely a conservative attitude. It is the heart of my trading and investment philosophy, and it has lead me to consistent profitability.

Consistent profitability is a corollary of the preservation of capital. Obviously, if there is no capital to invest there cannot be any profits. Capital isn't a constant—it is either gained or lost. To gain capital, you must be consistently profitable, but to be consistently profitable, you have to preserve gains. There is a trading rule that states, "Never let a profit turn into a loss." My rule is, "Never give back more than 50 percent of a gain." Assume you buy a stock at 40. If it went to 50 and then started to decline, sell at 45, if not before, to lock in the profit.

Consistent profitability requires constant balancing of the risks and rewards of each decision. By focusing on risk and scaling it according to accumulated profits, the odds of consistent success increase. For example, when entering a new accounting period (be it a month, a quarter, or a year) my initial positions are small relative to the capital available because there are no accumulated profits. If I initially begin to accrue losses, then I reduce risk by decreasing the size of any losing positions and scaling back the size of any new opening positions, and so on. That way, there is always capital available for investment—I'm always at the table. The converse is also true. When any accounting period accrues profits, I increase the size of each position, relative to the amount of profits. This process of constantly weighing risk is applied to each position individually and to the investment portfolio as a whole.

As profits accrue, I take this process a step further for the pursuit of superior returns. If, and only if, a level of profits exists to justify the aggressive risk required, I seek the higher returns by trading larger size of the instrument in play; the criterion used to assess the risk/reward of being involved in any market remains the same. Only a portion of profits, *not initial investment capital,* is exposed to higher risk. I continuously monitor the risk/reward factor and adjust the portfolio according to accrued profits.

The Implementation Process

How are these principles put into practice? There are three crucial aspects of implementation:

1. knowledge,

2. money management, and

3. emotional discipline.

Knowledge provides the raw materials necessary to make correct decisions. Money management is the means of determining when and how much to invest. Emotional discipline is the essential psychological requirement for executing your strategy based on knowledge and money management principles. Let me address the complex interrelationship of these three ingredients by discussing each of them in turn.

Knowledge

In our context, knowledge is the information required to understand the financial markets and make prudent investment decisions. To invest successfully requires knowledge of the economy as a whole, of the effects of government intervention, of the markets and their instruments, of statistical and technical methods, and of odds. With all this to consider, how can one possibly determine when and how to invest? The key is to reduce things to principles, to think in essentials at all levels. All things have a nature. Through observation and the exercise of Aristotelian logic, one can identify a thing's nature, isolate its essential attributes, and by that understand how it functions and predict its behavior under defined conditions. The economy and the financial markets are no exception.

The Austrian School

In analyzing the economy as a whole, I am in agreement with the Austrian School of Economics, whose most noted thinkers are Ludwig Von Mises and Frederick A. Hayek. Like the Austrians, I view the economy as a collection of individuals pursuing their goals through free exchange in the marketplace. Without government intervention, a free market results in an "evenly rotating economy" that experiences natural cyclic adjustments, with production and prosperity in an ever-increasing upward trend. Government intervention inhibits free trade, stifles the achievement of goals, and creates an arbitrary redistribution of income. It is the source of many minor movements within the marketplace and of most violent market swings in history.

By contrast, the policy makers in Washington are predominantly Keynesian interventionists. As such, they believe that economic intervention is not only a legitimate function of government, but also the key determinant of growth or recession, as measured by GNP. They think that by "fine tuning" the economy through careful management of taxation and monetary policy, stable and steady growth can be achieved.

A Doom and Gloom Scenario

However, the Keynesians have "fine tuned" us right into a $14 trillion U.S. debt load (Latin American, government, public, corporate, junk bond and consumer, etc.). They have deficit financed the longest "recovery" in history. We are now seeing the signs of potential inflationary pressures, and since 1913 there has never been a reduction in inflation (as measured by rising prices) without a recession or depression. The economy is so much more leveraged now than it was in the 1981-82 recession, that when the Fed finally restricts reserves, as it must, the world economy will suffer the most turbulent times of this century. All debts have to be paid, either by the debtor or by the creditor if the borrower defaults. Who will pay the price? Inflating our way out of this debt won't work today as it did in 1932. Instead, there will be rampant bankruptcies. Wealth will be destroyed to pay the price for what amounts to irresponsible loans against future production.

Look to the Fed

History supports my conclusions. I did a study correlating economic conditions and stock market performance to expansions and contractions of reserves by the Federal Reserve Board from 1949 to 1985. The results show that Fed policy largely determines both the direction of the stock market and the course of the economy. In addition, except during the past two world wars, the stock market is an almost infallible lead indicator of the effect of Fed policy on the long term economic trend. Every bull and bear market since 1949 is directly linked to the Fed's policy on reserves, and in every case, the reaction of the stock market anticipated the long-term trend of the economy.

The stock market is an accurate leading indicator because it reacts to changes in the Fed's policy more quickly than can the economy as a whole. It discounts the effect of Fed policy changes on future corporate profits. For example on July 24, 1984, Federal Reserve Board Chairman Paul Volcker testified before the Senate saying, "The Fed's [restrictive] policy was inappropriate . . ." That same day, the stock market had its low and a new bull market began.

Federal Reserve Board policy largely determines the long-term trend of the market. However, the Fed often attempts to mask its actual strategy. Consequently, I analyze the minutes of Open Market Committee and read between the lines, looking for subtle implications that reveal the true motivation of the Chairman or other key figures. Fiscal policy is inherently dependent on the character and intent of the men in positions of power and influence. I try to grasp the motives and intentions of these men by monitoring congressional hearings, press conferences, and political developments.

The Four Market Stages

As a "renegade" Dow theorist, I have determined that a market is always in one of four conditions: It is being:

1. accumulated (bought);

2. distributed (sold);

3. trending up or down; or

4. *waiting* to make a move (consolidating).

Further, three trends are always operating in a market: the short-term trend (which is from days to weeks and less than 14 days 99 percent of the time), the intermediate-term trend (which is from weeks to months, usually between 14 days and 6 months), and the long-term trend (which is from months to years).

The long-term trend of the market is by far the most important trend and the easiest to identify, classify, and understand. The intermediate- and short-term trends are subsets of the long-term. Once the long-term trend is known, the intermediate- and short-term trends can be measured and analyzed. Their nature and action become predictable in light of their position in the long term. For instance, intermediate bear market corrections are usually "V" patterns, where the low is made on high volume and the rally high is made on low volume; intermediate bull market corrections are usually "horseshoe" patterns where the low is made on low volume and the intermediate top is made on high volume. Intermediate bear market movements make higher highs that fail to carry forward above previous highs. Intermediate bull market rallies continue to make higher highs, and don't sell off below previous important lows. Ideally, by identifying the phase of the market and its status relative to all three trends, one can predict market performance. The major problem is how to go about analyzing and characterizing market moves so that the knowledge can be practically applied to the decision-making process.

An Actuarial Stock Market

The solution lies in statistical methods. Take life insurance companies for example. They use life span probabilities and adjust premiums to match the probability of payout based on the age and history of those being insured. I apply the same kind of methods to the marketplace. In 1974, I missed the October low in stocks and I wanted to know why, so I asked myself, "What exactly is a trend? What is its nature? How long does a trend normally last? How high or low does it normally go? What is the nature of a correction? How long does it normally last and to what extent?"

To answer these questions, I first had to define, measure, and classify all trends and corrections and identify a standard by which to define "normal." For two years, I pulled together every bit of recorded information I could find on the markets from 1896 to the present. Dow theory taught me that a trend is a significant market movement of measurable extent in an upward or downward direction over a definite duration. An upward trend is characterized by a series of higher highs and higher lows. A downward trend is characterized by a series of lower lows and lower highs. I then identified every trend since then, logging their extent and duration in actuarial tables. I classified each trend as short-term, intermediate-term, or long-term, and identified significant interrelationships. Using statistical analysis, I refined Dow's definitions and developed proprietary correlations between different types of trends, between trends and corrections, trends and divergences, and so forth. In short, I reduced the data to statistical terms applicable to my trading. Here are some examples.

Actuarial Markets in Action

To most people, a bull market is simply a broad, long, upward movement. For me, a primary bull market is a broad upward movement with a duration of months to years, lasting more than 1.8 years 75 percent of the time and lasting between 1.8 to 4.1 years 67 percent of the time. With regard to the Industrials and Transports, a primary bull market is interrupted by important declines or secondary corrections lasting weeks to months that never jointly penetrate previous primary low points. Based on this one observation, if in a four-year-old bull market the Industrials and Transports are in a secondary correction that reaches a lower low than the previous correction, I would look for the beginning of a bear market. Although not conclusive by itself, I would weight this factor heavily in my projections of the long-term trend. If it coincided with a high-volume acceleration and a tightening of reserves by the Fed, then I would speculate on this observation.

I also found that 99 percent of the time, short-term corrections last for a maximum of two weeks and their extent is 5 percent or less. Consequently, if the intermediate trend is up and the market sells off 3 percent in two weeks, then the short-term correction is acting "normally." As a result, there is a higher probability that the next move will be normal as well, and therefore the odds for speculating on the long side in the intermediate trend are excellent.

Before proceeding, I want to point out that it is absolutely a fool's game to use statistical profiles to predict exact future levels that the markets will reach. Levels don't produce tops and bottoms, they are the product of economic conditions, which are a function of the policy decisions of the government, especially the Federal Reserve Board. You can no more predict with statistics the exact top or bottom of a market than an insurance company can predict exactly when a specific person will die. Rather, with statistical profiles I calculate probabilities that are highly significant over a set of movements. For example, in a full market cycle (bull to bear and bear to bull), 85 percent of all movements fall within 5 percent of the extent and duration medians. Using such observations, you can determine what is most likely to occur.

Analogous to mortality tables, my actuarial tables provide a means to measure the statistical risk of holding a position at any point by comparing the current trend to similar trends using historical extent and duration medians. Using statistical profiles, I determine the probability of a trend continuing and adjust asset allocations according to the risk/reward factor, which is aligned with measured probabilities. Just as in the poker game example mentioned earlier, it is a way to manage odds, to always keep them in your favor.

I use statistics knowing that the outlook can change radically with a change in Fed policy or with the emergence of other new factors. I always couple my statistical approach with a continuing analysis of present conditions. I call this "recognizing the present."

Money Management

Money management is the second key aspect of implementation. It refers to the method of determining when and how much to invest in different markets. Since there are three trends that can be moving in opposite directions simultaneously, it is imperative to know which trend you are involved with and why. The long-term trend is for investors, the intermediate-term trend is for speculators, and the short-term trend is for traders. Accordingly, I could be either a trader, speculator, or investor, and often some combination of the three.

I use a tactical asset allocation approach to money management, with primary focus on the risk relative to the potential reward; that is, I always ask "What can I win versus what can I lose on this position?" To identify risk/reward in a concrete way, whether in cards or in the markets, you must know the statistical profiles.

Statistical Profiles

A statistical profile of a market trend has two principal components: extent, or how big the move is; and duration, or how long it lasts. When entering a market, I establish the percentage likelihood that the current trends are behaving according to historical extent and duration medians, and I adjust asset allocations according to the percentages. Consider the following example: Suppose we are in a primary bull market and I'm deciding how to allocate stock purchases that look good from a fundamental point of view. Fundamentals aren't enough. I also weigh the statistical risk/reward factor. In a primary bull market, the median increase for stocks in an intermediate move is 21.3 percent in 106 days. This means that from 1897 to date one half of all intermediate moves ended at or before these median points. Even though the stocks might be a good long-term fundamental purchase, to allocate 100 percent of one's assets when the market has already attained a median level is a poor statistical risk, because only 50 percent of all similar moves in history have lasted longer. A proper portfolio mix would limit equities positions to, at most, 50 percent of one's assets, no matter how good they look from a fundamental standpoint. That is what I mean about focusing on risk.

The Risk/Reward Factors

In managing money, I view risk differently than most people. Typically, "money management" refers to the portfolio mix — 1 percent in drugs, 2 percent in computers, etc. Many money managers evaluate risk in terms of the alpha and/or beta coefficients. These tell you only what will most likely happen to your portfolio based on past quality and volatility movements in stocks versus the market. If the market goes up or down 10 percent and your portfolio has a beta of 2, your portfolio will go up or down 20 percent. It does not tell you what the probability of the market going up or down will be. Beta tells you nothing about the risk of the forthcoming movement. I view money management in risk/reward terms, allocating assets according to the sum of my knowledge of all three trends, where the market stands in each, and a statistical risk/reward analysis. Looking at beta alone is analogous to a life insurance company issuing the same policy at an equal premium to both a 20-year-old man and an 80-year-old man. While a 20-year-old may, in fact, die before an 80-year-old, the statistical profile for male life expectancy suggests that this is highly improbable. Therefore, insurance companies "manage" their risk by charging a higher premium to the 80-year-old man. So by adjusting premiums to statistical risk, insurance companies are able to maintain their profitability over time. From this type of analysis, you can calculate the two aspects of risk: the risk-reward ratio of a price movement and the likelihood of a price movement occurring.

Stock market trends are subject to similar statistical probabilities; trends have quantifiable "life expectancies" and other consistently recurring characteristics. Adjusting asset allocations accordingly allows me to be aligned with these statistical probabilities, while constantly recognizing the present.

Within the context of this approach to measuring risk, I use a variety of technical methods to measure precise entry and exit points. In reality, technical analysis is just induction logic applied to price movements. Induction is reasoning from the specific to the general; it is the process of observing events, isolating similarities, abstracting the unifying element responsible for the similarity, and forming a generalization. For example, when IBM was a strong market leader in the 1970s, I noted that if it closed within $\frac{1}{4}$ of a point from its daily high or low, it opened in the direction of the close 92 percent of the time. Trading a portion of my own account on this one observation produced very handsome returns.

Can Trading Be Taught?

Can my overall approach to the market be taught? I thought it could, but over a seven-year period I instructed 38 people, told them everything I know, and only five were successful. There are many intelligent people involved in the financial markets, yet only a small percentage consistently outperform the averages. Why? What is the crucial difference between the successful and the unsuccessful?

Knowledge and method aren't enough—not in any endeavor. For example, consider the area of weight loss. Why is it so difficult to lose weight? If one goes into a bookstore, there are literally hundreds of books by experts on the subject that outline proven techniques. The knowledge component is no problem. Basically, all the books say the same things: eat less, don't eat fattening foods, and exercise. Yet, out of every 100 Americans who start a weight-loss program, only 12 actually lose weight, and of those 12, only 2 maintain their weight loss for more than a year. That is a 2 percent success rate; worse than the 5 percent success rate for commodity trading! The problem is not knowledge or method, but the ability to *execute.*

Emotional Discipline

If there is one crucial factor required for success, it is *emotional discipline*—the ability or will to execute knowledge. Emotional discipline is the least understood component of successful money management and the most difficult to acquire. Without emotional discipline, knowledge is worthless!

Emotional discipline requires self-awareness and the ability to segregate decisions from emotional reactions. For all but the last 8,000 years, the emotions of anger and fear and the response of "fight or flight" have been major survival tools. For modern man, however, the term "survival" means more than just sustaining life. It means long-term planning and establishing goals and purposes through use of reason and logic, which Aristotle properly identified and defined just a little over 2,000 years ago.

Unfortunately, two millennia hasn't been enough time for reason to be accepted as the primary means of human survival. Many still attempt to deal with modern events by responding emotionally rather than by exercising logic and reason. Consequently, the "fight or flight" mechanism still serves as the primary method of choice for some of us, even though the savage drooling beast it was once effective against is gone. On Wall Street we deal with facts; but without a carefully disciplined and logical approach to the decision-making process, numbers on a quote screen can appear just as vicious, and be just as deadly, as our ancestors' most dreaded monster.

When our ancestors faced danger, they had to be right . . . or they would die. By contrast, making mistakes is an unavoidable part of trading. It is the unwillingness to admit making mistakes that stops most traders from succeeding. It is their underlying psychology that undermines emotional discipline. We have a choice. We can let our emotions determine our behavior, while ignoring the facts of reality—the truth—including the consequences of our actions. Or, through self-understanding and knowledge of human behavior and psychology, we can "program" emotions to comply with reality. In choosing the latter, we can achieve emotional discipline and learn to consistently execute based on knowledge without interference from irrational emotions.

How can a trader lose a fortune by holding on to a position that is running against him? If he lacks emotional discipline, his false pride system won't let him get out of his position. Not only have fortunes been lost, but many have taken their own lives because they couldn't face being wrong.

How many people have bought stock, watched it lose money, and continued to hold on to it based on their *wish* that it would go back up so they could get out even? A wish is not a claim on reality!

Failing to Admit Failure

How many money managers employ the strategy of averaging down, which is nothing more than a camouflage for ignoring a mistake? If the object is to preserve capital, then when a position turns against you, the only reasonable thing to do is execute at a predefined exit point. Averaging down is just a way to say, "I'm not wrong." To buy a stock on an averaging down basis is a major money management fallacy. It's a way to avoid admitting an error.

The difference between consistent and sporadic success is the willingness to admit and analyze mistakes. If you ask a room full of people how many of them liked to admit making mistakes, maybe 1 in 100 would raise their hands. Yet, since human beings are neither omniscient nor infallible, making mistakes is a normal part of life and is an essential impetus to growth. Admitting mistakes is a positive human attribute. Trading and investing is a very competitive business. Wall Street is filled with gurus, letter writers, predictors. Everyone wants to be right all the time, but everyone can't always be right.

Setting, and Keeping, the Rules

By establishing a set of rules for entry and exit points, a money manager or trader is admitting that mistakes are possible. By executing those rules when a position goes against him, he is admitting making the mistake. He is also preserving capital. And if he analyzes why he made the mistake, then the odds of making it again are reduced. Without specific rules, it can be hard to admit you are wrong. In one intraday S&P trade, I watched my position move against me with incredible speed. I sat there trying to figure out what went wrong, but didn't act immediately. It cost me a lot of money, but I learned from the mistake. My existing rule of exit wasn't precise enough—it didn't put enough weight on the market's volatility. After that loss, I put a new rule into effect: after a one point loss in an S&P position (equal to $500 per contract), I get out. No questions asked, no excuses, no reasons, no wishes, no "I'll get out as soon as it . . ." I discipline my emotions, take the loss, and preserve capital.

Emotional discipline has been the key factor to my trading and investing success. Emotional discipline implies the ability to: (1) admit being wrong; (2) take the blame for one's own mistakes and; (3) analyze why the mistakes were made and take corrective action. Without these abilities, all the knowledge in the world and the best money management method ever devised are absolutely useless.

Scenario for a Disaster

How have I put these theories into practice? In a *Barron's* September 21, 1987, feature article, I was quoted as follows:

> There is a very good chance that this market has topped. . . . If the recent sell-off is followed by a rally that doesn't make new highs and that in turn is followed by new lows on high volume, the salad days are over for sure. . . . When the stock market does slip into a full-fledged downswing, program trading will exaggerate the move to such a degree that the sell-off may be the steepest on record . . . . The next bear market will crash so badly that the rules will have to change.

Many people have asked me how I made this call. Simply put, every analytical method pointed to a major down move. At the time, the stock market was like a very sick 98-year-old man on life-support systems. He might survive a while longer, but I wouldn't issue him a life insurance policy, not at any premium.

I first became cautious in March 1987. Because of program trading, there were huge amounts of "hot money" in the market. The program money was involved purely to make profits through various short term-hedge, arbitrage, and manipulative strategies; not because of the under-lying value of the stocks. I knew that if the Fed tightened or if the dollar fell significantly, the "hot money" would be pulled out, therefore accel-erating and exaggerating the resultant down move. On May 20, the Dow Jones Industrial Average stood at 2215.87 and began an intermediate up move. By August 25, the Industrials had increased 22.9 percent in 96 days, while the Transports had increased 21.3 percent 108 days. These were the exact median levels. In other words, the market had already achieved its "normal" median levels both in terms of extent and duration. In addition, from a technical point of view, there were divergences. The Dow made a new high in August, but the advance/decline ratio did not.

The market also was in trouble from a fundamental standpoint. It was overvalued by almost anyone's standards, selling at 21 times earn-ings, one of the highest PEs in history. Only in 1962, when PEs reached 22, was it ever higher. The book value to price ratio was nominally higher than it was in 1929. Adjusted for inflation, it was much higher. Moreover, the escalating debt caused me to fear for the health of the dollar and the economic consequences if something "went wrong." The question was not "if" but "when."

My predictions about the *what and how* of Black Monday proved themselves out. It was just a matter of determining precisely when the crash was going to occur. The first sign was on October 5, when I read in *The Wall Street Journal:* "Fed Chairman Greenspan said interest rates could become 'dangerously high' if inflation worries 'mushroom' in fi-nancial markets. Greenspan called such worries unwarranted but hinted the discount rate may have to rise to allay them." On the following day, stock prices plunged a record 91.55 points on interest rate worries. Then, on October 15, Dow Theory gave me a sell signal. One more straw would break the camel's back.

The Last Straw

Then along came the disagreement between James Baker and Germany on whether Germany should stimulate (inflate) its economy so the U.S. would not have to raise interest rates to protect the dollar. When Germany refused, Baker announced on October 18 that "he was going to let the dollar slide." At that point, there was no doubt in my mind that the financial markets would collapse because of this unknown dollar devaluation. I was looking for a drop in the dollar the next day. So, when the market gapped down on the October 19 opening, the question of "when" was answered. I proceeded to short a 200-point down opening, increasing my short position using futures. By the end of the day, that position alone had resulted in a $250,000 profit.

An Introspective Look

Whether trading firm capital or managing someone's money, I think it is incumbent on the trader/money manager to look within himself in order to identify his own strengths and weaknesses. This process is important because it lets the client know what to expect, and it helps the trader/money manager focus his strategy toward his strengths. Unfortunately, such disclosure is rare in this business.

Strengths

My greatest strength is the ability to consistently call significant market turning points. Beginnings and endings of long term movements are the product of economic conditions, which are a function of the policy decisions of the government, especially the Federal Reserve Board. I combine my knowledge of government policy with statistical methods to determine what is likely to occur. Then I examine the present market conditions closely: Where is the trend? Is it turning? That's what I mean by recognizing the present.

A second strength is my ability to play the short side adeptly. Even though bear markets aren't as popular as bull markets, I have done

161

exceptionally well on the down side (e.g., 1969–70, 1973–74). Bear markets, which have fewer participants, usually move more quickly than up markets. In September 1974 I doubled my capital in one month by being short. However, since 1974, there have only been two down years in the stock market, and even these moves were quite minor in nature. In the "bear market" from September 1976 to February 1978, the market dropped 20.4 percent, and from April 1981 to August 1982, it lost 29.4 percent.[1] By contrast, the 1969–70 and the 1973–74 bear markets were each down an average of 47.1 percent, and the worst bear market downleg in history occurred from March to July in 1932, losing 53.6 percent on its eighth and final intermediate down move. Most people today have not seen a true bear market and when they do they will not forget it.

I've never been caught long in a bear market or during any major correction in a bull market. Being invested in downswings is totally against my philosophy and my personality. Before taking any position, I determine my exit point—the point at which the market will be telling me that I was wrong. While I might lose money on short-term minor down swings, I don't believe I could ever be invested from months to years in major sell-offs.

In June of 1987, for example, my accounts were up only about 15 to 20 percent while the universe was up close to 40 percent. I just couldn't be bullish, for all the reasons I explained earlier. I don't compete with the averages, and this is a perfect example. The market was like a tubercular patient, apparently healthy, but sick fundamentally. I wasn't disappointed about my performance at that point because the risk was just too high to be heavily invested. Although my accounts ended the year up anywhere from 70 to 165 percent, I did have some doubts at the time. Since 1968—when I managed my first hedge fund—I have never missed so much of a top. But put into the same circumstances again, I

1.   These averages are computed by adding the percentage increase or decrease of the Dow Jones Industrial Average and the Dow Jones Transportation Average and dividing by 2 to obtain an average stock market movement as a whole. I use these two averages because they are the only averages which have been in existence since January 1, 1897 and consequently there is sufficient data to provide historically significant information.

can't say that I'd behave any differently. However, if you still have capital, there will always be another opportunity to make money. But, if you lose a great deal of money because of excessive risk, you cannot take advantage of future opportunities.

Weaknesses

One of my weaknesses is that if for some reason I miss the lows of a move, I find it exceedingly difficult to become aggressive in taking positions, even when I know that the move is probably going to continue. This occurred in 1986–87. I bought the September 1985 lows in size and then began scale selling from January 1986 through July 1986. This scenario typifies my style, which is to be very aggressive at low-risk market turning points and to begin reducing risk early in large up moves. The market was flat from July through December 1986, but I knew that if the Dow went above the 1975 point on high volume, the market would move up in a big way.

In January 1987 the stock market exploded, and I advised my corporate clients and pension funds to go long. Even though I knew that the market would move up, I simply could not participate in any significant way. Given the same circumstances again, I would invest my own money. I just felt that the market still represented too much risk, and I was unwilling to endure it. I had missed the fact that the rate of growth of the monetary base in the last part of 1986 and the early part of 1987 had increased 15.2 percent. That is the highest rate of increase in history, including World War II! I wasn't watching the monetary figures closely enough because I just couldn't believe that the government would be irresponsible enough to artificially extend the recovery by inflating. But then I wasn't thinking like a politician.

The reason I am cautious at entering a move once I've missed catching the turn is part philosophical, part psychological. In the philosophical sense, I don't like to jump into the market after a move has already started because the chances of getting caught long at the turn are enhanced. I know there will be other opportunities to catch a move at the turn and minimize risk. Psychologically, I don't want to be whipsawed. Buying strength and then selling weakness at a loss is not mentally good for anyone, but would be especially discouraging for me since I strive to catch the lows and highs with such a high degree of precision.

For instance, the 1990 drop in stock prices due primarily to the Kuwait invasion was a big problem for me. I was bearish in July 1990, expecting a cut in interest rates before going short. The Kuwait invasion was a surprise to me, and I was not short going into this event. The Dow dropped 9.6 percent from July 16, 1990, to August 6, which was the largest drop (except for the 1987 Crash), going back to 1984. The odds were poor to begin shorting, yet I love to play the short side of the market. I decided to stay in cash because if Saddam Hussein changed his mind and pulled out, the market would rally sharply. This was very difficult for me, but I was disciplined enough to live by the rules and the odds.

Ready for Black Friday

For example, I was out of the market from May to October in 1989. I was also concerned with the downside possibilities. I missed a significant percentage of the market's rise, but by October I was looking for a top. The median net appreciation of primary intermediate upward movements in bull markets (there have been 112 such movements since 1896) is 10 percent. In other terms, in 50 percent of all intermediate cycles in history, an up move of more than two weeks has ended in a down move of at least two weeks and the net median appreciation was 10 percent. In addition, only 15 of the 112 bull market up moves in history yielded more than 24.4 percent after the corrective down move took place. The primary intermediate up move from March 23 to October 9 was 24.4 percent in extent. In the same period, the Transports had moved up 52 percent, fueled primarily by takeover mania. Only 8 of the 174 upward movements in both bull and bear markets have appreciated more than 52 percent before failing. Measured by this statistical criterion alone, to be long in October was one of the poorest risks on record.

Statistical factors aside, there were other reasons to be cautious. As of Friday, October 13th, the Japanese and the Germans had raised interest rates. The Fed had reduced free reserves relative to previous reporting periods, and with the CPI increasing at a rate of approximately 5.5 percent, I didn't see much room for them to ease. The October 9th high on the Dow Industrials average had not been confirmed by the Transports. It was time to be building a short position, which I was, but not in any huge size.

I had a small short position going into October the 13th, and I was increasing size throughout the day as the market sold off. I was looking for a break on high volume to confirm my judgment of the coming correction, so as the market sold off, I had a close eye on volume. Rumors began to surface that financing for the United Airlines takeover had fallen through. Volume began to increase, and I began to buy puts aggressively. After 3:00 P.M. I couldn't get any more orders executed. By the close, the Dow had plunged 191 points—the second largest one-day drop in history. I nearly doubled the value of my managed accounts in less than eight hours. So even though I may have missed the primary movement from March to October, I made up for it on the short side.

Admittedly, I had no way of knowing the market would crash as it did. While program trading can accelerate market movements, especially sell-offs, I was looking for at least a two week sell-off and was hoping to increase size much more than I was able to when the market broke below the September 1 high on high volume. I was fortunate that the move was so large and fast and that I was able to time my buys and sells as I did. But the point is that being fully invested in the latter speculative stages of bull markets just isn't worth the risk. I would rather be looking for a top with cash in hand than see my profits get wiped out in a single day.

As a trader, the weakness of not following markets if I miss a turn is not terribly significant. But for the clients whose money I manage, it might be very disturbing if they don't understand the risk and see only what they are missing in profits compared to their friends. It might be difficult to understand why I am not participating if they don't consider my perceptions of the long term. I'll be very aggressive when the risks are low, and very cautious when the risks are high.

One of the most important things to remember is that it is the emotional aspect of trading and investing — rather than the lack of knowledge — that prevents people from making money.

Conclusion

On Wall Street, the need to eliminate emotions from the decision-making process is imperative for success. Moreover, from the standpoint of man's intellectual development, emotions have been considered basic for survival and part of man's nature for millions of years. To discipline one's emotions and make rationally based decisions is difficult to say the least. No one said survival or "staying at the table" was easy!

CHAPTER SEVEN

DENNY ENGELMAN
The Regional Floor Trader

Many people in the securities industry have been called innovators or merely opportunistic. Perhaps they are two of the most overused adjectives in the English language today. But no one can deny that Denny Engelman has created a niche for himself and his entire organization, Engelman & Company, which has been on the floor of the Midwest Stock Exchange for the past 25 years. Denny and his partners have siphoned off an ever-growing portion of the order flow from what many consider to be the primary market—the New York Stock Exchange—and contributed to an ever-increasing erosion of the NYSE's market share of total trading volume. They have done this with a combination of wit, cunning, and what many would call pure chutzpah.

This chapter spans four different eras: 1968, when he began in the business, through 1975; May Day, 1975 through May 1982, or what we would now refer to as the beginning of the great 1980s boom market; 1982–1988, which is post-crash; and 1988 to the present. For the purposes of this chapter, the regionals will encompass all the regional stock exchanges, but in particular Engelman is writing about the Midwest Stock Exchange, the largest of all the regionals and the second largest stock exchange in the United States.

In retrospect, 1968 was an important date because that was when the SEC abolished the give-up. The give-up was the ability for institutions and brokers to pay off soft-dollar claims with trades. 1975 signifies the most consequential date in the history of the rate structure of the securities business, when negotiated rates came into being. The spring of 1982 is important because it began the great boom of the 1980s. That May, with the Dow at 870, Joseph Granville publicly stated that the market would never go up again. The next day, it began to rise, and it has yet to reverse the trend. The 1988 post-crash environment is important for obvious reasons. The post-Black Monday environment demonstrated the importance that derivatives have had on the market-place, even though in reality they had little to do with the crash.

What We Do*

An institutional floor broker is a floor broker representing one or two institutional firms, (e.g., Goldman Sachs, Salomon Brothers, Jefferies, etc.). What the institutional floor broker attempts to accomplish is to take a customer's order to buy or sell shares of stock, and to successfully find the other side of the transaction at a price that is favorable to both customers. A floor broker can either be an employee of an "upstairs" firm, transacting only that company's business, or he can be an independent floor broker, where he or his other firm members work for a variety of clients.

The Investment Process

Let us review the investment process from the beginning. The mechanism really begins with the hourly worker who rivets bolts into a car at a Ford Motor Company plant. The cars are (hopefully) built year after year, and as he continues to work for Ford, he accumulates the rights to a pension. The actuarial staff at Ford Motor Company then allocate corporate funds to place into the pension plan and they determine that the money for the fund should grow at a given percentage each year. The pension fund staff then determines who should manage these funds to achieve this growth. The fund management process can be done either in-house or with outside managers.

The fund manager hires portfolio analysts, who make decisions about which securities to buy and sell. Say the portfolio manager decides to buy 90,000 shares of Union Pacific. The fund manager and his trader must decide which broker should execute this order. The broker now

*The building of a team that is number one year after year is the most gratifying feeling one can have. It couldn't possibly have been done without my two friends and partners Steven Silver and Jim Carney. I'm forever indebted to their work ethic and patience with my own shortcomings. Guys, you're the best. I also wish to offer special gratitude to Darlyne and Lauren for sticking with me through all the hard times.

gets an order to buy 90,000 shares of Union Pacific. He has one of two choices. He can go down and work the order on the floor of the auction market and buy it over a period of time. In this way the average price will reflect the ups and downs of the market during the day. Or he can say, "I want to buy my 90,000 shares, and I want to buy it now."

However, what the trader for the fund manager might find is that the market for the stock is "12 to a quarter up 1,000 shares." What does that mean? That means there are only 1,000 shares offered by the public at 12¼. And if he went down to the floor of the New York Stock Exchange and took a picture of all the activity, there might a total of 2,000 shares offered by various orders at 12¼. But he wanted to buy 90,000 shares.

Theoretically a good floor broker will probe the marketplace and ascertain what he will have to pay to get his 90,000 shares. He will do this by checking with the specialist and by analyzing the book of orders left by the public. At that point, the specialist should interject himself to help the broker buy the 90,000 by selling some of the stock short out of his own account. That is what creating fair and orderly market is supposed to be about. But what happened—because of the concentration of capital in the mid-1970s to the mid-1980s—is that the specialist's role as the fair and orderly market maker at the institutional level became obsolete. There were few specialists who wanted to sell 70,000–80,000 shares of any stock short at any given time. The specialist community became too undercapitalized for that responsibility. Also, what would occur if he decided that he liked the stock as well?

What happened was that the real power for institutional trading went off the floors of the exchanges and migrated upstairs so that Salomon Brothers, Goldman Sachs, and Merrill Lynch all interjected their own capital to smooth out the trading's ups and downs. The "upstairs traders" became the liquidity factor in the equity marketplace.

In the Beginning

In the late 1960s to early 1970s, we began a new process to execute blocks of stock (i.e., "size"). I recognized that the exchange floors were going to become obsolete and that the real markets were moving upstairs. To get the process upstairs, there needed to be communication among the upstairs brokers, because if they were going to risk their money to help the institutions have liquidity, they would have to have some sort of vehicle for understanding where various stocks were going to be bought, and where they were going to be sold. The New York Stock Exchange floor was inefficient at providing that information.

If you are a position trader for First Boston, how do you find 90,000 shares of Union Pacific when there are only 2,000 shares of public offerings at 12¼? You check the specialist's book on all the markets and you say, "Okay, maybe there's another 7,000 shares offered up to 13." In this day and age, and even before, the public is unable to grasp the actual supply and demand for stocks. If you look at any specialist's book on the New York floor, you don't see "stock." In equities, if you take the top 50 names out, there is not much liquidity left. While there are a lot of stocks left, there is not much liquidity in what we would call the secondary or tertiary stocks.

Assume that the institutional trading universe is made up of five firms: Goldman Sachs, Salomon Brothers, First Boston, Donaldson, Lufkin and Jenrette, and Merrill Lynch. Each one has a floor partner in New York and they all go to the Union Pacific specialist at any given time during the day. They are competitors, so they are not going to want to tell their rivals what they are doing. The other player in the game is a specialist, and he's not going to want to tell too much because his job is to buy stocks low and sell them high. However, we recognized that the specialist had one other job—putting the First Boston broker together with the Salomon broker to make a trade between the two of them. The specialist wasn't completing that job for two reasons:

1. He couldn't get the two competitors to talk; and

2. The floor brokers for each side weren't being told the entire story by the upstairs trader who was controlling the order, because the upstairs trader was afraid that if he told his floor broker everything he knew, the broker would relay that to the specialist. In turn, the specialist would cause the stock to move before the broker upstairs was able to complete his order.

Denny Engelman

This is all a little less true today than it was 25 years ago, for obvious reasons. The NYSE in recent years has realized that they went from 97 percent of the marketplace to 70 percent. They must have been doing something wrong, and if we make the assumption that in the last 15 or 20 years the marketplace has been taken over by the institutional investor rather than by the public investor, we can then lay the blame for their drop in market share, and their inability to control the institutional trader who decided either to trade off or on other exchanges, on the fact that the negotiated process and the ability to communicate various demand and supply pockets for stocks was lacking on the NYSE.

Our firm went from 50,000 shares a day in 1968 to 3-4 million shares a day in 1992, and we created a niche for ourselves by taking advantage of the inability of the NYSE's floor to function efficiently for the upstairs trader. We did that in a very easy way: we decided that if we stayed an impartial party, First Boston and others would talk to us if we were able to bring to the table the true picture of what was going on in a stock (in this case, Union Pacific) and offer some added clarity to the total picture. This meant that we did not care that there were only 7,000 shares between 12½ and 13. What First Boston wanted to know was if anybody else in the total structure of the marketplace might be willing to sell stock that was not showing a hand on the New York floor.

Let's assume that the Merrill Lynch trader had bought Union Pacific four days earlier at 11½, and decided that it was going to go to 12½, and was sitting on a position of 30,000 shares. He didn't want to tell that to the New York floor because he didn't want to depress the stock and keep it down. But in talking to him all day long, we garnered information. He told us, "Look, I really like the stock. I'm going to buy some stock at 11½ and if it gets to 12½, let me know. Maybe I'll start to sell some of the stock and take a profit." So First Boston comes to me and says, "Look, I want to buy 90,000 shares of Union Pacific and there's only 2,000 shares offered at 12¼. Where do you think I can find stock?" Well now, I have a reason to call Merrill Lynch and say, "Remember that 30,000 shares you bought the other day? If my buyer (who is actually willing to pay 12¼ for stock) is willing to pay 12½, would you be willing to sell your 30,000 shares?" If he says yes, and I go back to the buyer and say, "Look, there's only 2,000 in New York at 12¼ but, if you trade some stock at 12½, I can find you 30,000 shares." This method of finding 30,000 shares not offered on the N.Y. floor can be repeated several times over. For instance, perhaps Goldman Sachs knew of an institution that when Union Pacific was at 11½, told him that if it got to 12½ he would sell 35,000 shares. Because of our consistent daily coverage this fact was told to us. We noted it, and remembered to call Goldman as the Union Pacific trade unfolded. In the above case, as one of my guys called Merrill Lynch another called Goldman. If everything fell into place, Merrill will sell 30,000 at 12½. In this example neither broker had an order or indication of what he was willing to do with his NYSE floor partner. Thus, our firm supplied 65,000 of Union Pacific to First Boston at 12½, resulting in a sensible trade for him and his customer. Why? The buyer gets 90,000 at 12½. Each seller gets his price (12½). Each broker earns a commission or profit and First Boston is only short 25,000 shares out of 90,000. Significantly better than when the process started at 12 with very little stock offered up to 12½.

The Early Days

When I walked down to the Midwest Stock Exchange floor in the middle of 1967, the Exchange was executing about 250,000 shares a day, mostly in 100 to 200 share orders from local brokerage houses and some national houses, while the NYSE at that time was doing about 2,000,000 shares a day. It became quite evident to me that it took just as much energy for a person to pick up a phone, take an order to buy 200 shares of General Motors, put down the phone, walk to the specialist post, buy the stock, walk back, and report it to the customer on the other end, as it did for someone to pick up a phone, take an order to buy a 10,000 share lot or greater. This was the business that I wanted to be in.

It also became quickly evident that there was not a single specialist at any regional—and sometimes not even in New York—who would buy or sell 10,000 shares or more of a stock at any given price. We figured that the only way to buy and sell larger blocks of stock would be to have at least two customers—one buyer and one seller—to create the trade, so that we as floor brokers could accomplish two objectives: we could fill the order of the buyer or the seller (whichever initiated first), and we could charge a commission on both sides of the trade—an in-house cross by our firm.

The Four-Way Trade

When I came to the floor, the man who was executing most of that kind of crossing business was Bob Jablonski, along with his partner, Jay Mangan. The two men covered institutions directly. They not only talked to Salomon, Goldman, or the other large block houses; they also had lines into J.P. Morgan, Chase Manhattan, Putnam, Fidelity, and the other large institutions of the day. They performed as a broker between both the institutions and the institutional brokers upstairs.

At that time, they were doing what was called a four-way trade, or a give-up. These arrangements enabled an institution such as Morgan or Chase to execute a trade and pay off a commission, in what we now refer to as soft dollars, to houses without directly calling them. For example, Chase might buy 20,000 shares and Citibank might sell 20,000 shares of IBM. When Jablonski put through the ticket, the clearing house recognized the broker who was buying it and credited half the commission to another broker at the discretion of the institution that was the buyer. Similarly, the account on the sellside of the transaction made a similar direction, creating a four-way trade. The buyside received two commissions, the initial commission, let's say Salomon Brothers, and then half the commission would be credited upstairs in the clearing house, to Kentucky Corp., for example, as a payout by the buying institution. On the sellside, the same event would take place.

Will Weinstein and Peter Toczek (1968-1975)

However, in 1968, the give-up was abolished. The SEC determined that it wasn't lawful and at that time, Jablonski left the floor of the Midwest. As he walked out the door, he told me: "Son, I'm going to give you two accounts, Oppenheimer and Company and Arthur Lipper Corporation." At that time, Oppenheimer was run by a young guy named Will

Weinstein, and Lipper was run by the legendary Peter Toczek. While I knew that this was a great opportunity and the beginning of something that could become very substantial, I realized I would have to go to New York and introduce myself and, not knowing anything, tell them that it was up to them to help teach me the business.

The following week, I went to New York and met Will Weinstein. At that time, Oppenheimer was a fledgling block institutional brokerage firm, competing against the likes of Salomon Brothers and Goldman Sachs. Willy was one of the toughest competitors I have ever met, and he had one decisive advantage over his rivals: he had the huge order flow from the Oppenheimer Mutual Funds. The benefit of having the virgin merchandise of the fund to shop was combined with his own intuitive talent and the six young and hungry traders he had on his desk. I told Willy that I was setting something up on a regional, and he wanted to know the details. In time, we gave each other an ability we would have never achieved alone: my firm utilized his merchandise flow to get the call from the other brokers, and Willy utilized me to use that call to increase his capital base and thus reduce his risk in any given trade. For instance, if he had 50,000 GTE to sell from Putnam and he had to make a position bid for it, the NYSE floor was not able to distribute it, so he would call me. Why? In one call, I might be able to find two or three buyers he couldn't find in New York. He used me for my distribution system, and I used him for the names. Since Willy was one of my first clients, and had the virgin merchandise of the Oppenheimer funds and since he recognized the shortcomings of the New York floor in terms of risking capital to help facilitate the institutional business that was coming into play, he and I worked well together. He taught me how to be a good broker, and I taught him how to use a regional exchange. With one call to me, Willy could find out what five or six competitors were willing to do with a stock at any given time. Similarly, those five or six other upstairs firms could find out the other person was willing to do at a given price at a given time — something they couldn't do in New York.

Peter Toczek was a different story. At that time, he was the broker for Bernie Cornfield of Investors Overseas Services (IOS). When Toczek called, everybody trembled; when Bernie sold, everybody quivered. I remember Peter telling me the first time: "Start selling Merck."

I said: "How many Peter?" and he said: "Just start selling, and I'll tell you when to stop."

Three days later he told me to stop. The stock was down $11.

From 1968 to 1975, we built our business with a very small core of people. It was kind of like a wheel, with a hub, and spokes.

At that time, the block business was really made up of two people at the top and a host of other people scrambling to compete. Salomon and Goldman — Salomon with Jay Perry and Goldman with Bob Mnuchin — clearly led the way. Right behind them were Willy with Oppenheimer; Sy Lewis with Bear Stearns; Shields and Company, which was run by Danny Murphy and Louie Auer; and Dudley Eppel at Blyth. But our initial relationship was with Willy. With his capital and his names, we were able to use them as the hub of the wheel. The spokes then became all the secondary players in the marketplace at that time.

Friends Before Clients

Early on, we realized that in order to increase the number of people that we called the spokes of the wheel, we would have to do a lot of travelling to build relationships. It was not unusual for us to be in New York two nights a week. We would leave the Midwest floor at 1:00 in the afternoon, take a plane to New York, meet the guys at Oscar's or any bar down near Wall Street, drink until 8:00 or 9:00, make friends, take the red eye back at midnight, arrive in Chicago at 2:00 A.M., and be back on the floor again at 8:00 A.M., ready for business. Those were the days.

As these relationships were continuing to grow, we realized that a family spirit was an important part of what we were trying to accomplish. As we got to know the individual traders we also got to know their wives, and their children, both at conventions and on trips together. My first trip was going down the Colorado Rapids with my wife, Ralph Blair from Oppenheimer, and his wife. By the time that six-day trip was over, there wasn't a man on my floor who could have done business with Ralph Blair except for myself, because we had become close personal friends. I told my entire firm that the way to build this business was first to make friends with the traders and then build a relationship with their families because then business couldn't be taken away based on price. If our service was equal, we would always get the first call.

That concept of relationship building has been carried through for 25 years in my firm. Some of the friends we first made in 1968 are now running desks; others have retired. But those relationships have never waned; they will always be there in one form or another, whether or not we are in the business. Interesting enough, one of the problems of today's institutional floor brokerage is that the personality has gone out of the business.

Midwest versus New York Stock Exchange

There are several interesting stories that best typify what it meant to be an institutional floor broker on a regional exchange during this time. Remember: anything less than trading on the primary exchange, i.e., at the NYSE, was considered idiocy by many brokers and investors, so we had to be twice as good as our counterpart on the New York floor just to get the call. One story involves a guy working for me by the name of Jerry Markowitz, who had come from Oppenheimer, moved his family to Chicago and became a partner of my firm. Jerry was brilliant. Having once been an upstairs broker himself, he brought upstairs business mentality to the downstairs business. Three years after he came, he decided to move back to New York for personal reasons, and in doing so, decided to replicate our business on the NYSE floor, competing with Engelman Securities at its own game. I was a bit nervous. I told Jerry when he left that he couldn't accomplish in New York what he could achieve in Chicago. Six months later, when his operation folded, he called me up and I asked him: "Was I right?" He replied: "You were right." Why was I correct?

In New York, he had to deal with the partners of the various firms he was covering. For instance, he might be brokering for First Boston or Merrill Lynch, but they had their own floor brokers as well, also partners of theirs, thus creating a natural animosity between Jerry and the floor partners of these various firms. This created friction and jealousy. Jerry's upstairs client realized he was paying his own broker on the New York floor to get the same information that Jerry was supposed to be getting or vice-versa.

The sheer size of the New York floor as opposed to the Midwest floor made it impossible for him to do the job the way we could do it. For instance, if Willy called me up and said: "I think I have a seller of GTE; it's size, but I'm not sure how many," I could just hit a phone, talk to any one of a number of upstairs traders and find out if they were a buyer, put the trade together, and walk 20 feet to the post to cross it. In addition, I could walk to the post to find out any floor indications, whether or not anyone else on my floor was a buyer or seller.

On the other hand in New York, Jerry not only had to leave his phone, he would have to walk two minutes through the crowd to get to the post to find out if there were any other buyers or sellers. And during that time in transit, the price might move or the information might change. Additionally, the specialist wasn't his friend; he was his enemy. The other floor partners weren't his friends, they were competitors, so he couldn't find out very much from the floor. This all took him a lot of time, was inefficient, and clearly did not work.

All those factors are not true on the Midwest floor, my home turf:

1. There are no partners;

2. There are no specialists interjecting themselves; and

3. I am able—without moving—to hit a button in front of me to any one of 60 or 70 different upstairs brokers that are a factor in the industry to get the information I need.

The May Day Era (1975-82)

Before 1975, we were able to cover what we called the spokes and the hub of the wheel with two or three traders, simply because there were only six or seven players in the business that really mattered. In May 1975, the SEC decided to allow for negotiated rates.

The floor brokers didn't know what to expect. We knew one or two things were going to happen: we were receiving a commission of $3.00 per one hundred shares (3 cents per share) based on the old institutional rates, which adjusted to about 10 percent of what the up-stairs traders received from their institutional customers.

What was confusing to figure out was whether the decrease in rates was going to create an increase in volume that would compensate for our lost revenue. Luckily, history proved that the price was very elastic; the lower the rates, the more people traded. Institutions traded far and above the previous volumes, and at a greater rate of increase than the decrease in rates, creating significantly greater revenue.

Now all of a sudden they told us we were going to negotiated rates and I asked around the industry where they thought that would leave us and the industry at large. It ended up at between 7 and 10 cents per share, which was down about 60 or 70 percent from the old rates. Subsequent to that they went down to 5 or 6 cents per share. They were able to do that because of the incredible concentration of capital in the late 1970s and early 1980s.

The Institutional Force of Power

Despite the recession of the late 1970s, additional funds were being placed into the stock market. The drive to fund corporate and govern-mental pensions brought increased interest to the marketplace, while creating a greater concentration of this capital among the professional investing organizations. Clearly, the investing public, which used to purchase and sell stocks on their own whim—and using their own research—were now depending to a greater and greater extent on insti-tutions, thus making the institutional business the greater segment of the total marketplace.

In the early 1970s, the institutional business was about 30 percent of the total volume of the New York floor, with the remaining 70 percent being public orders. But within a few years, these figures reversed: institutions would account for 70 percent, and the retail would account for 30 percent. This was a fabulous boon to firms such as ours, that dealt only in the institutional business. With institutional business burgeoning, coupled with the decrease in commission rates, the need for capital commitment on the part of the institutional brokers became greater and greater. And with that increase in their commitment to facilitate and create liquidity for the institutions to buy and sell, our firm's role as a distribution center for stocks and as a *reducer of risk* for institutional brokers became greater and greater.

Playing in the Major League

As Goldman and Salomon clearly established themselves as the top two players in the institutional business, their percentage of the marketplace became greater and greater.

From the floor broker's point of view, the shopping of names became less and less important as there became a greater emphasis on the ability to provide a clear picture of what was in the marketplace at the time prior to the trade, and the ability to protect the customer after the print. Protection after the print became essential to making the business work. For example, if Goldman bought 200,000 shares of Merck a dollar down from the last sale and was going to have a long position of 50,000 of those shares, it was vital that when the next 20,000 shares to buy came to market, Goldman have the first shot at the merchandise. But if the 20,000 to buy went to the New York floor, where there might be another seller at the post, the specialist would sell 5,000, the other seller would sell 5,000 to 10,000, and Goldman would only get to sell 5,000.

If we could snag the buyer before he went to the New York floor, not only could we probably get the buyer a better price, Goldman would be able to sell all 20,000. Now, the question in Goldman's mind was, was he better off selling the 5,000 shares at one-eighth higher or all 20,000 at one-eighth lower? If a stock had printed at par and was trading a par and a quarter and 20,000 came in to buy and it went to the New York floor, the guy might pay a par and a half for all 20,000, with Goldman selling 5,000. But if we got the buyer on the Midwest floor, he would get to sell all 20,000 but he might sell it at par and three-eighths. While it might be a toss-up, we all believed — Goldman, our firm, and the rest of the brokers taking risks from the institutions — that they were better off selling all 20,000 at three-eighths and staying liquid than they would be getting the extra eighth of a point on only 5,000 and still being long 45,000. Therefore, for us to be effective, knowing who was long and *why*, *when*, and *where* was the paramount question.

Our firm also grew; we went from three to six brokers because of the increase in volume. We went from about 25 customers to 80, and each of our customers grew with the business as well, going from three to as many as seven or more traders on each desk.

Post May Day in Perspective (1975-1982)

Let's place the years of 1975–1982 in a more distinct and proper perspective:

1. The era of negotiated rates. Commission rates went from $3.00 down to between $1.00 and $1.50 per hundred shares. However, the expansion of volume more than offset the decrease in price, creating such an increase in revenue that brokerage firms experienced an explosion of the size of their desks.

2. The block trading business exploded, also bringing the advent of hedge funds, day traders, and fast money players. These factors, along with the beginning of stock options, created an intraday volatility that had never previously been experienced. Stocks that used to have a half-point range now experienced a 1½ point swing in a day. Again, the hedge funds, day traders, options players, the use of derivatives selling options, selling puts, shorting stocks — all the variations and permutations that arose through the advent of equity options — created an explosion in volume, which created a volatility that made day trading possible. Traders were now willing to buy 5,000 to 10,000 shares at any given clip in order to attempt to flip it for half a point.

3. Revolution in block trading. With the huge increase in market liquidity, instead of interceding our capital to buy 5,000 or 10,000 shares so the call would come to us and we could participate on the block, we had players at all times in almost all marketable stocks. This increased our call volume, which caused a large jump in share volume, necessitating the addition of four different traders, an increase in the number of accounts covered. All of this improved firm revenues and correspondingly, of course, profits. At the same time, the block traders now realized that they didn't want our capital to interface — they wanted us just to be a broker's broker — not a dealer — and to paint a clear picture of the marketplace. Being able to do this helped our bottom line immeasurably. Besides, at $1.00 to $1.50 per hundred, we didn't have much "juice" in the commission to offset the potential loss that we would take from positioning a stock.

The Consolidated Tape

During this time, the cry for consolidated ticker tapes was heard. We had felt all along that all of the U.S. exchanges had to be treated equally. Prior to the consolidated tape, trades that took place on regional exchanges never saw the light of day of the investing public. In fact, except for the people who saw the trade take place on the floor of the regional, nobody knew about the transaction except for the buyer and the seller. It was essentially an invisible market.

The first step toward consolidating tape was to ensure that if a trade printed on the Midwest, it appeared first with an ampersand, e.g., AT&T &M — with M for Midwest, P for Pacific Coast Telephone, X for Philadelphia Stock Exchange — so all stock exchanges were getting the same advertisement from their prints on a national tape.

Eventually the ampersand was dropped. But to accomplish that, Don Weeden, who had fought so long and hard for the right to be an independent third market firm, forced the New York Stock Exchange, the SEC, and all the regionals into the development of the consolidated network or the consolidated tape association (CTA). The dropping of the ampersand created the perception of a national marketplace.

If you were a market maker or a specialist on any exchange, the ability to display your quote and the desire for the public to get the best fill — whether it be on the Midwest, New York, Philadelphia, Boston, or the Pacific Coast was imperative. It allowed the small guys an equal chance to compete regardless of what floor they decided to work on. It created a great opportunity for regional specialists to get into the game. While they weren't big players, they were able at least to show their quotes and try to attract order flow at the same time. The regionals entered the beginning of the 1982 to 1988 period that I refer to as the *automatic execution era*, where the exchanges were competing for order flow not only by creating a good market but by reducing the cost of execution for the various firms. In that respect, I think the Midwest was in the forefront. The Midwest exchange went out to all the regional firms—not the big national wire houses but true regional firms—and attempted to attract their order flow by reducing their cost of clearing and execution. The natural result of that was increased small order flow. This caused the executing specialists' positions to become a little bit larger and therefore, their quotes to become a little bit tighter. The display of their quotes caused customers in the block business to call us.

For instance, if the specialist in New York was short 2,800 shares of 3M, the market in New York might have been a quarter by ⅝'s, 1,000 shares up. This meant that the specialist would sell the stock for the par plus 100⅝'s or buy it for 100¼, a thousand shares on each side. But if our specialist on the Midwest was short that same 2,800 shares, he might go up on the screen at 100⅜'s bid for 3,000. Let's assume that First Boston would have a seller who seeing the 100⅜'s bid, calls our desk and sells 3,000 shares. We would sell the 3,000 shares at 100⅜'s but we would also uncover some information that we previously didn't have: we would now know that First Boston was a seller of 3M.

What this whole process accomplished was to force the upstairs traders to look at the Midwest, thus creating a greater flow of information and a greater flow of indication, which made our jobs immeasurably easier. But it also caused dealers who previously had not dealt with us to get to know who we were. Once they knew us, we started to go back to our old ways of building our relationships, getting to know the people, going out, breaking bread, seeing eye to eye to eye. As Willy Weinstein used to say to me: "I never trade with anybody until I see the whites of their eyes."

Denny Engelman

The National Marketplace

This drive to have a national marketplace, which started in the early 1980s, really culminated in the late 1980s. The constant pressure that both the regionals and the third market placed on the NYSE and the SEC helped to create a national marketplace, one that wasn't divided because of somebody's ancient right to be in the marketplace. Instead a marketplace was evolving because people competed to make it better, competed to breed excellence, competed to bring liquidity.

This entire era peaked during a fight for a consolidated tape, the right of an exchange to display its quotes, the right of a specialist in Boston or the Pacific Coast or a broker of any one of those exchanges to display the fact that he had a customer who was willing to do something with him that, for any one of a variety of reasons, they weren't willing to do on the New York floor. The Securities and Exchange Commission, in their ultimate wisdom, saw that a consolidated tape in a national marketplace was in fact good for "the public."

But first, it started with the right to display trades on a consolidated tape.

At that time, it was only 7 or 8 percent of the national marketplace. So we fought hard for the right to display our quotes to our traders, and in the late 1970s, the SEC gave us that right. Now, where do you find out where the trade was traded? Brokers used the ampersand, our advertisement that we had the merchandise that the New York floor did not have. It provided competition to the New York floor. The question was, were the specialists on the New York floor who had been down there since the early 1900s and run by family operations going to wake up and say, "We better provide a service"?

Ampersand M following the name of a stock signified that the Midwest Stock Exchange, myself in particular, traded that stock. Now what does that do for me? One, it increases the information flow to the national marketplace, which makes the market more efficient. It also sends traders to me who I normally would not have dealt with. Here's how it might work. Let's say there is a trader out there who also is interested in the Union Pacific stock, who might not have been showing that he was interested. He might say, "It traded on the Midwest; I'd better find out what it means. The only person I know on the Midwest is Denny Engelman. I'd better give him a call." So he would call me and say, "Listen, I saw that you just traded 90,000 Union Pacific. I think I have a buyer." Well, this is wonderful. I've now got one trade and I've already got one guy who thinks he's a buyer. Now I've got to go back to the seller of that trade and say "Listen, our trade has created a possible buyer. Does your seller want to sell more?" And, all of a sudden, I'm into another trade. I couldn't do that before because there was no advertisement of my 90,000 shares.

Lesson #1: consolidated tape and automation of execution and all the things that were happening in the industry created more business for me. *Lesson #2:* our specialists, even though they're small, have the ability to display their markets. For instance, how many times does a broker push up a quote on whatever hardware he's using to see what the market is in New York? He sees one hundred by one hundred shares. In other words, there is no public order. It's 12¼ and three-eighths, 300 to 400 shares, and that's just the market that's in the book. Now, the Midwest specialist decides that he and his ultimate wisdom want to start 2,000 shares at 12⅜ because he thinks the stock is going low. So he puts his quote on the machine: 2,000 twelve and three-eighths.

Now when you push up the Quotron, you will see New York at 12¼ to ⅜, 300 to 400, Midwest 12¼, three-eighths, 100 by 2,000. Now you are willing to pay 12⅜ and you need 4,000 shares; you not only have to go to the New York floor to buy the three-eighths, you also have to go to the Midwest Stock Exchange to buy the three-eighths because this is where our stock is. Again, the buyer says, "I've got a key to Denny Engelman. I'm going to call him and he'll buy it for me." Now what has that done for me? It has created a trade at 2,000 shares at six-tenths a cent, which means $12.00 — not very much, but it has given me a guy who's willing to buy stock. I am not going to argue with that. I buy the 2,000 shares, but I'm smart enough to ask him, "Do you think you want to buy more?" And, since we're dealing in an institutional environment, we know that 2,000 isn't all the customer wants.

Of course, all of the activity during this 1975–1982 period could never have prepared us for what was about to happen in 1982. Although we experienced a recession from 1978 through 1980, our business was still solid, relative to 1975. But it wasn't anything close to what it was about to happen.

The 1980s Explosion

As we went through the late 1970s and the beginning of the early 1980s, we started to see more and more money chasing fewer and fewer stocks because we started to get the takeover boom of the 1980s, and when General Foods, RJR, NR, and RCA (to name a few) were removed from the marketplace, the relationship between supply and demand changed completely.

Secondly, Wall Street saw the advent of the day trader — the hedge fund guy, the guy who has found a way to make money by running in front of a big order, or by taking advantage of the various technology and derivative driven strategies being developed by the industry. The opportunity for someone with very little money to buy and sell stocks during the day for a point or a point and a half of profit created a lot of volume and opportunity. The combination of derivatives, the day trader, and more and more money chasing fewer and fewer pieces of paper created volatility; and volatility created the opportunity to make money, especially through exploiting the intraday highs and lows of any given stock.

These factors soon increased daily trading volume from 10 and 15 million shares a day to 100 million shares a day. I had to go from three people to ten people on my trading desk. At the same time, our rate structure was going down 70 percent. So we had to have a huge increase in volume to make up for the increase in costs and the decrease in rates. And it happened.

Another consequence of the change in the rate structure was the explosion in third-market trading. In this context, we'll talk about the third market being represented by Jefferies and Cantor Fitzgerald. These firms had the ability to interface themselves with the customer and beat the NYSE. Remember, in the 1970s they were not members of the Exchange; they had to pay commission to get to the New York floor, and they didn't have subsidiaries as they do now. These two firms were built because of the penetration of institutional investors into the area that we now call secondary stocks. Everybody can't just have General Motors, Dow Chemical, and Ford in their portfolio — they have to be able to own some of the secondary stocks. Secondary stocks do not have a lot of liquidity on the floor as do their blue chip brethren.

In the 1980s, the block traders realized that if they were going to provide more liquidity in the secondary stocks, they were going to have their heads handed to them because if investor number one decided he wanted to buy 100,000 shares of illiquid stock and Goldman Sachs provided the liquidity by shorting it to him that was fine. He might be able to get his short back in before his stock took off. But if four or five guys decided at the same time to buy the stock, and Goldman Sachs was the unlucky one to get the first call and Bear Stearns got the second call from the second buyer and Merrill Lynch got the third call from the third buyer, they'd all be short. They would all be chasing the same stock to cover their short, and their salespeople would do a good job of penetrating the institutions to find out where these secondary stocks were bought and sold.

Jefferies and Cantor made it their business to develop relationships with the institutions the same way we did, with the brokers and by concentrating on knowing where those secondary stocks' bodies were buried. In other words, they realized — just like I did — that it did not take a genius to buy 100,000 shares of Dow Chemical because both the public and the amount of shares that we were outstanding on the New York floor could provide that liquidity. In addition, in the early 1980s — through a little sleight of hand on their part — they were able to convince (just for example) Trust Company of the West that the third market was a marketplace completely different than the New York floor, which in some ways it was, but they truly convinced them the difference was night and day. For instance, they were going to the TCWs of the world and saying, "You have given orders to the New York floor to buy 100,000 shares of Union Pacific, but we on the third market are also trading Union Pacific, customer to customer; so while you're out there, why don't you at least tell us that you're there so we can at least find a seller. We can call you, and you can buy it from us because we're a different marketplace." Well they were in a different marketplace in fact, but they were calling the same institutions that the people on the New York floor were representing. They were just replicating the floor marketplace upstairs.

At that time, the various institutions didn't really realize that it is all one big marketplace, and so then, they would say, "OK, I'm buying Union Pacific on the New York floor and if you see it for sale, please let me know." That gave the salesmen at Jefferies an opportunity to make calls to potential sellers without having the actual buy orders on their desks, and to call another institution to find out if they wanted to sell a stock without having a buy order on his desk. Jefferies does not work orders like Merrill Lynch works orders. Jefferies does what we do—he creates trades with the illusion of having an order.

Nobody hands me an order to buy 90,000 shares of Union Pacific. What they say is, "If you know of a seller, I think I can buy 90,000 of Union Pacific." We go to a seller and say, if you're willing to tell me you're willing to sell stock, we think we know of a buyer who might be willing to purchase it."

In May of 1982, Joe Granville predicted that the stock market never go up again. History proved him slightly off-base in his prognostication. Instead, the Dow exploded going from 890 to 2700 between 1982 and 1987. I witnessed the most rapid expansion of equity trading in the history of the world. While the NYSE volume went from 150 to over 200 million shares a day, the regional volume went from 2 million to as high as 200 million shares a day. More people were day trading and the amount of institutional money managers (and thus traders for these managers) exploded. After all, the barriers to the institutional fund management business were negligible.

Additionally, institutional investment volume became the marketplace of activity, and retail volume essentially became an automated execution function through the DOT machines. Only institutional orders were now hand delivered by a floor broker to the specialist post, and the floor attracted many more specialists competing with the upstairs traders and the third market. As the floor of the Midwest became a totally institutionalized business, there evolved a concentration of capital in each specialist.

The Business That Never Was

In the mid-1980s I was approached by the chairman of the Boston Stock Exchange, Bill Morton (who also happened to be an old college friend of mine), to set up a brokerage operation on the Boston floor. The Boston floor was devoid of block competition, and they were relying on their smaller order flow execution. They were siphoning away crosses from New York, but were attracting very little block business—competitive order flow from the Salomons, Goldmans, Bear Stearns, and First Bostons.

As I flew up to Boston, the real question in my mind was were we as a firm now getting to levels with customers where they would or could not pay us? For example, when we billed them for 20,000 shares, they'd pay us for 20,000. But when we billed them for 40,000 shares, they'd still pay us for 20,000. My partner, Steve Silveroff, and I were basically trying to figure out how to squeeze more blood out of a turnip. It was my contention that if we were going to set up in Boston, it had to be something different than we had organized in the Midwest; otherwise we were just fooling our clients. Would Dean Witter pay us for 20,000 on the Midwest and for 20,000 in Boston to do the exact same thing? If they would, they were stupid, and I didn't want to treat them as if they were stupid.

My concept was simple. The Boston institutional trading community—Putnam, Fidelity, Boston Company, State Street Research and all the major firms were a very tightly knit group, and as whole, probably the most professional group of buyside traders in the business. I knew they were having trouble paying off their soft-dollar commitments, and they abhorred dealing with some of the soft-dollar brokers with whom they were committed to execute business. My gut feeling was that if I could convince them to let me open up a brokerage operation there using their soft-dollar commitments as a focal point of institutional order flow, then we might have something to talk about. I met with the Chairman and the Board of Governors of the Boston Stock Exchange and they were interested in the concept. For example, Putnam would come to us with a 300,00 share order. They realized we were capable of handling this business by shopping the indication, taking it around, and interfacing it with the system. We would then accomplish two purposes. We would find the natural other side of the order and at the same time allow Putnam to pay off 20 different brokers with this 300,000 share order, by designating other brokers with the commission credits.

The only problem was we would be helping the soft-dollar brokers do a better job of executing their business, even though they would not realize it. And with that recognition we realized that we would have to tell our brokerage customers, Salomon, Goldman, Oppenheimer, First Boston, Donaldson etc., what we were considering. I only got about four words out of my mouth with Bob Mnuchin of Goldman when he said: "No way. If you start going directly to my customer, then you are no longer going to be my broker."

That was essentially what every customer declared: if we were going to go into competition with our own brokerage customers, we were out. Well at that time, we had a $6 million a year business which was relatively riskless, and which afforded us a great lifestyle, and a lot of fun. It didn't take a lot of judgment to decide that this was not the thing to do. We simply could not go into competition with our own customers and expect to survive. The pie was not big enough, and we owed a lot more to our customers for seeing us through the 1970s and the early 1980s than to react to this opportunity. We decided not to do it. But it was to be an premonition. As I will discuss later, the idea of dealing directly with the institution would confront us again in the early 1990s.

In retrospect, the "roaring eighties" could be characterized as a time of incredibly high volume, increased day trading, the takeover craze, arbitrage, and incredibly lower rates coupled with greater volume.

The Conductor of the Midwest

It became a very competitive game. The first to fall were the rates, which were further reduced to a dollar per hundred shares transacted, or a single penny per share. In a period of three or four years, our gross pricing was cut by 70 percent while our expenses probably rose 50 percent, as we had to add more labor in order to service the volume.

It also became a rigorous and uncompromising task to walk that fine line between customers. It takes a constant vigilance to make sure that each of your traders is giving the proper information to each customer. If one person says the wrong thing, it can cause a lot of problems.

To place it all in a better perspective, running our firm made me more of an orchestra leader, with each section of the band made up of another brokerage firm. We had the percussion section, the strings, the brass, and the woodwinds. Not only did they play their tune, but together they had to perform a symphony, with each section playing from the same score. The tuba plays, the clarinet plays, the strings play, the drums play, and one person has to direct it. If they're playing in harmony, we do well. If they're not playing in harmony, then we have problems. We have First Boston mad at us because we told Merrill Lynch something we weren't supposed to tell them. This was the orchestra of which I was the conductor, making sure that the right call was made at the right time to the right person.

When a brush fire flared up (usually three or four times a day) I had to play fire fighter. For example, somebody wanted to buy 50,000 shares and we only had 30,000 shares for sale, or five people wanted to buy the 30,000 we had for sale. How would we split it up and divide it intelligently? Our business became trying to keep everybody happy, making sure customers understood that while we were working for ourselves, we were also working for them.

The Artful Dodger

The natural question is, how could we be First Boston's, Merrill Lynch's, and Goldman's broker all at the same time? Therein lay the art, the art of having someone believe in you, believe that you were their friend, that you were in fact working for them and we were. It was very seldom that someone accused us of playing favorites. When that happened we were always able to explain the situation. For example, the first call was always given the first call back; those people who treated us the best always got the best treatment.

When I used to talk at training classes at Goldman Sachs, the kids would ask me what kind of guys I was looking for. I would always respond, "What kind of guy do you think I'm looking for?" They'd answer, "Someone with a quick mind, a good memory, etc., etc." I would say, "No, you got it wrong. What I'm looking for is an Artful Dodger (a street-smart character from Dickens, *Oliver Twist*)."

What we do for a living is try to get people to do what they innately don't want to do, and that is to trade away from the NYSE, and away from their own partners in New York: "Trade with me, and pay me to trade with me. And come back and trade again and be happy with the job I've done." So to get somebody to do what they never want to do—do it, enjoy it, and come back and do it again—is, in fact, an art.

The Crossing Factor

Our firm is able to exist and thrive because we are able to cross trades on the Midwest Stock Exchange, something that can't be done in New York. Because the regionals only have a total of 30 percent of the marketplace, with the Midwest accounting for about 9 percent, there are not a lot of public orders on the books. Subsequently, there is not a big auction process going on and getting trades executed becomes a negotiated process. There are no brokers in front of the post with various buyers and sellers bidding an offer. For example, I would estimate that 30 percent of regional institutional activity are stocks being crossed by First Boston and Merrill Lynch in-house. In this example, both the buyer and the seller might go to the New York floor to say, "Please cross 90,000 Union Pacific at 12¼."

They found on the New York floor people who were willing to sell various stock at 12¼. But the specialist states, "You cannot do that on the New York without buying the stock of the people who were here before you got here." And the guy upstairs says, "Wait a minute. The buyer is willing to pay me a commission, and the seller is willing to pay me a commission. To do this, if I reduce the amount of stock my seller is selling on my particular print, and allow the New York floor to interject sellers, it reduces my revenue."

What this upstairs trader does is instead pick up the phone and call Engelman on the Midwest. For a minimal fee, he can cross 90,000 shares in-house, and the broker retains the commission. It's 100 percent of the buyer's commission, and 100 percent of the seller's commission, less my fee—which is very small because I have not really performed a function for him other than walking to a post, crossing something and walking back.

Why does he have to call me and not just call his own broker on the Midwest? Because nobody has their own partners on the Midwest— it is too expensive. You are much better off having someone like myself and my organization who talks to 15 or 20 guys, with each guy putting his own guy on the floor, offering that competitive flavor again. Additionally, by availing himself of my resources and contacts, he will put himself in a much greater opportunity to find the other side of a trade when he does not have both sides to begin with.

The Bottom Line

To make money in my business, you must do it on volume. Our charge for executing an order is only $1.50 per hundred shares. That is a penny and a half per share.

So to be profitable, I'd have to execute about two million shares of billable business, not in-house crosses. When First Boston calls me and says, "Cross 100,000 shares of stock," I am only paid $25, significantly less than six-tenths a share. The reason I only get $25 is that I am not really adding anything to the equation other than moving to the phone, to a place where I can trade the stock, putting it on the tape, and reporting it back. So, when I say "billable business," I mean business that isn't in house crosses. We do about three or four million of billable business on a good day and what differs between two million and the three and four million is my profit margin, which must be shared with thirteen other people.

The Tools in the Toolbox

What makes the markets and my job more efficient today is the variety of analytical, communication, and information tools that are out there. Technology plays a prominent role in this process. One of these products is AutEx. AutEx provides information about who is doing what to whom. It is another tool for traders to communicate to the institution what they want to do and institutions to find information and choose which person to use. From our point of view, reading AutEx allows us to find out who is buying and who is selling what stocks on the New York floor, or to obtain information that our customer isn't willing to give us.

I think that the information from AutEx is useful for the guy who says he buys 50,000 Dow. It just might be his way of keeping the name in front of the institution. You have to remember that AutEx is just a communication process that should have been done by the salesman. This is just another tool. When I go out to try to get a client to do business with me, one of my sales techniques is to explain why the broker should use me in the same way. You might use AutEx, i.e. advertising to the brokerage house what you want to do.

Somebody always needs a carpenter and a carpenter must use the right tools. Let us suppose that there were three carpenters in the world—First Boston, Merrill Lynch, and Goldman Sachs. First Boston has in its toolbox everything but a hammer and a saw. Merrill Lynch has everything but a saw, and Goldman Sachs has all of the items in its toolbox. At any given point in time, they might all be equal. But in the long run, the guy with the most tools in his toolbox wins.

We think that our firm is another important tool in a carpenter's toolbox. Therefore, if First Boston and Goldman Sachs use me, but Alex Brown and Merrill Lynch do not, we can convince Alex Brown and Merrill Lynch that they are at a competitive disadvantage to First Boston and Goldman Sachs. It's simplistic, but it works.

Finding the Buried Bodies

Remember, Mr. Broker must pay me for the right to do his business. Now imagine that I read on AutEx that Merrill is buying Union Pacific on the New York floor. Twenty minutes later Jefferies calls me up and he says, "I have an institution that might be willing to sell Union Pacific if you know of a buyer." Merrill hasn't told me they are a buyer because they want to keep the business on the New York floor and they don't want to pay me for the right to execute it, or their buyer just wants to work the order over a day or two. But I have the information that I got from AutEx, and now I have that call from Jefferies (these are all the things that wouldn't happen in New York) I then call the Merrill trader and say, "Listen, are you buying Union Pacific?" and he says, "Yes, how did you know?" And I reply, "I saw your reports on AutEx." Then I ask, "Do you have any size to buy, since you trust me?" He replies, "Yes I have some size to buy but I don't know if I can buy it all at once." And I say, "Well I think I have a seller."

"Who?"

"Jefferies."

"God, I've been making all the calls I can make to my salespeople and I can't find a seller. Maybe I ought to buy this guy's stock."

He also realizes that he is taking a risk if he doesn't buy it. He is taking the risk that Jefferies's salesman might find Merrill's buyer, that Merrill's buyer then would cancel with Merrill and do the trade with Jefferies. After all, half a loaf is better than no loaf. So he says to me, "Yeah, I have some size to buy; what do you think you have?" And I hang up the phone.

Denny Engelman

Now, I'm in the position I love to be in. I have two guys saying they want to do something. Both of them have size, but neither one wants to say how much. So I go back to the seller and I try to ascertain the number based on the information I have. Jefferies now calls their seller. "Well, if Merrill is willing to pay 12½, he will sell 100,000 shares," Jefferies tells me. I go to Merrill, tell Merrill what I know. Merrill comes back to me with, "The buyer really needs to buy 400,000 or 500,000 shares, but I'll buy your 100,000 now. I won't chase the stock up to make you look bad; I'll still continue to work. Are you willing to sell stock that way?" The buyer and seller are both happy.

An important factor in the everyday business is the seeming reluctance of institutions to accept a report regionally. There is basic mistrust if a trade is printed away from the primary market. For example, let's say Institution "A" calls Merrill Lynch and asks to buy 30,000 shares of Union Pacific. The market in New York is 12⅜−12½−50,000 by 50,000. Merrill Lynch wants to write a commission on both sides. On the one hand, Merrill could go purchase the 30,000 shares in New York at 12½. But if he calls another Institution "B," who wants to sell Union Pacific at 12½, he writes two commissions. The problem is, he can't trade it in New York because of the offering at 12½. So he crosses it on the Midwest with Engelman. The buyer wants to know why; because Merrill got commissions, that's why. The buyer paid the same price he would have in New York, so he should be happy. The seller is also happy because he sold something he wanted to sell. Everyone should win. However, the buyer is still skeptical. He assumes that he was treated unfairly just because the stock traded away from the primary market.

However, let's take the other example where it's not right to make that assumption. Say the market is at 12½, there's 3,000 offered, and a buyer comes in and wants to buy 10,000 shares even though there aren't three sellers in New York. I say, "But I'll sell you 10,000 shares at 12½," and Goldman says, "I'd buy but I can't trade regionally because my buyer is afraid." Then I say, "What is he afraid of?" He's afraid that Goldman had not probed to see if any of the 12½ stock would come in at ⅜ in New York, but he had. The fact of the matter was, I supplied stock that was not there. In fact, the buyer is lucky that I am there or

Denny Engelman

Now, I'm in the position I love to be in. I have two guys saying they want to do something. Both of them have size, but neither one wants to say how much. So I go back to the seller and I try to ascertain the number based on the information I have. Jefferies now calls their seller. "Well, if Merrill is willing to pay 12½, he will sell 100,000 shares," Jefferies tells me. I go to Merrill, tell Merrill what I know. Merrill comes back to me with, "The buyer really needs to buy 400,000 or 500,000 shares, but I'll buy your 100,000 now. I won't chase the stock up to make you look bad; I'll still continue to work. Are you willing to sell stock that way?" The buyer and seller are both happy.

An important factor in the everyday business is the seeming reluctance of institutions to accept a report regionally. There is basic mistrust if a trade is printed away from the primary market. For example, let's say Institution "A" calls Merrill Lynch and asks to buy 30,000 shares of Union Pacific. The market in New York is 12⅜−12½−50,000 by 50,000. Merrill Lynch wants to write a commission on both sides. On the one hand, Merrill could go purchase the 30,000 shares in New York at 12½. But if he calls another Institution "B," who wants to sell Union Pacific at 12½, he writes two commissions. The problem is, he can't trade it in New York because of the offering at 12½. So he crosses it on the Midwest with Engelman. The buyer wants to know why; because Merrill got commissions, that's why. The buyer paid the same price he would have in New York, so he should be happy. The seller is also happy because he sold something he wanted to sell. Everyone should win. However, the buyer is still skeptical. He assumes that he was treated unfairly just because the stock traded away from the primary market.

However, let's take the other example where it's not right to make that assumption. Say the market is at 12½, there's 3,000 offered, and a buyer comes in and wants to buy 10,000 shares even though there aren't three sellers in New York. I say, "But I'll sell you 10,000 shares at 12½," and Goldman says, "I'd buy but I can't trade regionally because my buyer is afraid." Then I say, "What is he afraid of?" He's afraid that Goldman had not probed to see if any of the 12½ stock would come in at ⅜ in New York, but he had. The fact of the matter was, I supplied stock that was not there. In fact, the buyer is lucky that I am there or

196

he would have to pay 12⅝. So, when he buys 10,000 from a regional, he is getting something because Engelman Securities provided an important service. I have represented myself as an agent for another broker. In that case, the buyer should be real happy that I'm in this process because I was able to find supply that was not there.

Trust

Being successful depends on trust—you just have to trust that your broker is doing the best job he can do. You will know pretty quickly if he is not because the price of the stock will move, and then you will be able to see it.

In order for me to be successful, I can rarely give up to a customer the identity of the other side of the trade. Still, they always ask for names. Ironically, it is not what you say to the other person on the other end of the phone; it is what they say to the next person that counts. You hope you can trust the person on the other end of the phone to be a professional and do the business the way it should be done, that is by the unwritten rules that were developed in the late 1960s and early 1970s by the people who helped build the block trading industry. You hope you can trust him to trade with a sense of both ethics and style, with knowledge of how to put a trade together, and to perform in the manner you yourself would. Then you can tell him anything because he understands what you do for a living.

But if he jeopardizes that trust, either inadvertently or deliberately; if he jeopardizes your relationship because of something you say; if he jeopardizes your relationship with one of his competitors, then he is in fact jeopardizing himself because he is cutting off your ability to give him information. Bob Mnuchin best understood this concept—he felt that the respect and the trust of his peer group was every bit as important as the trust and respect of his customer, even though his peer group is his competitor. That is a real important point—that's one of the things that separated Mnuchin and Goldman from the rest of the business at the time. Goldman believed that treating their competitors fairly and ethically was as important as treating the customer in the same manner.

Denny Engelman

The Ethical Way

Let me offer an example. Assume that Goldman Sachs has a 90,000 shared order of Union Pacific to buy. Mnuchin can not find any sellers through his sales force. He goes to the New York floor or the Midwest floor and he probes the offering side of the market to see what kind of volume is available at what prices, with the last sale being at 12¼. In that process, he comes to me and I—through my network—find out that at 12½, Merrill Lynch would be willing to sell 50,000 Union Pacific if Goldman Sachs traded a total of 90,000. But exactly at the time I communicate that information, one of his salespeople finds a seller of 90,000 shares at 12½. Mnuchin says he now has someone who's willing to buy 90,000 shares at 12½ and also has someone in Goldman Sachs's network who is willing to sell 90,000 shares at 12½, and therefore get 100 percent of the commission on both sides.

But now there is a problem, because in the process of trying to do that, Mnuchin has asked Denny Engelman to ask his network if there is anybody willing to sell stock at 12½. That creates an obligation. Now what is the obligation, to tell one of his own people that he's not going to be able to sell 90,000 shares because his competitor wants to sell some stock? That is not really servicing his operation. But he has created an obligation with me, because I have asked First Boston, or whomever my seller is, if they would be willing to sell some stock, and they've said yes. And in the time it took me to do that, Goldman Sachs has found their own seller. Mnuchin, would tell his own seller, "I'm sorry, you can only sell 40,000 shares because in the process of trying to find a seller, we found one through a competitor, and I owe that competitor the right to sell the stock even though I have a commission on both sides."

Mnuchin was one of the few people who would do that. Most people would say, "I'm sorry I have my own seller; you can't sell any." Unfortunately, that is the attitude of many clients today, who feel that the commission and the ability to get the commission on both sides is a more powerful influence than the ethics that were established over 20 years ago. There is a reason for that—most of the people who are running desks today or have power today didn't grow up in the business during the 1970s, where relationships — not machines — made the business. And the people who came into the business in the 1980s during the great boom were never placed in the position to work hard to find buyers and sellers because they were always present. In the 1970s, we tried to create trades out of thin air — and often succeeded.

Automated Delivery (1988-present)

The Age of the Dinosaur

What do you do? What can you say when the world is telling you that you're a dinosaur. Wow! How would we survive? "Quite well, thank you," said the dinosaur.

1988 to the Present

All exchange floors develop their own auto-delivery order systems. To the Midwest, it's MAX. To the Pacific Coast it's Scorex. To the NYSE it was DOT. Now it's called SUPERDOT.

Who cares? These are all systems to execute the retail order (let's say less than 5,000 shares). They will be filled on the best bid or offer on the exchange the order is delivered to. Therefore, the relationships the exchange has built up with the brokers (mostly within their own geographic region), and the exchange with the lowest cost of execution and clearance (there is no floor brokerage as the order is delivered via machine direct to the specialist) gets the business.

My Dad told me a long time ago you can't put flesh and blood in a computer. That is, you can't program emotions. Big institutional blocks take a lot of emotional pitch to execute. It takes dialogue and negotiation. Both are non-programable (I hope). In the last few years various automatic meeting systems like POSIT have been developed and have attempted to match price and size in a *passive* environment. This chapter is not the forum for a dissertation on passive block execution. Needless to say, my opinion is that *blocks* must be negotiated. This negotiation is an art form. It is true that the cost is lowered by automation and the broker may even add to his bottom line and some cost savings may in fact be passed on to the customer. However, my feeling is the end-user (pensioner) benefits more from the negotiated process.

As overhead was constant or increasing slightly, and volume and revenue fell, we determined to remain a broker's broker. Resisting the temptation to deal direct at discounted rates with the end-user, we had to work at establishing our relationships with the broker, meeting the new and much younger supertraders that were coming onto the trading desks, and most of all dealing with the fact that they were much better "informed" than the brokers of the past. Information systems built by the brokerage houses made their traders much more knowledgeable of data that heretofore *we* had provided. In addition, the block trading commission shrunk considerably as rates fell with volume, making the use of independent brokers (vis à vis your own house broker in New York) more appealing. But still the "core community" (6 or 7 houses who still told the institutions "we're here to provide the liquidity you can't find in the marketplace") felt that we were the only alternative to the NYSE floor, the only place they could "get" information and trust with their input.

Technology Comes to the Floor

Thus as the 1980s wound down, we were confronted with a clear "tiering" of the marketplace. The retail or public tier which in the 1960s and 1970s had accounted for 70 percent of the national daily volume and 90 percent of the daily tickets executed, now accounted for 25 to 30 percent of the volume and 80 percent of the tickets. The two-dollar broker became obsolete as he was replaced by the machine.

As the Midwest expanded its execution capabilities, it also had to enhance its trading technology structure. The floor of the Exchange became filled with quote terminals, overhang machines, and all sorts of computers. We had machines hanging on the post, around the post, on the post, and above the post. The change in the configuration of the entire exchange floor due to the impact of technology was extraordinary. Between 1965 and 1985, it looked like—and became—a completely different floor.

As a floor brokerage firm, we also had to reorganize our structure. We were now set up as a ten-person desk, three at each end and two at each side. This enabled a better flow of communication. This was critical, as the key factor to success—especially considering the amount of merchandise that was flowing, the volume we experienced, the speed with which the trades happened and had to be executed or shopped around—was to be extraordinarily efficient.

This meant that trader one had to be able to successfully communicate to trader nine at the other end of the of the table, 15 feet away: "I am a buyer of ABC, and use one ear to hear number nine's response, and his customer's instructions in his other in the other ear. My job was to orchestrate that flow of information. Once it came in the door, the goal was to close that trade. If there was any problem, we would make sure to allocate it properly.

Let me give you another example of how I had to be an orchestra leader. A guy comes in during the heyday of the 1980s, and he's not the kind of guy who covers arbitrage accounts. He has 100,000 shares of General Foods to sell, and General Foods at that time was in play. He's trying to give us business because it's well wanted in New York, and he says "Here, do this trade; it makes up for a lot of the tough ones you tried to do and couldn't." Well, everybody was covering John Mulhern, Ivan Boesky, and all the other arbitrage players at that time, so no matter who you called, they were going to make the same call to the same customers. So we try to be fair; if somebody said "I am a buyer of this and I have an order I am working it," he certainly got the first call. But we would always say "We have 100,000 for sale; you may not be able to buy it all" and then our staff would call a couple of other people we thought were trading the name that day or in previous days, and we would allocate it. Maybe 40,000 would go to the guy who told us that day that he had a working order, and then we would split the other

60,000 by 20,000 each, to three different accounts. But the orchestration of that and the fairness in the way it was distributed was significant, because each of our clients had to feel like he was being dealt with fairly. He didn't necessarily have to have the lion's share, but he had to come out of it looking like he was doing his job. For each account we covered we had to look like we were doing our job as well.

The old two-dollar brokers (those who were left) worked orders, as more and more institutions decided that there was so little liquidity and so many people were chasing so few (and the same) stocks, that working an order over the course of a day, attempting to match or better the mean-weighted average for the day, was a safer way to answer to a portfolio manager as to why the trader paid what he did for a stock. As we have said earlier, working the order that way is not what we did for a living.

1988 to the present has been a "good news/bad news" story. We had to resist dealing direct at discount rates with the end-user. We had to adjust and even change the way we worked an order. That was the bad news. The good news is that most of our competition (on the NYSE and other regionals) went by the wayside, leaving us in an enviable, but precarious, position.

In Conclusion

It has been one "helluva ride." How strange it is to look back now on how hard we worked to get a 10,000 share trade in the 1960s and 1970s to get paid 3 cents per share. I remember how many "road trips" it took in 1969 to establish relationships that still stand today and how little volume we had to do to cover our overhead. Today we work ten times harder to do the same amount of revenue at $\frac{1}{10}$ the old rates. Clearly, the business is going to continue to expand, especially as foreign capital seeks U.S. equities as a haven. They will do this as long as the low interest rates of the 1990s continue—with equities selling cheaper in relation to alternative instruments. This scenario portends great opportunities for the next several years.

What will our role be? Our role as negotiators, as seeing eyes for the upstairs traders, as great relationship builders, and as traders possessing a consistent work ethic, will guarantee us a prominent role in any trading environment of the future.

CHAPTER EIGHT

STEPHEN BODURTHA

*The Program Trader**

One of the most significant inno-
vations to hit the Wall Street trading world since May Day 1975 has been
the advent of program trading. Just the mention of program trading
can either bring cries of anger and agony from investors, while other
traders consider it to be one of the most creative and influential forces
in the market today.

In the early to mid-1980s, Kidder, Peabody & Co. served as a
hothouse of talent for the entire Wall Street program trading community. An entire generation of derivative traders, analysts, and theoreti-
cians on Wall Street—Steven Wunsch, Joseph Schmuckler, Joanne Hill
and others helped to turn what had been a proprietary trading strategy
into a useful tool for institutional investors. And among those at Kidder
was a young man fresh out of Harvard University's Graduate School of
Business named Stephen Bodurtha.

*The opinions contained in this chapter are the author's, and do not necessarily
reflect those of Merrill Lynch & Co., Inc. Under a policy adopted in 1987 and
broadened in 1989, Merrill Lynch does not execute index arbitrage program
trades either for clients or its own accounts.

Stephen Bodurtha

Since 1989, Bodurtha has helped to build a powerful program trading and derivatives effort at Merrill Lynch & Co. Bodurtha and his colleagues have developed a host of financial engineering techniques and strategies for its many institutional and corporate clients, further establishing its reputation as an innovative resource for its customer base. Bodurtha has been in a unique position to observe the emergence and rise of these technology-based strategies, and will relate his professional and personal observations about program trading from its inception to its current use.

A Continuing Controversy

Program trading has been both one of the most controversial and misunderstood practices in the stock market over the last decade. What has often gotten lost in the debate is the fact that program trading is not just a way to make arbitrage profits. It is a trading technique for institutional customers to implement their investment strategies. If the futures and options markets were to disappear tomorrow, program trading would still be practiced by these institutional investors, because it represents a cost-effective way for them to implement many of their investment strategies.

Fundamentally, there are two types of program trading. The first, and perhaps the best known, is the program trading that is related to stock index futures and options arbitrage. In this type of program trading, both institutions and professional traders are seeking to take advantage of mispriced futures and options. What they will do is sell futures contracts and buy a basket of stocks that will track that futures contract — or do the reverse: buy the futures contracts and sell a basket of stocks — in an effort to earn a low risk return in excess of the Treasury bill rate.

The second type of program trading has nothing to do at all with futures or options. It represents the buying and selling of portfolios of stocks by investment managers who tend to pick their stocks in groups, not one by one as a result of fundamental research. These portfolio managers are running models and identifying whole groups of stocks that they want to buy or sell. As a result, a program or a basket trade is the sensible way to implement those decisions.

Who Are the Program Traders?

Today, program trading is practiced by a variety of institutions and broker-dealers. Among the professional money managers, index funds were the earliest and continue to be the most regular users of program trading. In addition to the indexers, we have seen the growth of active managers in the program trading arena. These managers are identifying baskets of stocks that have certain characteristics — such as low price-

Stephen Bodurtha

earnings ratios or high growth rates, or stocks which are likely to produce earnings surprises—and then buying or selling them in bunches via program trades.

The Pension Fund Connection

Pension funds have also come to use program trading as a way to change their asset allocation. A pension fund may decide that in order to manage its liabilities more efficiently, it needs to be more invested in the stock market. In this scenario, the pension fund may sell bonds while simultaneously purchasing a basket of stocks via a program trade.

Pension funds also get involved in program trading when they change their outside investment managers. After the incoming managers have had a chance to review the outgoing managers' holdings to see which stocks they want to hold onto, there is usually a portfolio of stocks that needs to be liquidated and turned into cash for the new investment managers. These portfolio liquidations can be handled very effectively through a program trade.

The Proprietary Traders

Another class of users are proprietary traders. From time to time, there are opportunities that allow proprietary traders to earn excess returns by simultaneously trading baskets of stocks versus futures or options contracts. These opportunities will be discussed later in the chapter.

The Change in Technology

In its early days, a program trade was handled just like any other stock trade. Scores and scores or even hundreds of tickets in individual stocks were circulated on the floor of the stock exchange. When it came time to begin a program trade, all of these tickets were released for execution, which set off a flurry of activity on the floor of the exchange. Of course, the buying or selling put upward or downward price pressure on many of the market's blue chip stocks. The charged, frenetic atmosphere, combined with the pressure on stock prices, often prompted exaggerated rumors to fly which, in turn, often reinforced what was already happening in the market.

Of course, much program trading is now done electronically. Instead of being hand-delivered by floor personnel, hundreds of orders are routed electronically and directly to the specialist post for execution. Today, there are even institutions that have direct access to electronic program trading systems that allow a manager of an index fund or a quantitative portfolio to decide what stocks it wants to buy and sell, hit a few buttons on its computer and send a list of orders to the appropriate exchanges for execution. Many of these systems are equipped with a host of analytical applications that enable an institutional trader to make more intelligent trading decisions.

The fact that program trading has survived in spite of the controversy that surrounded it is perhaps the best evidence of its value to institutional users. It is simply the easiest and most natural way for an index fund or a quantitative manager to execute trades. The alternative would be to split up a basket into individual trades and try to simultaneously work hundreds of orders in the marketplace, something that could be very labor intensive, costly, and virtually impossible for a thinly-staffed money management firm to handle.

In addition, there are often economies of scale in trading stocks in program form. By hedging with futures contracts, institutions can often cut commissions, as well as the bid-ask spread and market impact expense of trading.

For example, a client wishing to sell a portfolio might find highly illiquid markets for each of the individual stock positions. But if the portfolio has some correlation with a stock index futures contract, then a broker-dealer might be able to hedge its market risk by selling those futures. Knowing it can hedge in this fashion, the broker might then make a higher bid for the whole portfolio than could be obtained by aggregating bids for the individual stock positions.

How We Got to Where We Are

Before going into greater depth on each of these topics, perhaps a little history on the origins of program trading is in order. Program trading received its start well before the advent of stock index futures contracts.

The 1970s saw the beginnings and subsequent tremendous growth in the area of passive index fund management. Index funds were evaluated—as they are today—by how well they tracked the performance of the index they were intended to mirror. As a result of this standard, index funds had a strong incentive to transact at or better than the closing prices that were used to calculate the performance of their target index.

For example, if an index fund manager were given $100,000,000 in new money to manage, they might enter the market at 3:30 P.M., a half an hour before the close, and purchase stocks. If the market fell after the time of their purchase, they would have incurred negative performance versus their chosen index. By contrast, if the index fund buys the index stocks at the closing price—that is to say, at the time that they will start being measured from—then they will be assured of getting off on an equal foot with the index.

The same is true when an index fund needs to liquidate funds and raise cash. For performance measurement purposes, the closing price of the index will be used to calculate what cash is owed to a customer or what performance has been generated. As a result, the index fund needs to liquidate at closing prices.

The Beginning of Index Arbitrage

So this first type of program trading really had nothing to do at all with futures or options arbitrage. It was not until 1982 when futures contracts began to trade on the Standard & Poors 500 and on other stock indexes that it became possible to use program trading for arbitrage purposes.

For example, assume that the S&P 500 index stood at 400.00, and the following market conditions prevailed:

S&P 500 Futures Price:	405.00
Time to Futures Expiration:	0.25 Years
Treasury Bill Rate:	5 percent per annum
S&P 500 Dividend Rate:	3 percent per annum

With these conditions, a proprietary trader could engage in the following strategy:

(1) Buy $10 MM worth of S&P 500 stocks at an index price of 400.

(2) Sell $10 MM worth of S&P 500 futures contracts at 405.

At futures expiration, the trader could unwind his or her long stocks and short futures position at the same price (it doesn't matter whether it's 400, 375, 425, or some other price), because the futures are deemed to expire at the opening price of the S&P 500 stock on expiration day. The S&P 500 stocks, for the most part, can usually be traded at that same opening price.

The proprietary trader has earned the following profit:

5 index points =   profit from convergence of futures and index (405-400)

plus

3 index points =   dividend yield for one quarter (3 percent annual dividend yield × index price of 400 × 0.25 years)

---

8 index point total profit   = 2 percent quarterly return on initial index price of 400

OR

8 percent annualized return.

Once set up, this strategy is basically risk-free, since the futures price must equal the price of an S&P 500 index portfolio at expiration. And yet, despite its risk-free character, the proprietary trader has earned an annualized return of 8 percent, or 3 percent more than the Treasury bill rate.

Stephen Bodurtha

When Treasury bill rates were in the 10 percent range, it was not uncommon for these arbitrage positions to generate 15 percent or 18 percent or more on an annualized basis. Naturally, program trading arbitrage attracted a fair amount of capital, and there were a wide variety of players. Professional trading organizations, broker-dealers and even the treasury departments of corporations would use program trading arbitrage as a way to generate above-market returns on their cash balances.

In addition, the index funds were also able to take advantage of mispriced futures contracts to boost their performance. But the index funds did not take the risk-free positions that we just spoke of. Instead, their goal was to own, at all times, the cheaper of either the futures contracts or the underlying basket of stocks. If the futures contracts were trading rich, they would sell the futures contracts and buy the S&P 500 portfolio of stocks. Conversely, if the futures were trading cheap to their fair value, the index funds would sell stocks and buy futures contracts.

Of course, all this trading was a competitive activity. With the amount of capital that was attracted to arbitrage related program trading, one might have expected the excess returns to disappear quite quickly, but they persisted for a number of years. Index funds continue to be some of the toughest competitors for the arbitrage opportunities, whereas a corporate treasurer might not want to bother with the execution detail in order to improve the return on his cash by 10 or 20 basis points. That margin of outperformance would be very valuable to any index fund and could indeed allow them to attract even more assets from clients. And so, the index funds fought tooth and nail to capture even the narrowest of mispricings in the futures market and they continue today.

It is also worth pointing out that this type of activity does not always require the futures contracts to be mispriced. Some traders put on long stock/short futures positions or short stock/long futures positions in anticipation of the futures contracts becoming mispriced. Sometimes these traders establish such risk-free positions even if they are only earning (initially) the equivalent of a Treasury bill rate. Their hope is that the futures will become mispriced later, allowing them to unwind the position and earn an attractive spread.

How the Game Has Changed

Since the mid-1980s, competition has gradually decreased the profit opportunities available in index arbitrage, and as a result, professional traders and index funds have done several things to continue earning attractive profits in this area. The two main steps they have taken are:

1. To take on greater risk in implementing these arbitrage strategies; and

2. To invest in advanced trading technology.

Legging

Arbitrage users have increased their risk profile in a few different ways. One of the more fundamental ways to increase the risk of index arbitrage is known as legging a trade. To take an example, if a trader thought that futures were trading at a slightly rich price, but thought they might become richer still, the trader might go into the market and buy the portfolio of stocks representing the S&P 500. Ordinarily, the sale of futures in an arbitrage strategy would occur simultaneously with the purchase of the stocks. But in legging, the trader essentially waits because they have a short-term view on the market that suggests that it will be profitable for them to wait before acting on the offsetting leg of the transaction. In this example, the trader might wait five minutes, a half an hour or even an hour before selling futures contracts against the long stock basket position.

Legging can and does get quite more complex. Today, arbitrageurs aided by workstation technology can detect trading patterns in various sectors of the market by analyzing the real time data that comes from the exchanges on trades as they occur and also bid-ask quote information from the market.

One example of how this data can be used is when a trader, instead of going long the entire basket of S&P 500 stocks, might choose to buy only half of the stocks in the index because he or she has been able to identify those stocks as being the cheapest to own at that given time. The trader might hold off buying the other half of the index until those stocks appear to be attractively priced. Typically, these strategies will be implemented over a relatively short timeframe, and rarely will they be carried over to the next trading day. But they provide a sense of just how competitive the arbitrage business is and the techniques the traders have used to keep the profit opportunities alive.

The Human Factor

There are several keys to success in the index arbitrage business. The first, of course, is having an experienced trader who understands the flow and the feel of both the futures market and the stock market. It is very helpful to be able to anticipate market swings over a very short time period. In addition, an experienced trader on the floor of the futures exchange is invaluable to the success and is a critical part of any successful index arbitrage program. A good floor trader will also be able to make judgments about the short-term direction of the futures market. They may have a sense of the levels at which there are buy and sell limit orders in the market that have not yet been executed, and which could either provide support or resistance to a market move in either direction.

The Workstation Advantage

Advanced trading technology is an indispensable tool in today's arbitrage activities. With today's trading room technology, it is possible to break down the S&P 500 into its industry groups and find out which are trading at attractive levels. It is even possible to anticipate the impact on the market that a program trade will have. Of course, it is invaluable to be able to anticipate with some accuracy what your net execution prices will be. It is one of the biggest unknowns in program trading when you go to the floor to execute a basket of stocks. Workstation technology by processing real time data on stock trades and bid-ask quote informa-tion—can give you a much better read on what your execution prices are likely to be. And improvements in accuracy of even a penny or two per share can make the difference between success and failure.

The technology available in the early days of program trading was paltry when compared to the powerful workstations of today. Program traders used to settle for watching two blinking numbers on a quote screen: the up-to-the-minute last trade prices for the S&P 500 index, and for the related futures contract. By the mid-1980s, they had stopped being passive observers of standardized quotes. They began to take in raw trade and quote data as it flowed from the exchanges, and manipulate it and display it on their own higher-speed personal computers. Ultimately, even the better PC's could not keep pace with the amount of raw trade data inputs and with the number of real-time calculations and displays that the program traders required. Today, almost all program trading desks are equipped with workstation technology.

Was Program Trading Really to Blame?

In terms of its impact on the market, index arbitrage has been blamed for the crash of 1987 and the mini crash of 1989. In judging whether or not program trading was the culprit, it is important to keep several factors in mind. First, when one notices that the stock market is going down and that there is a sell program in the market at that same time, there probably were stock index futures being sold in Chicago prior to that sell program. That futures trading could have been related to an investment manager trying to hedge its portfolio or in someone trying to take a market view that the stock market was going to be heading downward. In any event, before the sell program began, the institution in this example had effectively accomplished its selling and had removed its capital from the equity market by trading in the futures pit. Viewed this way, the sell program in stocks was simply a reaction to, not a cause of, lower equity market prices.

Second, index arbitrage typically neither adds nor subtracts capital from the equity market. Of course, a sell program may result in stocks going down. But when a sell program is going on, the arbitrageurs are simultaneously buying stock index futures contracts, which lends support to the market.

The Basket Traders

Now, let's turn from the world of index arbitrage to the other type of program trading which has been adopted by professional investment managers. The main practitioners of this type of program are index funds

215

and quantitative active money managers. As we have discussed, index funds need to invest or raise cash from their funds and a program trade provides the best means of implementing those decisions.

A quantitative active manager, instead of picking individual stocks, might be running a computer model, the output of which identifies 80 or 100 stocks that appear to be attractive. Now, the money manager might take those orders and split them up among five or ten different brokers, but this is very hard to coordinate and could lead to errors in execution later. So instead, many quantitative active money managers have adopted program trading as their preferred way of implementing their investment strategies.

There are three basic ways for a customer to implement a non-arbitrage program trade. One is to ask a broker to execute an agency program. The second type is an agency incentive structure. The third way is to ask a broker to commit capital, to take risk by guaranteeing execution prices. That is called a risk program or a principal program trade.

Agency Trading

The agency approach is just like any other "best efforts" stock trade. The institution will pay the broker anywhere from one to six cents per share and will ask the broker to get the best possible execution prices. One of the things that attracts institutions to the agency approach is the low commission rate that is often available to them. Sometimes though, the low commission is a false economy. If the broker is not motivated properly to pursue best execution, the customer will give back the commission savings and more in higher market impact costs. Market impact costs occur, for example, when your buy order pushes up a stock's price, resulting in a purchase price that is higher than the stock price either before or after your trade.

In particular, it is the quantitative active managers that need to be concerned about market impact, since such costs are a drain on their performance. (Since their goal is to beat, not just match an index, they can't be satisified by trading at closing prices). As a result, you will find these institutions continuing to pay higher commission rates for program trading execution services, because they believe the higher commissions will be more than offset by market impact savings.

When executing an agency program, a broker will use all the advanced workstation technology that it may have originally developed for proprietary trading purposes. The broker will use real time data to identify the most and least liquid positions in the customer's portfolio of orders. If the system is doing its job well, it will separate the easier orders and earmark them for electronic execution.

The tougher orders, the ones that would benefit from more patient working in the marketplace, can often be broken out and sent to the block trading desk. In fact, technology is sometimes overused to execute electronically some orders that in reality should be executed on the block trading desk. This overuse is tempting because it is cheap and easy to use electronic execution, but it may not result in the best trade prices. Very often, the only capital and only market making capacity that is available through the electronic execution systems is that provided by the specialist in individual stocks. So if one has a fifty or hundred thousand share order in a particular stock, it may make sense to take that out of the electronic execution environment and instead trade it on the broker's block desk.

A good broker will have the technology to do that analysis, to identify the tough orders to execute and will also have the willingness to separate those orders and not just blindly send them through the electronic execution channel. A sophisticated broker should be able to tell the customer at any time how much of its portfolio has been executed, what cost in terms of market impact has been paid and, if the customer were to complete the execution of its portfolio immediately, what it would cost in market impact. Not every broker is set up to know exactly where each and every one of the orders stand among the hundreds or scores of orders that are put into the marketplace on behalf of the customer.

Agency Incentive Trading

The second type of customer program trading is agency incentive trading. In this format, the broker and customer have basically the same type of agency relationship. The broker is acting in a best efforts capacity on behalf of the institution. However, it agrees that the commission it earns will be dependent on how well it executes versus a mutually agreed upon benchmark.

Often, that benchmark might be the prior night's closing prices, or it might be the average price of the trading day in each of the stocks. The point of this is that the broker will earn a base commission rate, usually a low one, if it does worse than the benchmark execution prices, and it can earn a higher commission rate if it beats the benchmark execution prices. Some customers prefer this method of executing because it, in effect, allows them to pay for performance. They reward good performance with a higher commission rate and they punish poor performance or avoid paying up for bad execution by having the agency incentive structure in place and having a low base rate commission.

Critics of the agency incentive approach suggest that it may encourage a broker to take unnecessary chances with the customer's order. For example, if the customer has given a broker a list of buy orders to execute and the benchmark is the prior night's close, the market may open up strongly the next morning. In that type of scenario, it will be tough for the broker to earn more than the base commission rate and the result may be that they are punished for an unfortunate market move that they had no control over.

Even in that context, it may make sense for the broker to begin executing the orders and avoid having the market move further against the customer. But if the broker thinks that the market might drop later on in the afternoon, it might take the chance and not begin to execute until later on in the day. The broker's hope is that the market will drop and that they will be able to earn a higher commission under the agency incentive arrangement.

However, in this example, the broker might be taking an unnecessary risk. If the broker is wrong, the customer's execution prices could be even worse. In spite of such considerations, the agency incentive structure continues to have a philosophic appeal to many customers and I expect it to be a permanent feature of the program trading business.

Principal or Guaranteed Price Program Trading

The last type of customer program trading is what we call the risk program or principal guarantee program. In this structure, the customer is asking the broker to take on the entire risk of execution. As a result, if implemented properly, the customer should know exactly what his or her total transaction costs are up front. Even though risk programs are more expensive than agency incentive trades from a commission standpoint, this certainty is what motivates many institutions to use the risk program approach.

There are a number of ways to implement risk programs. The approach that involves the highest risk is when, for example, a customer calls a broker before the opening of trading on a given day and tells the broker that he or she has a list of stocks of a certain size that he or she wishes to buy or sell at the previous night's closing prices. In this example, the customer has told the broker only the size of the portfolio, how many stocks are in the portfolio, and perhaps a few pieces of information about which industries are represented in the basket. The broker responds with a cents per share bid that is intended to pay for or charge for the risk that it is bearing, covering the costs of market impact and processing the trades, and also earning some profit.

The riskiest programs will command a fairly high bid. It would not be uncommon for a risk program to be awarded at a rate of 15 cents to 20 cents per share. On some risk programs, the lowest bid can be 50 cents to 60 cents per share. It all depends on the customers' portfolios. Knowing with certainty the cost of execution is one reason why customers choose risk programs to implement their investment strategies. Another reason is that they believe that it will be the lowest cost form of execution. The reason they think that is that they have kept secret their trading intentions from the marketplace.

While it may be desirable for an institution to avoid broadcasting its trading plans to the market, withholding information from the broker in a risk program will obviously increase the risk of the transaction to the broker. As a result, the broker's risk bid will be higher than it would be if the broker knew more about the contents of the portfolio.

Some institutions have become quite expert and have automated the way they provide detailed information about their risk programs to the street. Some institutions provide several pages of information containing risk characteristics on a portfolio, industry breakdowns and liquidity information. All of this is helpful to a broker who is bidding on a risk program, and if done properly, it should not compromise the secrecy of the institution's trading plans. An example of how that confidentiality can be violated in a way that will hurt the customer is where the institution provides the actual list of stocks to each of the brokers that may be bidding on a risk program.

In bidding on a program under such circumstances, each broker has a problem. If, for example, the winning broker ends up being long a portfolio of stocks that the customer wanted to sell, the winning broker has to liquidate that position. It has to sell those stocks knowing full well that the losing brokers know precisely what it must liquidate. Trading sizeable stock positions when the rest of the market knows exactly what you need to do can be a very punishing experience. But of course, the bidding brokers will anticipate that pain, so they will submit higher bids than they would otherwise. So in this case, the customer has provided too much information. As a result, its trading costs will go up.

As one can see, the customers who use risk programs wisely find a happy middle ground between keeping their trading intentions confidential, and providing as much information as they possibly can to the bidding brokers.

What It Takes to Win

To be effective in customer program trading, a broker needs to have some of the skills that are helpful in index arbitrage. But there are some unique attributes as well. Of course, it helps to have a trader who has a good sense of short-term market direction. Even though the customer program may have nothing to do with the futures market, knowledge of activity and the ability to interpret events in the futures trading pit can be helpful in executing packages of stocks for customers.

And of course, real time trading technology can be very helpful in anticipating and monitoring the cost of a program trade as it unfolds. It is critical to be able to get feedback in real time on a program trade and to be able to use that information to update and revise the execution strategy.

As mentioned earlier, it is also possible to rely too much on trading technology. Electronic execution systems are relatively inexpensive for brokers to use, but not all client orders should be executed through them. When a client wishes to buy or sell a meaningful percentage of a stock's typical trading volume, then it is important to get the broker's block trading desk involved, in order to achieve the best possible execution prices. Since many client-originated program trades contain such large individual positions, a good block trading desk is another indispensable resource to a superior program trading operation.

A Well Run Back Office

What is particularly important in customer program trades is having a reliable and efficient operations unit to report and settle the trades accurately. Many customers use program trading because it is a relatively simple way to get lots of trades done. To take a concrete example of this, instead of taking 100 execution reports from eight different brokers, a single worksheet showing all 100 executions can be sent from a broker to a customer electronically by modem. This worksheet can often be uploaded directly into the customer's internal accounting and settlement systems.

Typically, those trades need to be booked by a certain time each day. So if a program trading report arrives late, it is possible that the trades might not get booked until the following day, and thus the positions will not show up on the investment manager's books. Also, because you are relying on computers and computer programs to do this work for you, a simple mistake can be multiplied many times over in dealing with a portfolio of orders. So it is very important to have quality control and an accurate team of people who are reporting and settling program trades.

Stephen Bodurtha

Putting It All Together:
The Anatomy of a Successful Program Trade

At Merrill Lynch, we have had many opportunities to test how well we have put together the key ingredients to successful program trading. Few were more challenging than a $700 million manager transition we executed on behalf of a pension fund client in mid-1991.

This pension fund had decided to terminate a group of equity managers with subpar performance, and wanted to reallocate the assets to existing and newly hired stock managers. Slightly more than half of the $700 million transition was represented by buy orders. The balance consisted of sells. The pension fund's goal was to minimize the slippage, or total transaction costs, of executing these buys and sells. The fund chose an agency approach.

From the start, we knew that we faced some tough obstacles. Trade operations was the first one we had to address. The sell side of the transaction was quite straightforward operationally. The sell orders had been aggregated by the pension fund's custodian, and could be sold out of one account. The buys were a different story. For trading purposes, we needed to aggregate the buys for nine managers into one order per stock (there were a number of well-regarded stocks that several of the managers wanted to buy). But for trade billing and settlement, we needed to allocate each day's purchases in each stock to up to nine different accounts. Then, we had to determine the "leaves," or how many shares were left to buy of each stock for each of the nine accounts. Then, the execution and allocation process would begin anew. Without the right computer programs, these operational tasks would have been impossible. Fortunately, we had the right capabilities.

Another key task was to conduct our pre-trade analysis of the buy and sell portfolios, and to put together a trading game plan. Our analysis showed that many of the buy and sell positions consisted of more than 50 percent of the average daily trading volumes in many of the stocks. We knew that such high demands on liquidity created the potential for high market impact costs. We had developed a quantitative model of market impact, which was based on actual trades we had executed over the previous two years. We ran the detailed list of buy and sell orders

222

through this model, and found that the estimated market impact costs for this transition were 1.00 percent or more. Given that our client was hoping for a total cost of less than 0.50 percent, we had our work cut out for us.

If we were going to hit our client's cost target, we knew we had to do two things very well. First, we had to get outstanding execution prices on the largest, least liquid positions in the buy and sell portfolios. Second, we had to shrewdly balance our buying and selling throughout the transition. If we bought more than we sold on a given day (in aggregate dollar terms), then we would be exposed to a market drop the next day. In such a scenario, the loss on our larger remaining sell positions would overwhelm the fact that our remaining buys would be executed at lower (better) prices.

Having identified these keys to success, we broke the buy and sell portfolios into two categories: (a) those large orders which represented a substantial percentage of a typical day's trading volume, and (b) the more liquid orders which we felt could be executed through the electronic links to the listed stock exchanges and to our over-the-counter desk. The large orders would be given to Merrill Lynch's block trading desk, which specializes in finding liquidity and getting good execution prices for big stock positions. The smaller orders earmarked for electronic execution would help our buying and selling to stay in balance. If one of our block traders could execute a big buy order at a good price, for example, we would not want to be forced to execute an illiquid sell position just to keep our buys and sells in balance. Instead, we could electronically execute some of the liquid sell orders to maintain that balance, without incurring excessive market impact.

This plan was working well for the first two days of trading, but experience had taught us to expect the unexpected, and not to celebrate or let up before the last order was executed. This experience was put to the test when word arrived of an attempt to overthrow Gorbachev in the Soviet Union. This news brought about a precipitous drop in the market.

Our moment of truth came on the morning of the second day of the attempted coup, when the outcome was by no means clear. And it was here that our prominent role in stock and futures trading gave us the conviction to act when we had to. On that morning, there was a real possibility that we were entering an extended period of international instability, which could mean dramatic volatility and several trading days of steep market declines. In this environment, it might be tough to keep our buys and sells in balance at an acceptable cost, even if we wanted to.

Fundamentally, we viewed the U.S. stock market as being strong, and we thought the attempted coup was not likely to damage the conditions that had made it so. That view supported the idea that we should become aggressive buyers of stock, and slow down our selling. But world events can have an unpredictable effect on stock markets. If we adopted this approach and were wrong in our market outlook, our client would end up paying the price. The newly acquired stock positions might plummet in value, along with our still-to-be-executed sell positions, essentially doubling the client's loss.

As trading opened on that morning, we saw that many institutions were submitting large block orders to buy stock. In addition, our trader in the S&P 500 futures pit saw institutional bids for large quantities of S&P futures contracts. It became increasingly clear that the majority of market participants were looking at the coup-induced market drop as a buying opportunity. Armed with this information, we made a key judgment to do more buying than selling on that morning. It turned out to be the right choice. The stock market gathered strength. We accomplished numerous block buys at the market's lower levels, and several days later, we were able to sell many of our client's positions at the price levels that had prevailed prior to the attempted coup. Our active and skillful presence in both block trading and in the futures market made our decision possible and prudent. Without that presence, we would have lacked the insight to act swiftly when it was beneficial for our client.

The success of our strategy was revealed concretely when we produced the "Merrill Lynch Report Card," which is our special post-trade execution cost tally. The Report Card showed that our client's total execution costs—including commissions and market impact—were less than 0.35 percent, far better than our model's estimate of 1.00 percent or more, and better than our client's cost target of 0.50 percent.

What Does the Future Hold?

Looking forward, there are several important trends on the horizon for the program trading business. This may be speaking too soon, but it is possible that it will be a calmer and gentler world for program trading. One by-product of decreasing arbitrage opportunities with stock index futures is that there is less potential for program trading to be associated with, or even be seen in the vicinity of a substantial market drop. So we may see fewer charges that program trading is roiling the markets. At the same time, we can expect that the practice will continue to be exported as new stock index futures markets are set up around the globe.

Program trading has already been implemented successfully in Japan and in Germany. We can expect to see it emerge in other countries as well. Program trading is being extended even within the U.S. stock market. Until recently, most customers were able to obtain true electronic execution only on listed stocks, even though they might be submitting OTC stocks as part of their program trades. Very often, those OTC trades were broken out and handled in a conventional, non-electronic manner. Now, automation has arrived in the world of over-the-counter and smaller capitalization stocks. So now it is possible to obtain the same type of swift electronic execution in over-the-counter stocks as has been available for several years in listed stocks.

Program trading will also be used to help hedge the newer equity derivative strategies and products that have grown up over the last couple of years. For example, if an institution wishes to get stock market exposure by entering into an equity index swap, the derivative dealer agreeing to provide the equity return to the institution may hedge its obligation by purchasing a portfolio of stocks in a program trade.

Program trading gained prominence as a proprietary trading strategy, but it has evolved to meet an investor need. Whether futures, options and arbitrage come or go, program trading will continue to be an attractive method of implementing the investment strategies of certain types of money managers. If anything, these quantitative and passive strategies

Stephen Bodurtha

seem to be growing. We now see managers who seek to outperform by picking the best-performing mix of countries. When it comes time to switch from France to Germany, for example, a program trade will often be the transition method of choice. As long as portfolio managers continue to develop equity strategies that rely on techniques in addition to stock picking, program trading will be an important feature of stock markets around the globe.

CHAPTER NINE

EVAN SCHULMAN

Electronic Trading

Evan Schulman is president of Lattice Trading, a firm virtually synonymous with the development and implementation of electronic trading. Evan began his career with The Royal Trust Company in Montreal (it was here that he met his first computer). The company financed an account for Evan at the computer center at McGill University. Shortly thereafter, he moved to the Keystone Funds in Boston.

Before leaving Keystone for Batterymarch in mid-1975, he accomplished what is believed to be the first program (or package) trade in equities. Keystone was implementing an active/passive strategy in its high-risk fund, and the restructuring required the sale of a $100 million portfolio of stocks and the purchase of another $100 million of stocks. Evan finally convinced a broker to bid on this package blind; that is, the broker did not know the names of the securities involved in the trade but had to guarantee that the swap would not cost more than a fixed sum, including commissions and market impact. At Batterymarch Evan was also involved in the computerization of the firm. Here he helped to design, develop, and implement trading systems for both domestic and international securities.

Lattice is the logical outcome of Evan's interest in trading. Its goal is to provide institutional fund managers real-time control over their orders. To accomplish this, Lattice has developed an electronic broker that provides access through a single terminal to most electronic markets. It is a single footprint for managers (in that orders can be submitted to those markets through most brokers), and a kit of trading tools, including the ability to make orders conditional on other market events. The result is that managers can fashion and implement their own proprietary trading techniques.

This chapter attempts to outline the forces pushing us towards an electronic implementation of continuous auction markets.

My First Computer Date

Words and phrases change their meanings over time. My first "computer date" was not arranged by a computer but was a date *with* a computer. In 1963, The Royal Trust Company in Montreal sent me to see the McGill Computing Center to evaluate use of their IBM 7020 model for investment research. That machine was enough to attract any red-blooded youth; elegantly reposing in air-conditioned splendor, she hinted of great untapped prowess by blinking her panel lights in mesmerizing patterns. I was in awe.

Over the next five years we developed programs (later repatriated to the Trust Company's Honeywell 400 computer) to measure the investment performance of client portfolios, to allocate the weighting of investments in portfolios using linear and quadratic programming algorithms, and to remove seasonal and other factors from market data time series. It was in this later activity that I learned my first lesson about the relationship between computers and the market: the market was always faster. By the time the machine had enough data to confirm that something was happening, that event was well underway; indeed, the statistical programs used could give no assurance that the event had not already run its course by the time it was identified. No matter how fast the machine was, it could tell us only what had happened, not what was going to happen.

Implementation Costs

Somewhat dismayed by these results, I moved to the United States. Maybe the Americans had a better understanding of how the world works. I accepted the position of Director of Computer Research at Keystone Custodian Funds in Boston, then and now one of the leading U.S.-based fund managers. One of my first jobs was to evaluate the disappointing performance of one of their funds. Pawing through the reams of paper used to document investment decisions, I discovered that these portfolio managers actually kept a record of the price of a security at the time they made their decision. I decided to compare that price to the actual cost or proceeds realized by the ensuing transaction. My second lesson concerning markets was that delays between decision and

execution led to implementation costs or slippage. Evidently, the information that prompted the buy or sell decision became available to other
market participants, and the price adjusted. This price gap, which we
will call *information cost,* was aggravated by the market's lack of liquidity,
i.e., if the investment manager was in a hurry to build up (or liquidate)
a position in a security, he or she would push the price of that security
beyond where the value of the information would move the price without
that portfolio manager's reaction. This is termed *market impact.*

Implementation costs include the information costs, market impact,
and commissions. They are measured from decision to implementation
price and dwarf commission costs. Prior to the advent of negotiated
commissions in May of 1975, commissions alone ranged from ½ of 1
percent to 1 percent of the amount traded. Total implementation costs
were estimated by Jack Treynor, then editor of the *Financial Analysts
Journal,* as 10 percent. He arrived at this figure by noting that paper
portfolios tended to outperform standard indexes by 10 percent, while
actual portfolios had great difficulty matching the performance of these
indexes. Given lesson one, that part of the cost resulting from commissions and market impact cannot be recovered if the investor was reacting
to publicly available information.

At Keystone we used the computer not only to measure portfolio
performance but also to disaggregate that performance into its various
parts: security selection, sector bets, market timing, transaction costs,
etc.[1] We also attempted to evaluate the significance of the over- or
underperformance so measured. This work was refined to such an extent
that it was actually used as part of the bonus formula for Keystone's
money managers.

The third lesson concerning markets and the computer became
clear to me: in the chaos of markets, humans crave certainty equivalents
so badly that a printed number, no matter how suspect the underlying

---

1.   This is a neat trick, especially if one doesn't know how to accurately measure
overall portfolio performance in the first place! Institutional investment performance is
measured monthly or quarterly, while investment strategies are in place for periods of
time measured in years. Observations of shorter duration than the strategy being
measured are incomplete, and disaggregating an incomplete measurement is unlikely to
generate information.

calculations, carries a weight far in excess of its worth. Does that explain the raison d'etre of technical analysis services? The reader may consider the latter a glib remark. It is not meant to be. Technical analysis has many, many staunch adherents, in spite of innumerable academic studies that indicate no forecasting power. I know this, just as I know that astrology's truth is in the eye of the beholder. For example, when faced with a most important event over which I had little or no control—a judge was to decide custody of my children—I entered a bookstore and looked up in an astrology book the date that the custody hearing was to take place. There in black and white I saw that the omens were good; I felt somewhat relieved and slept well that night. I understand that such a service (creating a semblance of certainty where there is none) provides real psychic support in the period during which we await the outcome of a particular process or event. I should note however, that I did not buy the book; I'm not that irrational.

The First Program Trades

Before leaving Keystone, we combined the first three lessons—and the result was the first computer-generated package trade in equities. Keystone divided the world of securities into different risk pools. The unmanaged, or passive performance, yardsticks of those pools had an unfortunate characteristic: they tended to outperform the actual portfolios selected from those sectors. It was clear from the performance data that the fund managers did not have sufficient information to invest the bulk of their assets, less implementation costs, to better advantage than that sector of the market in which they were required to work. We argued that it was possible to get very close to that yardstick performance with certainty—simply purchase everything in the risk pool. We realized that the Index Fund concept applied to a benchmark other than the S&P 500.

The Board of Directors bowed to the third lesson—they accepted the concept of certainty and authorized the investment department to index the bulk of one of their portfolios to its respective risk pool. The portfolio managers were instructed to use their skills and information on a small portion of the fund to see if they could indeed disprove the first lesson and adjust the smaller securities positions, for which they were responsible, before the market discounted the new information or analysis.

Our goal was to determine whether or not the amount of assets managed was the problem causing underperformance. If the portfolio managers were successful, that is, if they could beat the index with their actively managed portion, they were to be given more money to run. Restructuring of the portfolios involved the sale of $100 million of stocks that were overemphasized in the portfolio and the purchase of an equivalent $100 million of stock that was not represented or underweighted. The second lesson concerned transaction costs: these were to be minimized.

We received permission to undertake this project in the spring of 1975. The actual transaction was to occur shortly after commissions became fully negotiable on May 1, 1975. The fund selected to be rebalanced first was that which invested in the highest-risk equities. It also contained more than its share of stocks with limited liquidity. To say that I felt challenged would be an understatement. We started to negotiate the transaction with brokers. This was not something that one could get executed in Boston. Therefore, we made several trips to New York. One, in particular, was memorable.

We stepped off the Eastern shuttle in New York, to be greeted by the longest, blackest, shiniest limousine that I had ever seen. We were whisked downtown (the only missing element was the motorcycle escort). A magnificent lunch was spread before us. Our hosts told us that theirs was truly a great firm, one with legendary trading skills. We were then asked to indicate just how they could help us. I noted that we were looking for a firm just like theirs, one with real trading expertise. I added that based on my studies, brokers, with only a modicum of trading expertise, should be able to make 1 percent from trading if they controlled both sides of a portfolio switch such as we were about to undertake. If the brokers went long what we wanted to sell and short what we wanted to buy, they would be hedged against market moves. They could gradually unwind these positions over time as prices moved in their favor. I suggested that a firm with real trading expertise would do better than the 1 percent and should be willing to pay our clients for the privilege of executing our orders. The amount to be paid should be stated before the trade began — in fact, before they saw the orders. To appreciate the boldness of this request one has to remember Jack Treynor's estimate of implementation costs, mentioned above, at the 10 percent level.

I took a taxi back to the airport.

However, we persevered and eventually found a broker who bid on the program without seeing the orders. He did not pay for the privilege of executing the orders, but he did offer a fixed all-inclusive cost to be based on the price of the securities immediately before he saw the orders.

I am told that a true student of life learns until the day he dies. Personally, I find it humiliating to be taught lessons at this late stage, but this particular program trade was indeed a learning experience. First, the broker removed from the list those names that were too illiquid (they cared not whether we were buying or selling). So much for their legendary trading expertise. And what had our portfolio managers bought? Next, they requested us to break the program into five pieces, one to be given to them each day of the week. My big splash in the market was becoming more like an anemic dribble, and dribbles are not macho.

Finally we started. At market closing I would turn up at the broker's office with a set of buy and sell orders amounting to roughly $15 million for each side. These trades were then printed at the opening price the next morning at prices that were within the negotiated parameters. I expected a swelling in volume as others reacted to the obvious increase in liquidity in these stocks. It did not happen. Other traders, worried that they did not know what was going on, retired to the sidelines. So much for expectations. The broker's inventories — rather than the trading volume — swelled, and we had to put delays in the program.

Nevertheless, the program was completed. Our clients benefited from a fast transition to the desired portfolio along with transaction costs well below those recently experienced, and the broker made a profit of about 0.7 percent on the total package — very close to the forecast of 1 percent derived from our simulations.

Before I leave the Keystone experience, it is important to note that, initially, the computer's involvement in the package trade was not for speed. The buy and sell lists were part of a portfolio management function; the delivery of these lists to a broker was to extract economies of scale from that broker and to cut down on the errors generated by humans facing a sea of data. In 1975, there was no electronic routing of orders, such as a DOT system, taking trade instructions directly from the institutional money managers to the floor of the New York Stock Exchange.

Brokers were encouraged to bid aggressively for this business because of the way we acted. While we did not tell them the names of the securities involved, we did give them the flavor of those securities and the concentration levels of each list. We also allowed the broker some leeway in determining when to trade. These actions were to assure the broker that we were not involved in a trade based on security-specific information. Investors who have information about a company that others do not have — security-specific information — tend to trade in a hurry, as they try to establish or unwind a position in the stock before others discover what they know. Those who trade with such investors tend to find that they have sold too low or purchased too high in the short term. By allowing brokers leeway in timing the transaction and trading portfolios as opposed to individual names we were signalling that we had no security-specific information, we were simply restructuring our portfolios.

The computer's function in the first program trades was accounting, the error free transmission of orders, and as a signalling device to assure the other side of the trade that we were merely involved in portfolio restructuring.

Batterymarch

The application of computers had significantly altered the investment process at Keystone. More changes were unlikely to be implemented in the short run. It was time for them to consolidate and evaluate. It was time for me to move on.

The move to Batterymarch was traumatic. I was leaving a firm with $2 billion in assets under management to join one with but $100 million. My employment discussions with Dean LeBaron, the owner, did not concern salary; I did not expect a small firm to pay more than I was getting from one of the established industry giants. But I did need a computer; by now I was hooked. Our discussions concerned the size of the computer budget.

Batterymarch did not have a computer. We rented time from a commercial time-sharing service. To make our limited funds go farther, we selected the most "cost effective" service — my associates noted that it was the cheapest. Our brokers, believing that quality of service was important, selected other services. There was no way of moving data from one time-sharing service to another. That generated problems.

Batterymarch provided an index fund service, passive investing, which it offered to its clients. We undertook to invest in the 250 largest capitalized firms in the S&P 500 in such a way as to mimic the full index. Because we registered with the SEC as an investment adviser and not as a mutual fund manager, each client had to have his own account. An overweighting in one portfolio could not be used to offset an underweighting in another; purchases and sales had to be broken down into orders by account. We had five or six accounts, each with cash flow. The computer would generate some 200 to 250 orders for each account.

At that point in time, it was not an easy matter to move data from our "cost effective" computer time-sharing service to the time-sharing services used by the brokers. Punch cards were the medium of choice. Tape was available, but in those days getting one machine to read another's tape was an arduous challenge. Besides, I could count my cards to see that I had the right number of transactions. Acquaintances still tell stories of Madman Evan running (literally) from the low-rent district of Boston (where else would a "cost effective" purveyor reside?) to the business district with bundles of computer punch cards held together by elastic bands. The stories have since been embellished to include snapped elastics and dropped cards.

Again, we should note that the computer performs two functions in these trades, physically separated by my mad dash through downtown

Boston. Our computer was used for its ability to manage portfolios, an accounting and balancing function, and to transfer the results of that process to a machine-readable medium. Thereafter, we used another machine to transmit those results to the brokers without using error-prone humans. Overall, this rather clumsy process signalled to the other side of the trade that we were not exploiting any proprietary information. Speed, at least in terms of nanoseconds, was not of the essence; accounting and accuracy of data transmission was.

Electronic Trading

We learned from this three-phase process. Brokers would fight for order flow, and the use of computers allowed us to process a relatively large volume of orders with surprisingly few errors. Could we obtain similar results for our active accounts? Active investors manage portfolios based on forecasts of risk and return and, in Batterymarch's case, neglect of these stocks by other money managers. We thought that we could utilize the computer to trade active accounts, and we obtained our first general time-sharing computer by the end of 1975. The Batterymarch electronic trading program struggled into existence during the second quarter of 1976.

To state that the initial goal of this computer-based trading program was unimaginative is being too kind. We were not motivated by dreams of artificial intelligence and new trading strategies. We expected to increase our business; that meant more staff, both for the trading desk and the back office. If by using computers we could avoid this increase in staff, the increased revenues would flow directly to the bottom line. Further, the business risk was minimal because once the programs were written, there would be no additional costs if the growth did not occur as anticipated. This was a very attractive aspect of the project; as opposed to adding staff for growth and then facing layoffs or overhead if the growth did not materialize, we bore only the cost of writing a program.

We even touted the concept of using our computer to trade as a cost saving for the brokers. They did not have to respond when we called them. They could call the computer when they had some spare time and needed some work or when they had the other side to an order they had seen on our machine. We argued that this business had zero marginal cost and/or was providing them with liquidity for their other clients. We asked only that the savings be passed back to our clients in terms of reduced commissions.

And it worked! A friend of mine in the brokerage community claimed that if one were to draw an iso-commission map of the United States, there would be a deep dark hole centered in Boston: that would be Batterymarch.

As in the case of our index transactions, the computer was being used for its portfolio accounting and balancing ability and to communicate clearly with the brokers, clients, bank custodians, and the back office without errors. The only business risk was whether clients would feel that Batterymarch eschewed its fiduciary duties by turning over trading authority to the computer. We solved that by having a trader, in fact our head trader (our only trader), monitor the program continuously during trading hours.

The design of the trading system reflected our narrow goals. A limited set of brokers was allowed to log onto the system, which was secured by program control and a password. Every few months the broker or brokers who had done the least trading was asked to leave the system, and one or two new brokers were added. This competitive spur gave brokers the incentive to trade as opposed to just look.

Once they were under control of the trading program, they could look at the book of Batterymarch orders, which included a limit price for each order. At this point they could either execute an order directly or put one or more on "hold" while they tried to find the other side.

If a broker indicated that a trade had been executed, the program updated the shares remaining and allocated the shares traded among Batterymarch clients. The allocation reflected our philosophy of being fully invested. The client with the largest cash balance in terms of portfolio percent received priority in purchases; those with the lowest cash balance received priority in sales. The program also prepared the data for the portfolio accounting system, wrote the information into a file for the client's custodian bank (retrieved by the bank at the close of business that day), and informed the broker of the delivery instruction for the clients participating in that trade. Clerical errors resulting from data entry were eliminated.

Time-Sharing Mysteries

While the computer we purchased and programmed was a general time-sharing machine, our business did not warrant more than one telephone line for the brokers. A broker would call the machine, look at the list, select what he wanted to do, and sign off. As he signed off, the machine would update its files and be ready for the next broker.

However, as we gained clients, we increased our trading volume, and the brokers required additional lines. We installed more lines, and I learned something about time-shared computers. As before, a broker signed on and selected what he wanted to do. However, while he was making his decision, another broker could sign on. In all likelihood, the second broker would make the same decision as the first one. As each broker signed off, the disk files were updated to reflect each decision. But other brokers had read the old disk files into their sector of the computer's memory. The program, as I had written it, was unaware of the other brokers' selections. The computer recorded the last one to sign off as having the order, but as far as each broker was concerned, the machine allowed him to put that order on hold. The first day we had the new lines, six brokers turned up at the same post on the NYSE with the same order. They quickly realized what had happened and gave me a call.

We immediately closed the system, and I spent the next thirty-six hours wrestling with the program, putting flags and locks on stocks that brokers had under consideration so that another broker could not get at that order until the first broker was finished. I learned a great deal about time-shared programs quickly and decided that we should hire experienced programmers. The programmers who wrote and maintained the subsequent versions during my tenure—Beverly Cancelliere, Douglas Holmes, John McCormack, and Andrew Von Baird—transformed a crude working skeleton into a sophisticated, powerful piece of code.

In accordance with our goals, the system virtually eradicated errors in our back office. It also solved the staffing problem mentioned above; we added very few extra staff as we expanded. A dramatic example of just how free we were from the normal office procedures occurred during the great Boston blizzard of 1978. Batterymarch was the only manager in the area that continued to trade. Portfolio managers could sign on to the machine from their homes to review and authorize orders. Brokers could call our computer from around the country and execute orders. For a few days, the office ran by telecommuting.

The International Arena

Shortly thereafter, Batterymarch decided to offer an international service. Could we use our trading system internationally? International brokers were quite clear in saying, "No! Do not use technology as a Trojan horse. Keep the American disease of competitive commission rates at home." It was also argued that these markets were less efficient than the American markets; investors needed the services of a broker to represent them. Simulations indicated costs of 3 percent from decision to execution price, assuming that the decision price was the close of the night prior to the trade and execution was the highest price the following day for purchases, the lowest for sales. We were assured that using a broker to represent us would greatly improve upon these results because any broker worth his salt would be able to purchase stock below the high and sell above the low.

Without the experience to argue against this, I agreed to do our first international trade as advised. We rented the international trading desk of a large New York broker. During the day we ran our portfolio-balancing program to select the issues to be purchased, based on the closing prices of the previous session on the foreign markets. I then got on the New York Shuttle and arrived at the broker's desk in time for the Japanese market to open—8:00 P.M. our time, 9:00 A.M. their time. We traded all night using telephones to bellow orders and changes to those orders. I use the word bellow advisedly. It is most natural, although somewhat embarrassing to relate, to shout in an attempt to get an individual who barely speaks your language to understand what you are saying.

The next morning, with worn out vocal cords, I returned to Boston. We calculated the cost to our clients of our trades, using the previous night's close as our decision price. The cost was 3 percent—exactly the cost suggested by our crude model of getting the worst price of the day. That settled it. By using the machine I would at least be able to sleep at night.

We told brokers that the only way that they could get orders from Batterymarch was to get a terminal and log into our computer system in Boston. The business would be there. Enough of them did and we were able to manage money internationally, getting orders executed at the prior day's close. The one exception was Spain. They would not log on to our machine, and the London brokers did not step in to fill the void. While I volunteered to fly to Spain (in February, as I remember it), Dean LeBaron objected on the basis of a ten-second cost/benefit analysis. We sent telexes to Spain.

Program Modifications

Trading by computer at Batterymarch was a big step forward. To do so allowed the manager to integrate portfolio management and trading. No longer need these be two different processes separated by a mad dash through town or by the flow of written buy and sell tickets from the portfolio manager to the trader. Each night our portfolio balancing program surveyed all portfolios under our care to ensure that they reflected our current judgments in light of the day's closing prices. Given the price limits attached to each order, a trade may or may not be executed, but the order was generated and, if approved by the assistant portfolio manager, advertised to market participants the next morning. We then set to work to see if we could improve its ability to execute at prices that were more favorable for our clients.

The "hold" option changed dramatically over the years. Initially, this feature gave the broker the exclusive right to execute up to three orders at any time during a two-hour period at our price limit. However, the broker was not obligated to execute the trades. In the event that the order was not executed, or only partially executed, by the end of the hold period, that order would again become part of the general pool of orders. It could only be executed and not be placed on "hold" for the next 15 minutes. Later, brokers undertook to execute 1,000 shares or more if they put a stock on hold, the time period of the hold was reduced from 2 hours to 15 minutes, and the hold feature was restricted to the afternoon trading hours. All of these changes recognized that the "hold" feature was really nothing more than an option, that options have value, and that we were giving our brokers these options for free.

We changed the way the limit price was calculated. Initially it was the close of the market on the day prior to generating the order. Technology improved and we obtained a real-time price feed for our computer. We were then able to "market adjust" our limits and to make them the most favorable (for our clients) of the last sale or the market-adjusted limit.

Batterymarch's approach to trading became known as "R2D2" by the trading community, referring to the personable robot in the famous Star Wars movie series. Our "wish list" of trading intentions became a regular item for the morning meetings of most large brokers and money managers.

Market participants began to step in front of our orders, using the Batterymarch order as a stop-loss mechanism for their trades. Thus, if Batterymarch was buying (selling), traders could buy (sell) ahead of us. If the stock moved as we expected, they would make a profit, if not, they could cover their position by hitting the Batterymarch order, which acted much like a floor (ceiling) for the price of that stock as long as we remained interested. The result was that we were affecting the price of stocks without obtaining our desired positions. Trading became more complex than envisaged by our limited goals mentioned previously. A trading strategy had to be superimposed on our trading mechanics.

To hinder these frontrunners, we decided to implement substitute orders. Our investment strategy was based on factor exposure. Usually several stocks would fit our needs; we rarely had information that was specific to any one company. As a simple example, say that we wanted $5 million worth of exposure to oil stocks. There may have been as many as five stocks that met our needs. Using substitution, we could put orders for $5 million for each of the five stocks into the trading system for a total of $25 million of orders. The program was instructed to stop trading once it had spent $5 million on any one stock, or any combination of the five stocks. We worked hard to ensure that there was no double execution.

Now it was more difficult to run in front of our orders. If we executed a substitute order, the floor or ceiling was abruptly removed for all related orders. It became far more risky, far more difficult to game the system. Further, because we had greatly increased our chances of finding the other side, we could be firmer on our price limits.

One final innovation was made for our work in international markets. Not only did these markets trade when we were home asleep, but many of these markets did not even broadcast a price feed. How could we ensure fair prices for our clients? We were no longer satisfied with prices as set by the previous night's close. Illiquid international markets handle this problem by having call markets as opposed to the continuous auction markets utilized by the more liquid American markets. A call market is just that: everyone trades a particular stock at one point in time, and then they move on to trade another stock. All the interest is focused on a stock, there is one price determined by the supply and demand at that time.

We felt that this was a reasonable model for trading our international lists. The computer would advertise our orders and accept bids or offers from foreign brokers during local market hours. Brokers were free to change their input until the moment of our call market. At that point the program selected the best bids or offers that met or exceeded our reserve price and notified the brokers within seconds whether and for whom they had done the trade. Competition was to ensure that our clients got the benefits of any price improvement that occurred when the foreign markets were open. As of this writing, Batterymarch still uses the call market system for international trades.

Under the system, international brokers work during their local hours. They execute the trades at prices set by the money manager; they cover the clients' foreign exchange liability and report the executions to the machine in U.S. dollars. The process leaves little room for surprises. In the morning (Boston time), there was little left to do except to see how the stocks had closed that day (most of the foreign markets complete trading by lunch time in Boston).

Surprises were generated primarily by the arrival of significant new information during the trading day overseas. Although there were several such events, the one I remember best occurred early in the system's life. We were still trying to convince brokers that we had no special information on the companies in which we were trading. Batterymarch purchased a block of Broken Hill Proprietary in Australia. The transaction occurred in the morning, Australian time. That afternoon the company announced that they had struck significant quantities of oil in a new field. When I arrived at work that morning we were inundated with calls from Australian brokers calling from their homes just before they went to bed. What did we know, when did we know it, what were our sources of information? It is difficult for an investor to argue that he was uninformed, especially after a success.

Evaluating the System

The hallmark of the Batterymarch computerized trading system was openness, or honest disclosure of our trading intentions, with a reliance on the forces of competition for protection. The question is, did it work? Professor Andre Perold of the Harvard Business School and I addressed this question in the following discussion.

We examined some $3.5 billion worth of trades done by the system while the firm was restructuring client portfolios over the period November 1984 through March 1985. The results of the analysis are somewhat ambiguous because, to date, no other money managers have allowed their transaction data to be examined in the detail that Dean LeBaron, the owner of Batterymarch, let us examine Batterymarch's data.

We looked at the data first from a short-term perspective. On average, where did our transaction lie with reference to the bid/ask spread at the time of the trade, and what happened to the price of the stock immediately prior to and after our trades? In particular, we checked to see if other traders set market prices in order to take advantage of our advertised intentions. If this was the case, we expected to find small spikes in stock prices, up in the case of our purchases, down in the case of sales. Certainly if we were always executing on the wrong side of the bid/ask spread we would expect to find a cost averaging some 6 cents from the midpoint of the bid/ask and roughly the same from the stock's average price in the short run. Since a graph of what we were searching for looked much like a pimple, we termed this analysis "Acne."

At first glance, our fears were unwarranted. On average, our transactions occurred just on the wrong side of the midpoint of the bid/ask spread, and between 0.02 percent and 0.08 percent on the wrong side of the average of prices 30 minutes, or even an hour, either side of our trades. Both measures indicated a price disturbance of 1 to 2 cents per share on a $30 stock, a credible performance given that the minimum spread on such stocks is 12.5 cents.

However, much information had already been divulged by our program by the time an execution took place on the system. Had our advertising affected prices? Was there an implementation cost? Since we had divided the securities to be traded into groups, some of which would be off the system when others were on, we could check the price behavior of stocks for trade with the behavior of those no longer being advertised.

The results of this analysis were enough to warm the heart of any advertising executive, but not mine. The very fact that a stock was advertised on the system affected its price by roughly 0.2 percent. That is, if Batterymarch indicated that it wanted to buy a stock, the stock's price rose by 0.2 percent on average; an advertised sale would push the stock's price down by some 0.2 percent. Once a stock was removed from the system, its price would revert, but by less than one half the distance of the disturbance caused by advertising. The effect of advertising on the first day was three to four times the effect described above.

While this was interesting in and of itself, our system of limit prices protected clients from the implementation costs generated by advertising. That is, the program controlling the trades would not chase a stock that moved away; rather it would patiently wait for stock to come to it. Simply stating the algorithm that way raises the specter of adverse selection because we were, in reality, offering the other side an option. It would be exercised only when it was in their interests to do so. The question now was what happened to the prices of securities after completion of a trade, not what happened after the order had been partially executed, because the remainder of the order was still being advertised on the system and acted like a floor or ceiling for subsequent price moves. But what happened after the order had been completed?

The results were disquieting. On average, the prices of stocks completely sold, as opposed to partially sold, rose 0.5 percent equally weighted and 1 percent value-weighted by the end of the day of the completed trade. The prices of stocks purchased to the full extent of the order fell some 0.4 percent.

As mentioned earlier, there are no comparable figures for other money managers. We expect that the procedure of using market-adjusted limit prices and counting on competitive forces is reasonable. But the analysis did uncover areas that systematically generated trading costs: advertising and order completion. Both were aspects of the same underlying problem; it would be difficult to address these from within the confines of a large money manager.

Advertising interest in a stock as a money manager firmly attached that manager's label to the stock — "XYZ is a Batterymarch stock," or "Batterymarch is selling XYZ." Others can then frontrun the order, trusting in Batterymarch's analysis or market impact to give them a profit. Substitution did help blunt these effects, but there was no anonymity. Without other managers on the system we could not hide in their order flow.

The transparent nature of the system also gave rise to the order-completion problem. Even if we had not displayed our overall intentions, traders had access to records of our positions in each stock. Once we started to sell, they knew how much we would sell; once we started to buy, they knew the size of our average position by type of stock. When they saw that the order was about to be completed, they knew that the cumulative effects generated by our advertising were about to be removed; the support was to be withdrawn from stocks we purchased, the cloud removed from stocks sold. The time to frontrun had ended, the correct strategy at that point was to help fill our order and benefit as market prices returned to their unadvertised state. To cure these problems required a new company. Lattice was born.

Lattice

We had come a long way at Batterymarch. While the system had started out as a simple labor-saving device, it ended up with strategic features such as substitution and market-adjusted limits. Further, these were under program control and therefore controllable in real time. To divert orders to a conventional broker in order to hide in the flow generated by his other business was to throw out an intriguing set of tools — and at just the wrong time. Analysis of the market crashes of October 1987 and 1989 indicated that our equity markets desperately needed liquidity.

Figure 1.1 is an attempt to show this need. The figure is a simple representation of limit orders in the book of a specialist or market maker. Within +/- 5 percent of the current price, there are limit orders for roughly a day's trading volume, on average; one-half a day's volume on each side of the bid/ask spread — beyond that, little or nothing. If, for any reason, we get beyond a 5 percent move, it is as if a running back has broken deep into the secondary defense of the opposing football team. Not only has he made yards, he is going to make many more — with no one in sight to stop him.

It may be productive to view this lack of depth and liquidity in the book as a structural problem — a by-product of asymmetrical deregulation. The fixed commission structure was discarded in 1975, and after fits and starts, commissions became competitive by 1980. However, the self-regulating organizations that control access to the markets, particularly the NYSE, left unchanged both institutional access to those markets and the mechanisms (specialists, upstairs market makers, etc.) that provide liquidity to the markets. Under this system, the individuals who are specialists, and have a net worth measured in millions of dollars, are expected to supply liquidity to institutions with assets measured in the

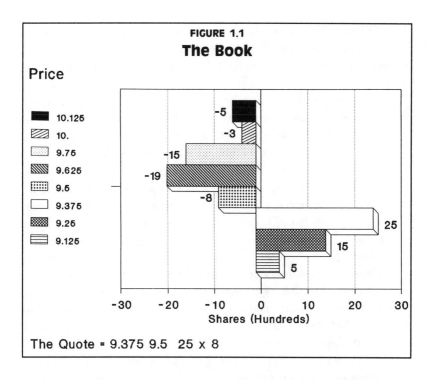

FIGURE 1.1
The Book

Price

	Price
■	10.125
▨	10.
▤	9.75
▨	9.625
▦	9.5
▭	9.375
▨	9.25
▤	9.125

Shares (Hundreds)

The Quote = 9.375 9.5 25 x 8

tens of billions of dollars. At the risk of stating the obvious, it does not and will not work.

The point here is that lack of liquidity is not a behavioral problem, but one of institutional structure. This structure prevents money managers from having real-time control of their orders. This generates an agency problem in that managers cannot get conditional orders or, indeed, any complicated orders to market with any degree of precision. The portfolio manager issues instructions to his trader, the trader to the broker, the broker to the floor and the floor to the specialist. Each person listens, interprets, and compresses the information for transmission, much as the clerk in an old-fashioned grocery store would listen to and interpret a client's order. The clerk would then go back to the store's inventory and fill the order to the best of his ability. Service and customer satisfaction greatly improved with the advent of the supermarket. Armed with a full information set, the supermarket customer can search the store's inventory, responding to new products and events. We want Lattice to give institutional portfolio managers the same freedom and increase in customer satisfaction that supermarkets provided their customers.

Currently portfolio managers, who execute on the floor of an exchange, have the choice of three basic order types; limit, market, and participate. A market order is one to purchase at the asked price or sell at the bid. In both cases the quantity that can be moved at those prices is limited. A limit order is an order to buy or sell at a specified price. Here there is no limitation as to the size of the order, but there is no guarantee that the order will ever be fully, or even partially, executed. An order "to participate" instructs the trader to participate in trades as they occur on the floor; it, like the market order, gives up price control for volume.

These are blunt instruments with which to engage in price discovery, a primary function of markets, and the only order that supplies liquidity to the market, the limit order, exposes the client to the possibility of being picked off by other traders. Indeed, limit orders can be viewed and valued as near-the-money options. Because it takes minutes for an institutional money manager to change or cancel an order on the floor in response to new information, the use of limit orders exposes clients to costs equal to, or greater, than the commissions charged and, as discovered in the Batterymarch data, gives valuable information to other market participants.

Money managers are, understandably, reluctant to expose themselves or their clients to the costs associated with such agency problems. The result is a huge pool of potential orders that never see the light of day.

Can we estimate the size of this pool? Table 1 attempts to set a value, in terms of cents per share, for a $40 stock on the option implied by a limit order. We use the Black/Scholes formula for an at-the-money option on stocks with different levels of volatility. These values are calculated for both a five- and a one-minute time span. The agency cost associated with a five-minute retrieval capability appears equal to the present institutional commission rates. Assuming that the elasticity of

---

TABLE 1.1
Value of Real Time Control
Cents/Share

Annual Standard Deviation	20%	30%	40%
5-Minute Values	2.3	3.4	4.6
1-Minute Values	1.0	1.5	2.0

At-The-Money Option: $40 Stock; 250, 6.5 Hour Days

---

demand for commission-based services approximates unity (the marginal cost of getting an order to market approximates zero, set marginal cost = marginal revenue, and we have a unit elastic demand curve), removing this agency cost should just about double trading volume.

But it may be even better than this. With agency costs approaching zero, money managers could attempt to extract more revenue from their asset base. They can supply liquidity to the market as opposed to always demanding liquidity from it; and they can game the markets. Fischer Black, the legendary MIT professor and partner at Goldman Sachs, has noted in a recent paper that there is an incentive to bluff in the market to obtain the difference in costs between liquidity-generating trades and information trades. To size the potential order flow is much like asking how much of the adding machine market electronic calculators would capture. An estimate of 100 percent would have been a gross underestimate because the small, versatile electronic calculators were as different from the heavy mechanical adding machines as real-time control of orders is to current trading practices.

Unrestricted Access

The signs of orders to come are already observable. We are aware of pairs, index arbitrage, substitution, spread jumping, etc. These are all orders that are executed as a function of the prices of one or more securities, and they are profitable enough that some members of the trading community either absorb the agency costs involved or go to the expense of building their own trading systems to control the agency costs.

Now allow electronic access to these markets in such a way that portfolio managers and traders have real-time control of their orders. The result will be a flood of orders, conditional on a wide array of possible events, passively waiting execution. This ever-changing sea of orders will provide depth and liquidity to the market. No longer must the specialist stand alone, no longer must the security analyst walk the streets, unable to profit from his insights because the market is too thin. Other orders will be attracted by this new-found liquidity. Fischer Black will be there, bluffing; market technicians will be there, averaging; and artificial intelligence buffs will also be there, in all probability.

What I am forecasting is a set of networks collecting and managing orders to be arrayed in a centralized book. Those who bear performance responsibility will have real-time control over them. These transaction systems of the 1990s — and beyond — will constitute a seamless integration of the investment management process and trading. The result will be billion-share days, not because of a crisis, but every day, day in and day out.

Superficially the structure of the markets will be the same. There will still be exchanges, although they may be but nodes on a worldwide network. We will probably access these nodes through a broker; credit checks still need to be performed, transactions still must be settled. But here the resemblance to our current markets begins to fade. We will have a far more level playing field; that is to say, the intermediaries — the broker/dealers and the specialists — will no longer have an information advantage. With computerized access to the news wires and their orders, investors will know as much as soon and be able to react as quickly as anyone else. Those with trading expertise who now, with precious few exceptions, reside almost totally on the broker/dealer side of the desk, will move towards the buyside of the street. After all, the buyside has the assets. Whether this happens literally or by the broker/dealers subcontracting their trading expertise remains to be seen.

Probability and pattern-recognition theory will become the traders' tools of trade. Pattern recognition algorithms sitting on powerful computers will sift the incoming flow of market information, looking for relationships over time and/or among securities that appear to be unusual. Once these are found, the machine will search its historical fundamental and news data bases, asking the question, What is the probability that the observed abnormality in price behavior is due to information or an impatient trader? Based on the answers, the machine may itself respond to these price patterns or present the information to a trader/portfolio manager. Again, as the playing field becomes level, removing the distinction between the buy- and sellsides of the street, the distinction between portfolio manager and trader will fade.

While not being overly flattering, I view the trader/portfolio manager of the future as a spider sitting at the center of a web. He has literally hundreds of orders sitting out on various nodes of the worldwide trade net. The computer is trying to buy on the bid side of the market and sell on the ask. Orders executed will immediately trigger an offsetting order, whether in that security or another like it. The computer will be providing liquidity to the market, trying to extract the bid/ask spread from the market for its client as a reward for so doing. The manager's computer reacts automatically to trades, trying to keep the holdings of its portfolios aligned with each portfolio's strategic goals as it provides liquidity to other market participants.

Should the price patterns become more extreme or the computer program have trouble holding the portfolio close to its desired factor exposures, the trader/portfolio manager will be notified of all the relevant information. And that is the point: both sides have participated in the series of transactions leading to the current bid/ask quote. By buying and selling at different prices, they have generated information in the price-discovery process. Each side has thus paid for the information generated. There is something of a free lunch, in that others can see the trades and try to glean information. But if the bid/ask spread is narrow and the trading algorithms sophisticated, only the traders will know for sure.

Some of this is going on now. Managers who want factor exposure, say to oil stocks, may be indifferent to which of five or more stocks they want. Setting the five as substitutes and using tight price limits, these managers can glean information about the firms and/or their shareholders' intentions by watching which of their orders get taken. Even more information can be obtained if the system reacts to trades with incremental price changes. This is also true in pairs trading and most arbitrage transactions. Pairs trading is based on finding two stocks that have a relationship, say, IBM and DEC. When that relationship degenerates, buy the laggard and sell the one that is outperforming. If the relationship is fundamental, they will eventually resume it, and the trader can unwind his positions for a profit. Both of these types of trades are conditional trades. Both are small subsets of what will be possible when institutional managers, with real-time control of their assets, provide liquidity to the market, rather than demand it.

Summary

We have lived through the early days of electronic trading. As its use has grown, its functionality has changed. Technology is now capable of directly connecting the institutional asset base to our markets, giving the money managers real-time control over their orders. This access will mean a flow of orders to market that never made it before because such orders tend to be conditional on other market events.

What are the implications for the trader? The result will be deeper and more liquid markets as institutional money managers submit a sea of short-lived limit orders triggered by price moves in any number of related securities. To use an analogy, lack of real-time access to the markets acts as a shackle on those who have the capability to provide liquidity and depth to our markets. Our money managers must be empowered—they must be set free from their shackles.

Index

Index

Index

Index

U
Union Pacific, 171-173, 184-185,
    187-188, 192, 195, 197-200
United Airlines (UAL), 20, 138
U.S. Steel, 118, 131

V
Value Line, 38
Volatility, 6, 20, 25-28, 85, 145, 181

W
Wall Street Journal, 26, 160
Weeden, Don, 124-126, 131
Weinstein, Will, 174-176

About the Editor

Alan Rubenfeld is Vice President of Sales and Marketing of ITG Inc., a New York-based broker-dealer that offers a group of fully integrated trading tools that enhance decison-making, increase trading efficiency, and strengthen the link between investment strategy and execution. Previously, Mr. Rubenfeld was a Vice President of Merrin Financial, where he was in charge of developing their InterMarket Trading Network, an electronic trading interface between institutional traders and broker execution systems.

Mr. Rubenfeld was also a director in the Conference Division of Institutional Investor, where he was the Director of TraderForum, a private membership organization devoted to the professional development of the buyside equity trader. He also served as Director of International Markets, where he devolped programs that brought institutional investors to foreign financial centers. He received a B.A. in English and an M.B.A. from the University of Michigan, Ann Arbor.